SOUTH AFRICA'S FOREIGN POLICY
1945–1970

JAMES BARBER

SOUTH AFRICA'S
FOREIGN POLICY
1945–1970

London
OXFORD UNIVERSITY PRESS
NEW YORK   CAPE TOWN
1973

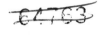

Oxford University Press, Ely House, London W. 1

GLASGOW   NEW YORK   TORONTO   MELBOURNE   WELLINGTON
CAPE TOWN   IBADAN   NAIROBI   DAR ES SALAAM   LUSAKA   ADDIS ABABA
DELHI   BOMBAY   CALCUTTA   MADRAS   KARACHI   LAHORE   DACCA
KUALA LUMPUR   SINGAPORE   HONG KONG   TOKYO

ISBN 0 19 215651 9

Printed in Great Britain by Hazell Watson & Viney Ltd Aylesbury, Bucks

For J and J and M

CONTENTS

TABLES

ILLUSTRATIONS

MAPS

FOOTNOTE ABBREVIATIONS

H of A South African House of Assembly Debates (Hansard)

IRR South African Institute of Race Relations—Annual Surveys of Race Relations in South Africa. Compiled by Muriel Horrell

IDAAF International Defence and Aid Fund—Information Service Manual (Southern Africa)

ACKNOWLEDGMENTS

I should like to record my thanks to the following:

Jennifer Potter who carefully and meticulously worked through the manuscript improving, reordering, and clarifying it; Jack Spence, Christopher Hill, and Adrian Leftwich who all read sections of the first draft and made useful comments which I was able to use in revising it; Marina Goddard and Jean Halsey who undertook the burden of typing and retyping; John Hunt who supplied the maps; and to Richard Brain and Ena Sheen of the Oxford University Press who carried out their editorial tasks so efficiently.

I should also like to thank the Nuffield Foundation for its generous support, particularly in providing funds for a trip to South Africa.

1

INTRODUCTION

I set out to write a book about relations between Britain and South Africa since the Second World War. As I am English, I thought it would be the South African view of the relationship that I would find more difficult to understand. Therefore I began by building up my knowledge of South African attitudes and policies towards Britain. In doing this I soon discovered that relations with Britain were so important that they intruded into almost every aspect of South Africa's foreign policy, especially in the years before 1960. Once I recognized this I decided to concentrate my energies on this wider study, although doubtless signs of my original interest in the bilateral relationship show through.

In examining foreign policy the main focus of interest falls on the government, and within the government on the ministers who have direct responsibility for the conduct of foreign affairs. As a consequence other groups, institutions, and organizations are examined only in so far as they influence the government policy-makers. This imposes substantial limitations in terms of relevance on the range of political activity which is examined, and in South Africa's case the restriction is especially noticeable for non-whites. No black or brown South Africans have any direct voice in government decision-making. The status and activities of the African, Coloured, and Asian peoples play an important part in this study, as they must in any study of South Africa, but they are not treated as central issues. Equally, within the structure of white politics, the parliamentary opposition is seen principally in terms of its influence on the government.

In any government there are relatively few key figures who have responsibility for foreign policy. It tends to be a specialized, discrete area of activity. The major policy-making is concentrated in few hands, partly because of the procedures used for processing foreign policy business, partly because it is the concern of senior members of the government (and usually the chief executive) and partly because the government aims to present a united 'national' front. Certainly responsibility is concentrated in South Africa. The ministers are advised and served by permanent civil servants, but the public face of foreign policy-making has very largely been restricted to the Prime Minister and the Minister of Foreign Affairs.

While they are few in number, the South African policy-makers usually hold views and pursue policies which reflect a broad consensus on external affairs within the white society. The policy-makers play an important part in building up this consensus, but in doing so they must not offend too sharply against strong and widely held attitudes especially on questions of race, and it is on questions of race that external challenges have been directed against South Africa. The white consensus on racial issues can, therefore, be seen both as a support for the government as it has met these challenges but also as a constraint on its flexibility in responding to them. (To write of a 'white consensus' does not imply that all whites share the prevailing views on racial issues. There has always been a small minority which does not.)

Policy-makers are greatly restricted by the circumstances in which they work—by economic, geographical, and social considerations, by questions concerning internal security, available resources, the attitudes of foreign governments, and the thousand and one other factors which are compounded together to create the limiting framework in which foreign policy is made. The South African Government has faced these common constraints, but in addition it has been constrained by the particular circumstances in which internal and external pressures have often been directly contradictory. South African society has a complex pattern of race relations, based on norms of behaviour which shape the daily lives and political decisions of the policy-makers, but these same norms are rejected outside South Africa. Because all South African government leaders have been committed to retaining exclusive white control of government they have often revealed a similar pattern of response to external pressures. Yet despite this, some stamp of the individual does come through. This is particularly noticeable in the cases of Smuts and Verwoerd. They dominated their governments. Their strong personalities set them apart from their ministerial colleagues, and their ideas had a distinct and personal quality.

In understanding any state's foreign policy, it is impossible to divorce external affairs from their domestic base. The question is not whether internal affairs are to be examined, but rather how much attention is to be paid to them, what sectors are to be covered and in what depth. In South Africa's case the relationship between internal and external affairs is strong and obvious, both in terms of external response to internal development and the influence of the domestic situation on the attitudes and perception of the policy-makers. Domestic and foreign policies overlap continuously so much of South Africa's foreign policy is a product of, or a response to, internal affairs.

In approaching South Africa's foreign policy there are certain common assumptions that are so widely held that they are easily accepted without thought, while in fact they are open to considerable doubt. For example, it is almost instinctive to say that in world affairs South Africa has become increasingly isolated. 'Isolation', 'the white laager', 'withdrawn into themselves', are words and phrases that slip out very easily, and plainly with some justification. But it is only partial justification. In terms of diplomatic relations South Africa did face considerable isolation between 1945 and 1970, but at the same time she enjoyed one of the fastest economic growth rates in the world. This simply could not have been achieved without extensive international contacts and co-operation.

The contrast between diplomatic and economic contacts calls into question the basis on which South Africa's international relations should be examined. Should we, for example, concentrate on activity at the United Nations, or should we rather examine the flow of trade and investment? Obviously it would be a mistake to concentrate exclusively on one form of contact to the exclusion of all others, and in South Africa's case particular caution must be exercised in accepting too easily that the widely reported, public, diplomatic reactions represent the whole picture.

In examining South Africa's foreign policy over a twenty-five-year period there is available a diverse mass of evidence. I cannot pretend that I have been able to examine more than a fraction of it. I interviewed extensively in South Africa, but my main sources have been written documents. Many of these come from the

South African Government itself—the parliamentary records, government reports and statistics, government propaganda. These government records present particular problems, for plainly they are very selective, much is left unstated, and the best light is put on any government action or policy. Yet there is no choice. Heavy reliance has to be placed upon them in discovering government views and attitudes, and however slanted the flow of information, the government must, in trying to gain the support of its own population and in trying to influence foreign governments, articulate its foreign policy. It must explain to a diverse audience many of its attitudes, its objectives, and the methods it is using to achieve these objectives.

I decided to start the study in 1945 rather than 1948 (when the National Party came to power) because there are common characteristics in South Africa's international position and her foreign policy which stretch across the whole post-war period. These characteristics were not substantially altered by changes of government inside South Africa.

In terms of the structure of the book I have used a chronological framework. I did this because policy-making has to respond to constantly evolving and changing circumstances, and by examining the development over a period a pattern of change both in decisions and attitudes can be traced. Within the chronological framework I have distinguished four separate periods. Each of these has distinct characteristics based on the changing circumstances faced by the policy-makers and their perception of and response to these circumstances. The divisions between the periods are necessarily arbitrary with considerable overlapping, and in some cases common characteristics run across every period. For example, economic development clearly jumps over the chronological barriers. Also the divisions I have identified differ in their character. The first represents the change of government from the United Party to the National Party. The others do not represent changes of government, but changes of circumstances, attitudes, and perceptions in a continuing government situation. These changes are often cumulative and cannot be tied down to a single point in time. Yet, with these difficulties accepted, the division into periods helps in understanding the evolution of South Africa's foreign policy, and is especially helpful in showing the relationship between internal and external developments.

PART ONE

THE AFTERMATH OF WAR
(1945–1948)

2

SMUTS'S VIEW OF
THE POST-WAR WORLD

At the end of the Second World War the South African Government had no suspicion that in the years ahead it would face persistent and increasing international hostility. In May 1945, as the
first session of the United Nations was assembling at San Francisco,
Jan Hofmeyr, the Deputy Prime Minister, said that among the
good that had come from the evil of war was 'the enhancement in
our prestige and honour of our country amongst the nations of the
world. . . . There is no lack of evidence of that in San Francisco
today.'[1] The South African Government's optimism was based on
its wartime experience. It had stood firmly by the allied cause
through the long, dark days of German and Japanese success until
victory had been secured.[2] Like the other allies, the South
Africans entered the post-war world anticipating the fruits of
success.

In South Africa itself the war had caused little physical hardship. The battlefield had been far away, and the South Africans
who stayed at home had faced few privations. The war had even
brought the advantage of increased economic activity and wealth.
Professor Houghton in an analysis of South Africa's economy
based on Rostow's stages of development identified the period
between 1933 and 1945 as that of the 'take-off' into sustained
growth. He argued that the war gave a stimulus to many South
African industries because goods previously imported were no
longer available, and so both the volume and variety of goods
manufactured in South Africa increased. 'The end of the war', he

---

[1] H of A, 3 May 1945, col. 6947.
[2] Roughly 200,000 South Africans had joined the armed forces, and of these
6,840 had been killed, 1,841 were missing, 14,363 had been wounded, and 14,589
had been taken prisoner. Nicholas Mansergh, *The Commonwealth Experience*
(London, Weidenfeld and Nicolson, 1969), p. 296.

wrote, 'left South African manufacturing industry larger, more
diversified and with enhanced technical skill and confidence.'[1]

Although South Africa had made these economic gains, in
another way the war had imposed a particular domestic burden on
the Union. The decision to go to war had split the white society,
deepening and sharpening old wounds and even dividing the ruling
United Party and its Cabinet. Immediately Britain declared war
General Hertzog, the Prime Minister, introduced into the South
African House of Assembly a neutrality motion. In this he was
opposed by eight of his cabinet colleagues including the Deputy
Prime Minister, General Jan Smuts. Smuts countered Hertzog's
move with an amendment proposing participation in the war. In a
dramatic parliamentary confrontation it was Smuts who triumphed
by 80 votes to 67. He then formed a new government and led
South Africa into the war.

Smuts had no doubt that the decision was right but equally he
had no doubt of the sacrifices involved. The memories of a bitter
past came flooding back—a past in which Boer had fought against
Briton, and in which there had been deep divisions among Afrikaners themselves. It was these old memories and wounds that
Smuts and Hertzog had tried to heal by their political union. The
two men had formed the United Party in the early 1930s, at a time
when South Africa faced grave economic crises, but they had
hoped for more than an economic recovery. They had hoped for
the reconciliation of Afrikaans- and English-speaking whites.
Hertzog and Smuts, both themselves Afrikaners, rejected the
suggestion that South Africa should be dominated by the Afrikaner section of the white population. Instead they set out to
reinforce the ties between the two main white groups, to solve
what was then called the 'race problem'.[2] It was these hopes of
reconciliation that in part had prompted Smuts to subordinate his
own personal ambition and serve under Hertzog, and it was these
hopes that were gravely threatened by the decision to go to war.

While Smuts and Hertzog had been united in their ambitions
for reconciliation, they had not been as united in their attitudes
towards foreign policy. Foreign policy was then largely a question

[1] D. Hobart Houghton, *The South African Economy*, 3rd ed. (Cape Town and
London, Oxford University Press, 1973), pp. 16–17.

[2] The 'race problem' at that time was seen as the relationship between the
Afrikaners and the English-speaking whites, as distinct from the 'native problem'
which was concerned with the black man's position.

of relations with Britain—the old 'imperial factor' in South Africa's history. Britain was the major colonial power in the continent, the central member of the Commonwealth, and the mother country of many white South Africans. Smuts was a great Commonwealth man. Over the years since the Act of Union in 1910 he had become increasingly convinced that South Africa's interests, both externally and internally, were best served by staying close to Britain and by retaining the British Commonwealth and Empire as one of the major forces in international politics. Hertzog had never shared these ideas. He was not, like the Nationalists, a bitter opponent of the strong British connection, but he accepted it rather than enthused about it. In his view, South Africa had to decide its interests independently of Britain, although very often these interests would coincide.

To Hertzog, and even more to the National Party, the decision of Smuts and his followers to take South Africa into war was a glaring and disastrous example of the Union yet again holding on to Britain's coat-tails and becoming involved, as in 1914–18, in a major war which was of no direct interest to her. This view was rejected by the vast majority of English-speaking South Africans. The division was not a simple one of Afrikaner versus English speakers—Smuts himself was an Afrikaner—but it had enough of the Boer and Briton split in it to reopen the old wounds.

The chief opposition to the war came from the National Party, led by Dr. D. F. Malan. The Nationalists, who had stood aside from the Hertzog–Smuts coalition, saw themselves as the bearers of the 'true' and 'pure' Afrikaner traditions—traditions which emphasized the unique position and rights of Afrikaners in South Africa, and the need for a republican form of government built on the principles of the old Boer republics. These traditions had originally been built up by a rural people who often caricatured the English speakers and their Afrikaner allies as soulless business and commercial exploiters.

Following his failure to keep South Africa out of the war, Hertzog and some of his Afrikaner supporters left the United Party, sharpening further the division within the white society. For the future the United Party, although it retained Afrikaner leaders and minority Afrikaner support, had to rely more heavily than ever on the English-speaking section of the population. The dispute over the decision to go to war had given shape to the major

white political parties of the post-war years. This division, although it later became overshadowed by the question of relations
between whites and non-whites, has never disappeared. During
the war the Nationalists kept up strong and persistent criticism of
South Africa's involvement. Not only did they brand it as Britain's
war but there was considerable sympathy with Germany. Even
among the more moderate Nationalists, there was a certain satis-
faction in the early German victories, in seeing 'the old bully
being bullied himself'.[1] Among the more extreme Nationalists
there was overt support for Germany, and while these factions
were disowned by Malan and their leaders imprisoned by the
Government, they had in their ranks future Nationalist leaders
including a Prime Minister, B. J. Vorster.

For a time Hertzog joined the Nationalists but he never settled
there. They were too stern and inflexible for him, while, on their
part, they were suspicious of him as a compromiser. But it was
Smuts who was the chief Nationalist ogre—the man, and an
Afrikaner man at that, who had once again 'sent South Africa's
sons to die for England',[2] and who was the creature of Hoggen-
heimer, 'that cartoon conception of profit-seeking economic
development devoid of all non-economic motivation'.[3] To some
Nationalists Smuts was no better than a traitor. In contrast he was
idolized by his own party. He was held in such awe that the traces
remain even today. Go into a United Party office and the chances
are that a portrait of Smuts will be hanging as a centrepiece. His
authority was accepted almost without question, and yet in retrospect it is possible to see that he may have been too dominant, too
awe-inspiring for the future health of the United Party. There was
too little criticism, too little original thinking in the party. Beneath
the protective shadow of Smuts's last years there was little light
for vigorous new plants. The one plant that might have flourished
was Jan Hofmeyr but he died before Smuts, leaving the party
bereft of outstanding young talent.[4]

---

[1] Quoted in conversation by an ex-Nationalist minister.
[2] Quoted in conversation by another ex-Nationalist minister.
[3] Ralph Horwitz, *The Political Economy of South Africa* (London, Weidenfeld
and Nicolson, 1967), p. 4.
[4] For the major biography of Smuts, see Sir Keith Hancock, *Smuts:* vol. I,
The Sanguine Years 1870–1919; vol. II, *The Fields of Force* (Cambridge University Press, 1962, 1968). For that of Hofmeyr see Alan Paton, *Hofmeyr* (Cape
Town and London, Oxford University Press, 1964).

While at home Smuts remained a controversial figure, abroad he had enormous prestige. This was another reason for the South African Government's confidence in its international position at the end of the war. Before the war, the Union had seen herself as a small state with no great international pretensions, but in Smuts she had produced a statesman of world repute. Like previous South African Prime Ministers he acted as his own Minister of External Affairs, an arrangement particularly suited to his interests. The National Party complained that this deep involvement in world affairs introduced alien and unhealthy values into South Africa, that Smuts was too ready to sacrifice the Union's interests for those of his international ambitions, and that he spent far too much of his time and energy in pursuing these ambitions instead of dealing with South Africa's internal affairs. If a monument were erected for Smuts, said Malan, it 'should stand next to that of Jan van Riebeeck at the place he landed, but ... while the monument of Jan van Riebeeck had its back to the sea and faces South Africa, the monument [of Smuts] should have its back to South Africa and face overseas.'[1]

During his Premiership, Smuts so dominated South Africa's foreign policy that there is a temptation to see the policy being shaped by his individual will. There is partial truth in this, for Smuts was not only the dominant decision-maker, but with his philosophy of 'holism'[2] he brought to South Africa's policies a breadth of vision and aims which were personal and quite distinctive. As his interests lay in the whole structure of the international system, he related South Africa's interests to that broad framework. Under him South Africa's stated objectives had a grand, panoramic sweep which his successors never emulated, or perhaps never had the opportunity to emulate. Smuts fixed his eyes on far horizons. Those who followed bent their heads to search the ground around their feet.

Yet, for all the grandeur of his views, what became plain in the post-war years were the constraints imposed on Smuts. These were not only such constraints as geographical circumstances, limited resources, and limited information, which face all policy-

---

[1] H of A, 27 Jan. 1950, col. 244. Van Riebeeck was the leader of the first Dutch settlement at the Cape.

[2] Smuts's philosophical views are discussed by Hancock, *Smuts*, vol. I, ch. 15 and vol. II, ch. 9.

makers, but the particular restrictions surrounding South Africa. In the post-war years it was Smuts the South African and not Smuts the world statesman who emerged most clearly. Whatever his past fame and his future ambitions, he was a part of white South African society. He shared in its ambitions, its values and attitudes, and it was these values and attitudes which increasingly came under pressure in the post-war years. Under this pressure the policy Smuts pursued, or was forced into pursuing, merged imperceptibly into policies which any white South African leader would have followed. He was forced away from his grand designs to defend the structure of his own society. A clear contrast emerged between Smuts's ideas of what *should have been* in the post-war world—the issues he thought important, the international values he wanted to preserve or to create—and the policies he was able to pursue.

Smuts's sense of values and his image of a reordered international community came out most clearly in speeches he made towards the end of the war, or immediately after the war, before the pressure was on South Africa. One of the most powerful of these speeches, 'Thoughts on a New World', was made to the Empire Parliamentary Association in London in 1943. In this, his 'Explosive Speech', Smuts covered such topics as future power relations, Britain's role as a leader in Western Europe, and Commonwealth reorganization.[1] Characteristically, his ideas were sketched on a grand scale. When he spoke of the future he was concerned with such issues as the structure of the United Nations and the rebuilding of Europe, and if this appeared pretentious to his opponents it never seemed that way to Smuts. For him it was impossible to distinguish and separate the part from the whole, and so it was a misconception to speak of South Africa's interests as though they could be isolated from overall international developments. South Africa's future, as indeed the future of all states, depended on the stability, peace, and progress of the whole international community. This was Smuts's reply when his opponents accused him of sacrificing South Africa's interests to his grand designs.

Smuts had always been respected for his foresight, yet, when he attempted to identify the major problems of the post-war world, he naturally looked to the past and drew on his immense experi-

[1] See J. C. Smuts, *Jan Christian Smuts* (London, Cassell, 1952), pp. 440–9.

ence. Within this experience, international relations had been dominated by two world wars, both of which had had their origins in Europe. This coloured all Smuts's thinking. For him the over-riding task in international affairs was to prevent a third world war, and to achieve this he supported three major objectives: first, the creation of an international organization designed to preserve the peace; second, the restoration of a peaceful and prosperous Europe; and third, the reinforcement and expansion of the British Commonwealth of Nations. These objectives, as seen by Smuts, were not mutually exclusive but knitted together to reinforce each other.

Smuts was committed to the idea and the ideal of an inter-national organization, but he never underrated the difficulties of creating a new world order from the ruins of war. When he arrived in San Francisco to help establish the United Nations he said: 'The last great battle of the war is not being fought in Britain or anywhere else, but right here in San Francisco . . . any document which concludes this war and starts the future ought to include a statement of faith.'[1] Smuts played a leading and active part in the formation of the organization. He was appointed President of the Commission on the General Assembly, and he made the first draft of the bold declaration of aims and ideals contained in the preamble to the Charter. The ringing phrases of the preamble are largely Smuts's phrases. It was he who suggested that the members 'reaffirm faith in fundamental human rights, in the dignity and worth of the human person, in the equal rights of men and women'.[2] Ironically these very words were soon to be turned against him and his country as a new idealism, the search for equality between black and white, was taken up. It was an idealism that Smuts had not foreseen and which white South Africans had not been conditioned to accept.

The structure of the United Nations which emerged from the San Francisco conference in 1945 did not satisfy Smuts entirely. There had been too much wrangling, too many compromises to make. Among other things, he regretted that the veto of the Great

[1] Quoted by J. C. Smuts, op. cit. p. 470.
[2] H. G. Nicholas, *The United Nations* (London, Oxford University Press, 2nd ed. 1962), Appendix, p. 196. The actual draft made by Smuts read: 'To re-establish faith in fundamental human rights, in the sanctity and ultimate value of human personality, in the equal rights of men and women.' (Quoted by J. C. Smuts, op. cit. p. 478.)

Powers had not been restricted to war prevention.[1] But usually he kept his doubts private, while publicly emphasizing the virtues and strengths he saw in the new organization, especially on the over-riding issue of securing the peace. 'The great question', he said, 'is peace and how this can be preserved.'[2] To achieve this, Smuts, unlike the other old dominions of Canada, Australia, and New Zealand, accepted that the 'Great Powers' must have a special status. While Mackenzie King of Canada stubbornly stated, 'We were fighting to prevent two countries from dominating the world, and we do not now wish to see any one, two, three or four countries dominate the peace',[3] Smuts accepted the Great Power status as a necessity of life, as the only way of inducing them to co-operate in the organization. Without them the United Nations would be meaningless, he said. Yet Smuts never saw the United Nations as a super state. For him it was a conference of sovereign states.

His National Party opponents were sceptical of the organization from the beginning. With their more confined, inbred view of foreign relations they criticized specific aspects of the United Nations. For example they said that Smuts had accepted too readily the special status of the Great Powers, for past experience showed that it was the powerful states who were the most aggres-sive. They asked what would happen if one of the Great Powers broke the peace. Who then would guard the guardians?

Although Smuts had high hopes that the Great Powers would work for peace, he was unsure of the future roles of the two super powers, the United States and the Soviet Union. Despite his belief that Europe, and particularly Western Europe, was the heartland of international relations, he recognized that the war had changed permanently the strengths and relationships of the leading states, and that the Soviet Union and the United States were now the two strongest powers. But because of his uncertainty about their behaviour, he hoped that their dominance could be mitigated by the quick recovery of Western Europe. Smuts saw the United States as a young giant full of promise and hope, but somewhat unsophisticated and unsure of itself. He said: 'The

---

[1] H of A, 6 Feb. 1946, col. 1165.   [2] ibid., col. 1156.
[3] Quoted by Nicholas Mansergh in *Commonwealth Perspectives* (a collection of seminar papers published by Duke Univ. Press and Cambridge Univ. Press, 1958), p. 39.

United States is the land of hope, unaware of its own strength, inexperienced and sometimes fumbling, but beyond doubt the greatest country in the world and just beginning.'[1]

The Soviet Union was, of course, a greater enigma. Smuts realized the difficulties of working with the Russians but thought it worth a price to ensure their co-operation.[2] He waited, hoping that if the Soviet Union's major status was recognized she would work with the Western states to ensure the peace. In 1943 when Smuts suggested that the restoration of Europe could best be achieved by regional development, he proposed that the Soviet Union should take the lead in Eastern Europe, while Britain led in the West.[3] When other Western states were becoming increasingly antagonistic Smuts, although strongly anti-communist, was slow to condemn. Even after Churchill's 'Iron Curtain' speech at Fulton in 1946, which brought a chorus of approval from the National Party, Smuts called for patience, saying that war motives should not be attributed to others and that all states should work together to make a success of the United Nations.

Peace was so much the overriding consideration for Smuts that when he explained that the United Nations, unlike its predecessor the League of Nations, would interest itself in social and economic questions, he justified this in terms of eliminating the causes of war. He told the House of Assembly in Cape Town:

It is some new light which has come in our human path which may help to banish the shadow of war. It is not merely a case of war being concerned directly, but also of the factors which indirectly bear on war and probably social and economic conditions are one of the most prolific and fruitful and dangerous sources of war. The attack on war is now being made on a much broader front than ever before.[4]

Smuts's concern with the United Nations was closely related to his concern for the rebuilding of Europe. 'The restoration of Europe', he said, 'is the supreme problem of the coming peace, and beyond all doubt, the most urgent problem before the world.'[5] In the past Europe had been the focal point of international activity and also the flashpoint for two world wars. For Smuts it remained central to international politics. When it was decided to locate the United Nations in America he said:

[1] *The Times*, 23 June 1945.   [2] Hancock, *Smuts*, vol. II, p. 431.
[3] *The Times*, 23 June 1945.   [4] H of A, 6 Feb. 1946, col. 1168.
[5] *The Times*, 22 June 1945.

To my mind the problem of the world for a long time, the problem of world defence, the problem of peace and war will be a European question and the departure of the United Nations to North America seems to me like sending the general far away from the field of action where the armies may have to do the fighting.[1]

Concern for world peace and order explains a part of Smuts's commitment to Europe, but there was more to it than that. Like many white South Africans, Smuts felt a special tie with Western Europe. South Africa is a part of Africa. There is no escaping the geographical fact, and most white South Africans readily identify themselves as 'Africans', but they identify and are identified as Africans with distinct differences. Racially they are a small minority in what has often been an alien continent. They carry with them a civilization whose roots lie in Western Europe, and, whatever the disagreements and frictions which have arisen and continue to arise between them and the 'mother continent', they still draw many of their cultural norms from Western Europe. They see themselves as a 'Western' society, which has transplanted a European civilization into Africa. Smuts voiced this feeling when he said: 'It [Europe] is the old mother continent of the world, it is the motherland of our civilization. It is now down and out in many respects [but] . . . Europe will resurrect itself and it ought to have a chance to do so.'[2]

One of Smuts's greatest hopes for the future was the continuing strength of the British Commonwealth. In a world of great uncertainty and potential instability, he saw the Commonwealth as a rock on which harmony and peace could be built, and which would support and not compete with the United Nations. In 1945 the Commonwealth was a small, tight-knit body, in which full membership was confined to five white members.[3] In this intimate group each member had a powerful voice and could genuinely feel part of the inner circle of one of the most successful international organizations. Perhaps the sense of common purpose had not always been as strong as it sometimes appears in retrospect,[4] but certainly the Commonwealth emerged from the war confident of its strength and ability.

---

[1] H of A, 6 Feb. 1946, col. 1172.   [2] H of A, 6 Feb. 1946, col. 1172.

[3] Britain, Canada, Australia, New Zealand, and South Africa. South Africa was not a 'white' state in the ethnic composition of its people, but its government was exclusively 'white'.

[4] See Mansergh, *The Commonwealth Experience*.

Smuts took immense pride in the Commonwealth's past achievements and had high hopes for its future. For him the Commonwealth, as it had been built up over the years and as it had been tested in the fires of two world wars, had achieved an almost spiritual quality. It was, he said, bound by 'unbreakable spiritual bonds which are stronger than steel'.[1] He thought that it could and should stand as the third 'Great Power' between the United States and the Soviet Union. In a broadcast in June 1946 he said that the emergence of two mighty powers was in some ways a frightening situation but 'In between them [America and Russia] lies scattered sprawling over the seas, the British group which may yet prove the saving grace of this vast power constellation—the area of stability between the two power poles.' He saw Britain as 'some vast geographical nervous system . . . spread over the globe, drawing and supplying energy and power everywhere'.[2]

On occasions such as his 1943 speech, Smuts associated ideas of European recovery with a powerful Commonwealth. He hoped that Britain would lead the recovery and suggested that she could strengthen her European position 'by working closely together with those smaller Democracies in Western Europe which are of our way of life, and in all their ideals, and which in many ways are of the same political and spiritual substance as ourselves'.[3] At another time, he suggested the establishment of a European Union on Commonwealth lines, so that 'we might at long last see the noble old mother continent of our common civilization emerge from its confusions and miseries and realize its freedom and place in a new renaissance more glorious than any in its great past'.[4]

As well as the Commonwealth's general advantages as an international organization, Smuts could see particular benefits for South Africa. As a 'small' state in isolation she could never play a significant role in the great issues which captured his attention. But the Commonwealth gave each member a strength and a voice greater than itself, and for Smuts personally a stage of international dimensions.

[1] Nicholas Mansergh, *Documents and Speeches on British Commonwealth Affairs 1931–1952*, 2 vols. (London, Oxford University Press for the Royal Institute of International Affairs, 1952), vol. I, p. 568.

[2] *The Times*, 1 June 1946.

[3] Mansergh, *Documents . . . 1931–1952*, vol. I, p. 571.

[4] *The Times*, 31 Oct. 1946.

South Africa's defence arrangements had been closely associated with the Commonwealth. As Smuts had felt impelled to lead the government into war alongside Britain, he had no doubts that Britain felt responsibility, almost guardianship, for South Africa. This interlocking defence arrangement was not based on any formal agreement, and the South African Government was firmly opposed to any formality. In terms of internal politics it was essential for the government to stress again and again South Africa's independence of Britain. Yet there was the reassuring assumption that the relationship between Britain and the old dominions was so intimate that it did not require formal agreement. As in other Commonwealth matters, Smuts believed that defence arrangements were bound by those spiritual bonds stronger than steel. When, in April 1946, Mr. Eric Louw questioned Smuts on press speculation about a Commonwealth defence scheme proposed by Mr. Chifley of Australia, Smuts assured him that South Africa had undertaken no commitments, that he personally was against formal agreements, and that the government would never enter any defence scheme without Parliamentary approval.[1]

While Smuts was always careful to emphasize South Africa's independence of action, he probably found it impossible to imagine the Union becoming involved in hostilities without Britain and the rest of the Commonwealth. He spoke of the Commonwealth 'seeing to its defences' and working together on defence discoveries in technical and scientific fields as though it was a unified organization. He feared for world peace if Commonwealth communications were 'ruptured or endangered' by closing Suez.[2] When he came to realize that it was impossible for Britain to shoulder all the commitments he had originally envisaged for her, he concluded that the other members of the Commonwealth must contribute more to their own and Commonwealth defence.[3] For Smuts independence and commitment were compatible, for South Africa's interests lay in working with and for a strong Commonwealth.

Smuts's emphasis on independence within the Commonwealth was rooted in South Africa's history. The Commonwealth link overlapped into internal politics. For Smuts, reconciliation between Boer and Briton could best be achieved by a South Africa within

---

[1] H of A, 17 Apr. 1946, col. 5774.   [2] *The Times*, 20 June 1946.
[3] H of A, 14 Apr. 1947, col. 2661.

the Commonwealth and under the monarch, while for the Nationalists the monarchy emphasized South Africa's continuing subordination to Britain, and it was a subordination that spread over a
wide range of activities including business and trading interests.
The passion and bitterness of the dispute was captured in the
clash of symbols—the Union Jack against the Republican tri-
colour, 'God Save the King' against 'Die Stem'. In 1940 Johannes
Strijdom, later to become a National Party Prime Minister, said
that South Africa's involvement in the war had shown that she
had a free constitution but not a free government. The only way
to change this 'terrible state of affairs' is 'by doing away with the
British connection and getting a free South African Republic.
Then we could not be dragged into such a war.'[1]

While for the United Party the Commonwealth had the great
positive advantage of a close connection with Britain, it had also
had what can now be seen as the negative advantages of not being
too concerned with race relations and strongly respecting the
tradition of non-interference in internal affairs. Relations between
whites and non-whites had been a topic of interest for the Commonwealth, as was inevitable with Britain's colonial involvement,
but it had never been seen as an issue which could seriously
challenge South Africa's membership. In retrospect the seeds of
future discord can be identified,[2] but in the 1920s, 1930s, and on
into the early 1940s it was easy to disregard them or to believe that
racial issues could be played down. This certainly seemed to be
Smuts's attitude. The future Commonwealth he envisaged in 1945
was a projection of the Commonwealth of the past—close-knit,
intimate, avoiding friction over internal issues, and still predominantly white.

The spread of South Africa's influence into other parts of
Africa was another potential advantage Smuts saw in Commonwealth membership. All South African governments have
shared this ambition. In 1923 Smuts had tried unsuccessfully to
persuade the white Rhodesians to join the Union, and at the same
time he had been anxious to build stronger links with Mozambique. He had written: 'It would be a great thing to round off the

---

[1] Quoted by Nicholas Mansergh, *South Africa 1906–1961: The Price of
Magnanimity* (London, Allen and Unwin, 1962), pp. 53–4.
[2] For example the Indian challenge at the 1921 Conference. Hancock, *Smuts*,
vol. II, p. 139.

South African state with borders far flung into the heart of the continent.'[1] And he had sometimes tied this to a vision of a great 'white' belt stretching through Africa, with the Union as its leader. Smuts's vision of a great white belt had faded by the 1940s, but he retained the belief that the Union had a prominent if as yet undefined role to play in continental developments. In southern Africa in particular the government was eager to extend its responsibilities. In the early days of the war, Smuts had asked Britain to hand over control of the three High Commission Territories of Bechuanaland, Basutoland, and Swaziland. Britain refused, and Smuts neither pushed the issue nor publicized the refusal. He had no wish to sour South African relations at such a difficult time, but the ambition to extend the Union's influence and responsibilities remained. When, in March 1945, he was urged by a member of the House of Assembly to help create a massive federal state of South Africa, consisting among others of the Union, the Rhodesias, Kenya, and the High Commission Territories, Smuts confirmed that he had always striven to knit together 'the parts of Southern Africa that belong to each other, parts that must necessarily work together for a stable future on the continent of Africa'.[2]

South Africa's broad if vague ambitions in Africa had also appeared in Smuts's 1943 speech when he called for a Commonwealth reorganization in which the Dominions would play a more prominent role. He wanted them to become 'sharers and partners in the Empire' and 'to take both interest and pride in the Colonies within their sphere, and in that way to create, in our great worldwide Commonwealth, a new "esprit de corps", a common patriotism, and a larger human outlook'.[3] Smuts was, of course, principally thinking of South Africa's 'sphere of influence' in Africa.

It soon became apparent that Smuts's broad ideas and assumptions were irreconcilable with the constraints surrounding the Union after the war. In international affairs Smuts's instinct was to seize the initiative and ask others to follow. In the post-war world he was never allowed to do this. He was attempting to work on a different plane, but he was forced away from his grand designs to a defence of his country's internal racial policies.

[1] Mansergh, *Documents . . . 1931–1952*, vol. I, p. 571.
[2] H of A, 19 Mar. 1945, col. 3720.
[3] Mansergh, *Documents . . . 1931–1952*, vol. I, p. 575.

The South African leaders who followed Smuts had no option but to accept a circumscribed role. From the beginning they perceived themselves as defenders of the white society; they could never afford the luxury of seeing themselves as leading figures on the international stage. Smuts's experience demonstrates and emphasizes the narrow limits imposed on those who followed him. He was the one post-war South African leader who could call on immense personal prestige and who had no foretaste of the constraints under which his country would have to operate, but even during his period of office the pressures had begun.

3

SMUTS CABINED AND CONFINED

Smuts had failed to anticipate the tough reality that South Africa's relations with other states would increasingly be shaped by her internal racial policies. It seems ironic that of all people a South African leader should underrate the importance of race relations. It was not that Smuts was unconscious of the problems—as a South African that would have been impossible—but he never saw it as a major issue of international relations. In reading Smuts's speeches there is a feeling that he turns to race relations reluctantly, that in international politics he had hoped to escape from the persistent and intractable racial problems of his own country, and when he was forced to respond he always argued that the problems, whether within South Africa or the world in general, were exaggerated and emotionalized. For men of Smuts's generation international politics had been concerned with other things than race relations. It had been dominated by white states, many of whom had empires, and so were themselves inclined to avoid racial issues. Also Smuts was wise enough to sense that any increase in attention to racial questions would be detrimental to South Africa.

Smuts was not insensitive to the problems and dilemmas of racial divisions. He could appreciate the points made by South Africa's critics that injustice and discrimination grew from these divisions, but while he could display this degree of objectivity he offered no solution. 'I am suspected of being a hypocrite', he wrote, 'because I can be quoted on both sides. The Preamble of the [United Nations] Charter is my own work and I also mean to protect the European position in a world which is tending the other way.'[1] He wrote this about relations with India over the treatment of Asians in Natal, but it captures his attitude to racial

[1] Hancock, *Smuts*, vol. II, p. 450.

questions in general. He could see both sides of the problem, but unlike his hopes for white unity, he could see no clear path to reconciliation. He tried to push it away as a problem to be settled by future generations. But in doing this he made a clear decision, a decision for the *status quo ante bellum* which within the Union committed him 'to protect the European position'.

Inside South Africa Smuts and his United Party were prepared to show some flexibility on racial issues—they never displayed the same dogmatic certainty as the men of apartheid who followed. For example in 1947 Smuts tried to restore confidence in the Native Representative Council, a Council composed of Africans which had refused to transact business because it was given too little responsibility. Smuts held talks with Z. K. Matthews and other African leaders in which he suggested the possibility of an all-elected Council which would be able to spend its own revenue and have some executive authority in the development of the Native Reserves. He also held out the possibility of the recognition of African trade unions. Matthews and his colleagues rejected the proposals as they wanted to see a reorientation of policy recognizing Africans as citizens, 'and not a mere tinkering with the framework of our existing Native policy'.[1]

Smuts and his colleagues were never prepared to force through policies which ran against the broad stream of white opinion, an opinion which accepted racial discrimination as the norm. They always argued that to challenge white opinion on this issue was to court political disaster: there was no point in having liberal policies if there was no hope of carrying the white voters along with them. The United Party saw itself as a pragmatic party, accepting what was, and 'what was' in South Africa was white domination. In a society that bristled with divisive issues the relationship between white and non-white was the most divisive of all. Smuts's instinct and political experience steered him away from grasping the nettle. Hofmeyr, the deputy Prime Minister, was much more forceful on this issue. His message was that South Africa should and must rethink her racial policies, and he risked his political career and endangered his party in saying so.[2]

[1] Quoted by Gwendolen M. Carter, *The Politics of Inequality* (London, Thames and Hudson, 3rd edn. 1962), p. 358. See also Hancock, *Smuts*, vol. II, pp. 488–9.

[2] Some United Party supporters thought that Hofmeyr's opinions lost the party the 1948 election.

Unlike Smuts, Hofmeyr was prepared to bring racial issues to the
fore. When he spoke to the Royal Empire Society in 1945 he said
that South Africa, as a diverse society, should play a leading role in
building up a common purpose within a diverse Commonwealth.
It was a problem for which a solution 'must be found for the sake
not only of the countries immediately concerned but for the sake of
humanity'.[1] Smuts admired Hofmeyr's ability, but on racial
issues he thought him unpractical, too much the idealist. Hofmeyr
died in 1948, after the United Party's electoral defeat, but subsequent developments indicate that it was Smuts and not he who
understood more clearly the temper of white South Africa. Yet
Smuts himself could never escape the mistrust created by his
ambivalence on race questions. 'On the colour problem he has
never sounded a clear note', said Malan, and because of this he
always had problems with the white electorate despite his obvious
personal distinction and eminence.[2]

Outside South Africa Smuts and his ministerial colleagues were
attacked on different grounds. It was at the United Nations that
these attacks were launched with the greatest vigour. From the
beginning the opponents of the Union's racial policies, from inside
as well as outside South Africa, saw the United Nations as an
important sounding-board for their opposition. At the meeting of
the General Assembly in 1946 Smuts was embarrassed by the
appearance of Dr. A. B. Xuma, the President of the African
National Congress, who came to lobby delegates against the
Union's policies.[3] Xuma was the first of a long line of South
Africa's critics who have found their way to the international
organization. At first there were two main issues—South Africa's
administration of South West Africa and the treatment of Indians
in the Union. These were precise issues, but even in these early
days, when the attacks lacked the persistence and bitterness of
later years, it was clear that behind the precise questions was a
general challenge to the whole racial structure of South Africa.

At the United Nations the challenge to South Africa became

[1] *The Times*, 25 Oct. 1945.
[2] Quoted by A. Vandenbosch, *South Africa and the World: The Foreign Policy
of Apartheid* (The University Press of Kentucky, 1970), p. 129.
[3] See Jack Spence, 'South Africa and the Modern World' in the *Oxford
History of South Africa*, vol. II: *1870–1966* (Oxford, Clarendon Press, 1971),
p. 509, and Peter Walshe, *The Rise of African Nationalism in South Africa*
(London, C. Hurst, 1970), pp. 329–32.

associated with the drive against colonialism, which received support from the United States and the Soviet Union as well as from the
newly independent states. The Great Powers, in which Smuts had
placed such faith, simply refused to play the parts he had written
for them. Even the United Nations, the stage for international
action, soon became unrecognizable as the one that Smuts thought
he had helped to build. It became, in Smuts's words, 'a cockpit of
emotion, passion and ignorance'.[1]

Smuts's reactions to the attacks were characteristic of those
which have been refined and developed by South African governments over the post-war years. He protested at attacks on South
Africa's internal policies, and immediately drew attention to
Article 2(7) of the United Nations Charter. 'There', he said, 'is
my veto.'[2] This article states that:

Nothing contained in the present Charter shall authorise the United
Nations to intervene in matters which are essentially within the domestic
jurisdiction of any state or shall require the Members to submit such
matters to settlement under the present Charter; but this principle
shall not prejudice the application of enforcement measures under
Chapter VII.[3]

Smuts was particularly indignant because he believed that those
who led the attacks were prejudiced and ill-informed about South
Africa. When he replied to an attack by India in November 1946
he asked if there was anywhere where more discrimination and
prejudice could be found than India. He spoke of the discrimination of caste and community and religion and then accused Sir
Maharaj Singh, the Indian representative, of giving a 'completely
distorted picture [of South West Africa] based perhaps on
ignorance as well as prejudice'. No mention, said Smuts, had been
made of the education and social services which had been provided,
and the large degree of native self-government.[4] Change the small
details, and this could have been a speech made by a South
African representative at any time over the next twenty-five years.
Under attack, Smuts had revealed another of the characteristics
that was to persist—the belief that criticism comes from those who

---

[1] E. Walker, *A History of South Africa* (London, Longmans, 1968), p. 762.
[2] Information gained in conversation with Mr. Douglas Mitchell.
[3] Nicholas, *The United Nations*, 4th edn., p. 215 (Chapter VII deals with
'Action with Respect to Threats to the Peace, Breaches of the Peace, and Acts of
Aggression').
[4] *The Times*, 11 Nov. 1946.

are biased, who do not understand and usually do not want to understand South African conditions.

It was Smuts also who, in response to these attacks, first attempted to narrow their range by setting them in a legal framework. This was a natural defensive position for South Africa. If it succeeded it avoided a debate on wide-ranging moral and emotional issues, and instead concentrated on precise points which could be met in the formal, legal terms of international law, with its inherent bias towards the *status quo*.

South West Africa had come under South Africa's administration after the First World War as a League of Nations mandate territory.[1] Because of its small population, its geographical proximity to South Africa, and its lack of development it was designated as a 'C' class mandate, whereby it was to be administered under the Union's laws as an integral part of its territory. But South West Africa remained an international territory, and as mandatory South Africa undertook certain obligations. She agreed to 'promote to the utmost the material and moral well-being and the social progress of the inhabitants'.[2] She was obliged to make annual reports. She had subscribed to the general objectives in the League's Covenant by which, in the ex-German and ex-Turkish territories, 'which are inhabited by peoples not yet able to stand by themselves under the strenuous conditions of the modern world, there should be applied the principle that the well-being and development of such peoples form a sacred trust of civilization'.[3] Even in the time of the League there was controversy over South Africa's behaviour, with criticism of her administration and her interpretation of the 'sacred trust of civilization'.[4] But in general the League's yoke had been light and

---

[1] Mandated territories were those territories previously administered by Germany and Turkey which were transferred to allied countries. In the case of a 'C' class, the administration was given to 'advanced nations who by reason of their resources, their experience or their geographical position can best undertake this responsibility'. R. W. Imishue, *South West Africa: An International Problem* (London, Pall Mall Press for the Institute of Race Relations 1966), p. 5.

[2] Article 2 of Mandate. Quoted by Spence, in *Oxford History of South Africa*, vol. II, pp. 505–6.

[3] Article 22, League of Nations Covenant.

[4] See Spence, op. cit. p. 506, in which he discusses the accusations of maladministration.

South Africa had administered the vast, harsh territory with little outside interference.

Following the Second World War and the dissolution of the League, Smuts went to the United Nations to seek approval for the incorporation of South West Africa into the Union. In this, said his Nationalist critics, he made his first mistake. They said that he should have incorporated the territory by right, that by going to the United Nations he had given the firm impression that the incorporation was open to dispute and required United Nations approval. In fact, said the Nationalists, the United Nations had no rights or claims over the territory. A firm, positive statement of intent by South Africa was all that would have been required. It is easy to understand Smuts's decision to go to the United Nations. In the first place he was reasonably confident of success, for like most white South Africans he thought the case for incorporation was irrefutable. And secondly, there was his commitment to the ideals of the international organization. He was anxious that he of all people should not be accused of ignoring the new body, when all the other mandatory powers had accepted a United Nations voice in the future of these territories. Smuts argued that there was no *compulsion* on South Africa to make a trusteeship agreement, but there was a moral obligation to try to reach an agreement. If this failed, then the *status quo* would be retained.[1]

At the United Nations the South African delegates argued that it had always been accepted that 'C' class mandate territories could be incorporated, and that of all these territories South West Africa was the most suited for incorporation. It was, they said, unique. It was the only mandated territory having a common border with the mandatory power, and was in fact geographically indistinguishable from the remainder of the Union. Also it was thoroughly integrated economically, and once doubts about its future status were removed capital and business would flood into the territory. It was further argued that control of South West Africa was essential for South Africa's security. In both the world wars it had been a danger to the Union as a centre for pro-German activity, and in each case only quick, decisive action had prevented a serious situation from arising. The whole momentum of the South African case was that South West Africa was a 'natural'

[1] H of A, 15 Mar. 1946, cols. 3676–80.

part of South Africa, that it would be both difficult and dangerous to have the territory separated from the Union. It was, they said, only the dilatoriness of the early Cape Government that had prevented its absorption before the Germans had seized it. That dilatoriness had been rectified by the occupation of the territory by the South African Government in the First World War. If on no other grounds, the territory could be claimed by right of conquest.[1]

The South African Government further argued that if United Nations principles for the Trust Territories were applied, the Union's record was clear, for in the tribal areas, which then covered about a quarter of the territory, the 'native tribes' already enjoyed a large degree of self-government under their own chiefs.[2] As a final crowning argument for incorporation, the government claimed that the people of South West Africa wanted it: the territory's all-white Legislative Assembly had passed a unanimous resolution supporting incorporation, while the government announced that African tribal opinion had been sounded and was also overwhelmingly in favour of it. At tribal meetings the question had been put, whether you 'would like to remain under the Union flag and form part of the Union, and retain all your privileges or whether you wish to be controlled by any other Power or by the nations whose names are mentioned and who now belong to the United Nations'.[3] According to the South African Government there was 85 per cent support for staying under the Union flag and only among the Hereros had there been a majority against it.[4]

In November 1946 the United Nations 4th Committee rejected

[1] For an outline of South Africa's case see *United Nations Year Book 1946–47*, p. 206.

[2] South West Africa was divided between the 'Police Zone' in which European laws were enforced, although a majority of the population were Africans, and the Tribal Areas which were ruled indirectly through traditional chiefs. See Imishue, *South West Africa*, p. 10. For the redivision of South West Africa with the introduction of Bantustans, see ch. 15, p. 239.

[3] *The Times*, 29 Nov. 1946.

[4] The actual figures given by the South African Government for the referendum of 'natives' was 208,850 in favour and 33,520 against (*Round Table*, March 1947, vol. xxxvii, no. 146, p. 133). A majority at the United Nations criticized the referendum, but the British Government accepted it. Attlee told the Commons: 'I take this opportunity to say that His Majesty's Government in the United Kingdom are satisfied as to the steps taken by the South African Government to ascertain the wishes of the inhabitants.' He stated that Lord Hailey, who had been in South Africa, had been satisfied with the way tribal opinion had been sounded (Commons *Hansard*, 23 Oct. 1946, col. 1666).

South Africa's request to incorporate South West Africa. Three reasons were given: first, it was said that the discriminatory policies of the Union were likely to be against the interests of the African inhabitants of the territory; second, that incorporation would be contrary to the United Nations trusteeship system, which in the eyes of most states had directly superseded the mandate arrangement; and third, there was the doubt whether the Africans had understood the issues involved or heard of the advantages of the trusteeship system. Prompted by the 4th Committee, the General Assembly accepted, by 37 votes to 0 with 9 abstentions, a resolution stating that it was unable to accede to South Africa's request and recommending that South West Africa be put under a trusteeship agreement. South Africa was invited to follow the example of all the other mandatory powers by preparing such an agreement. The General Assembly resolution came after what was to become the familiar pattern of 'militant' and 'moderate' draft resolutions from which a final 'compromise' resolution was drawn.

What is significant is that as early as November 1946 South Africa was facing widespread criticism on issues concerned with her racial policies. She was not yet isolated but she was already becoming an embarrassing international friend. On the South West Africa issue even the moderate resolution did not support South Africa's case but left her with the initiative to remedy the situation, as against the militant motion which insisted that the United Nations *impose* a solution. The width of international opinion which was already prepared to tell South Africa what she should be doing is shown by the sponsors of the compromise resolution—the United States, Denmark, India, and Cuba.

An impasse which has never been broken had been reached as early as November 1946. Since then the South West Africa issue has dragged on and on. There have been slight shifts of emphasis, there have been various strategies attempted by both sides to break the deadlock to their advantage, and certainly there has been increasing bitterness, but at base the situation has not changed. South Africa has claimed the right to absorb South West Africa. The United Nations have denied that right and claimed that the territory is one in which the United Nations has a direct interest. This was the situation which confronted Smuts, and which has taxed every subsequent South African Government.

The initial clash over South West Africa coincided with India's first attack on the Union Government for its treatment of the more than a quarter of a million Indians[1] who lived in South Africa. Nehru declared that: 'In South Africa our honour is assailed: there is rampant racial discrimination against our nationals.'[2] At the United Nations India sponsored a resolution which stated that South Africa's policies to the Indians of South Africa were a denial of human rights, and that they impaired friendly relations between two member states (i.e. India and South Africa).[3] Again South Africa was thrown on to the defensive—into a position which she has never succeeded in escaping, of finding herself continually harried and attacked, and forced to defend herself on issues which she regards as exclusively within her domestic jurisdiction. Since these first attacks in 1946, their range and intensity have increased but again the basic position has not changed. A majority of states at the United Nations said that South Africa's racial policies were against fundamental human rights as outlined in the United Nations Charter. Therefore they were a matter of international concern and not merely of domestic interest to South Africa.

With the question of the Indians, as with South West Africa, the South Africans miscalculated. Initially they thought their case was so incontrovertible that they failed to anticipate the opposition which lay ahead. When India brought up the question of the Asiatic Land Tenure Act the South African Government was certain that this would be recognized as an exclusively domestic issue. Heaton Nicholls wrote: 'We felt our case to be so judicially secure that it had only to be stated to be recognized.'[4]

Smuts, while attending the United Nations, agreed to discuss the Indian resolution 'without admitting the right of the United Nations to intervene in this matter'. When he addressed the United Nations Legal and Political Committees, he said that the vast majority of Indians in South Africa were South African nationals, and therefore outside the competence of the United Nations. If the United Nations interfered in such matters it was 'bound to lead to ultimate disaster for the organization and the peace of the world'.[5] He denied that racial discrimination as practised in

---

[1] I have used 'Indian' and 'Asian' as interchangeable.

[2] *The Times*, 8 July 1946.   [3] *UN Year Book 1946–47*, pp. 146–7.

[4] Heaton Nicholls, *South Africa in My Time* (London, Allen and Unwin, 1961), p. 320.

[5] *UN Year Book 1946–47*, pp. 145–6.

South Africa had infringed any elementary human rights, and claimed that, on the contrary, the distinctions drawn between the races were a safeguard for 'the more backward sections of our multiplex society'.[1] This was true, he said, of legislation which had been designed to separate Asians and Europeans and therefore avoid friction between them. There was, he continued, no exact definition of 'human rights' in the Charter and therefore there could be no specific obligations to meet them, but certainly 'political rights and freedoms . . . were not fundamental'. Such an argument 'was tantamount to saying that the most progressive races should be retarded by the less progressive if the latter were in a majority. Equality in fundamental rights and freedoms could be assured in a multi-racial state only by a measure of discrimination in respect of non-fundamental rights.'[2] He concluded by saying that the United Nations had no place in this dispute, but suggested that an advisory opinion be sought from the International Court of Justice about whether this was an internal issue as covered by Article 2(7) of the Charter.

South Africa's reaction to the Indian attack had been to emphasize legal rights. As with South West Africa, it was the natural defensive position, and similarly it failed to gain majority support. At a plenary session in January 1947 the General Assembly passed a resolution stating that friendly relations had been impaired between India and South Africa, that they were liable to be further impaired unless a solution was reached, and that the treatment of Indians in South Africa should be within the provisions of the Charter, and in conformity with an agreement reached by the two countries at Cape Town in 1927 (which South Africa denied as a binding international treaty).[3] The resolution called on the two countries to reach a satisfactory solution. When the General Assembly met for its next session in September 1947 India immediately complained that not only had South Africa failed to implement the resolution, but that Smuts had abused the United Nations and had denounced the idea of human equality.

The clash with India implied more than a conflict of interests

---

[1] *The Times*, 22 Nov. 1946.   [2] *UN Year Book 1946–47*, p. 146.
[3] The 1927 agreement was that India agreed to arrangements for the voluntary repatriation of Indians, while the South African Government agreed to improve educational and other facilities for those Indias who stayed and became part of the permanent population. (See *Oxford History of South Africa*, vol. II, p. 449.)

between two states. In the first place it revealed that particular aspects of South Africa's internal politics would be discussed at international gatherings whether South Africa liked it or not. This has faced all post-war South African governments with the dilemma that, while their internal strength rested on the continued commitment to white domination, in international circles their country would be abused and attacked for the very policies which were the life-blood of their political survival. Despite their interest in achieving good international relations, when the conflict position arose Smuts and his colleagues in the United Party naturally chose the values of their own society and defied the international challenge.

The treatment of the Indians in the Union brings this out plainly. The Indians are largely concentrated in Natal,[1] a stronghold of the United Party, with a predominantly English-speaking white population. During the war the government had come under strong pressure from the whites of the Province to restrict further the rights of the Indians. Until 1943 there had been no formal restriction on Indian ownership of land, but their settlements had been grouped together so that there were distinct Indian areas. In Durban, the major city, the whites complained that the Indians were spilling out and occupying traditionally European areas. Under pressure from within his own Party, Smuts introduced the 'Pegging Act' which made interracial property transactions in Durban illegal. Bitter objections followed from the Natal Indians and the Indian Government. An attempt at compromise, the Pretoria Agreement of 1944, failed. Then in March 1946, under further white pressure, the government introduced the Asiatic Land Tenure and Indian Representation Act, which it was recognized would meet opposition from India. While this Act delimited the areas in which Asians could buy property, it contained changes in electoral arrangements which it was hoped would appease the Asians. For the first time they were offered the opportunity to choose representatives for the House of Assembly, the Senate, and the Natal Provincial Council, but the representatives had to be *white*. The offer was rejected, and the South African Indian Congress called on India to take the issue of discriminatory legislation to the United Nations. India did this and further displayed

---

[1] At the 1946 census of the 282,000 Indians in the Union, 228,000 lived in Natal.

its opposition by breaking off its small trading contacts with the Union.

The difficulties which South Africa faced at the United Nations during 1946 were the first skirmishes in a clash of values which has characterized South Africa's external relations ever since. Much to the indignation of the government, South Africa has often been seen as part of the world's 'colonial' problem. The General Assembly had declared its awareness 'of the problem and political aspirations of the people who have not yet attained a full measure of self-government and who are not directly represented here', and had stated that members who accepted responsibility for non-self-governing peoples should 'recognize the principle that the interests of the inhabitants of the territories are paramount'.[1] This was a principle which many states thought should be applied to South West Africa immediately, and it was increasingly argued that it should be applied for the benefit of all the non-whites of South Africa. The white South Africans fiercely rejected the implication that they were colonialists, or alien rulers. They were Africans, their homeland was South Africa but they also happened to be whites.

The clashes within the United Nations over South West Africa and the treatment of South Africa's Indians left Smuts a disheartened and disillusioned man. The change came during 1946. In the early months of the year he remained reasonably optimistic although there were signs even then that he saw dangers ahead. The optimism did not survive 1946. It was a year that confirmed a deep division between the Eastern and the Western allies of the recent war. The South African Government, like other Western governments, became much concerned with the dangers of communism. As the hopes of Great Power co-operation had been lost, the dangers of the cold war had to be faced, but (as already described) even more important for South Africa, 1946 saw the first serious attacks on her racial policies at the United Nations. Smuts's letters to Hofmeyr 'reveal that he went to Lake Success with trepidation',[2] and he had good reason for it. 'We found', said Smuts, 'a solid wall of prejudice against the colour policies of South Africa. ... Inflammable issues of race and colour swept over the multiple Assembly in a flood of emotion

[1] *UN Year Book 1946–47*, p. 80.   [2] Paton, *Hofmeyr*, p. 436.

fanned by mischievous propaganda and created a situation which only calm reflection can bring to reality and proper perspective.'[1]

When he reported to the House of Assembly early in 1947 he was, if anything, even gloomier. He told the House that 'the past four months have been some of the most difficult of my life', and when he was asked what would be the situation if the United Nations applied sanctions against South Africa, he did not dismiss it as an absurd, impossible idea. 'We know', he replied, 'that sanctions constitute a war measure. Sanctions are war measures and South Africa must treat this matter very seriously in the position the world finds itself today. . . . We are in a delicate and even dangerous situation.'[2] He spoke of a new stream running through world opinion that could be a death blow to the United Nations. South Africa had been the first to be attacked on internal affairs but others could follow. 'I have learnt', he continued, 'during the past few months that South Africa is in a much more dangerous and much more difficult position than ever before. We have built up a community in the southern part of the continent which is not without its dangers. This is a unique experiment in the world and that is why the other nations in the world cannot understand it. . . . As a minority [i.e. the whites] we have maintained our position here for three hundred years. We have built up something in this country, which, in my opinion, is a monument among the nations, something that we cannot sacrifice.'[3]

Again, without seeming out of place, the substance of this speech of January 1947 could have been repeated by any South African minister over the next quarter of a century. The South African case—the refusal to contemplate radical change, the assertion that there was 'something that we cannot sacrifice'—had been made. The 'something' was white rule.

While the United Party government had to endure great disappointments in the immediate post-war years, the international picture was not entirely gloomy. Although the South Africans thought that the international pressures on them were harsh and unwarranted they were not nearly so strong or persistent as they became later. Nor was South Africa as diplomatically isolated.

[1] *The Times*, 19 Dec. 1946.
[2] H of A, 21 Jan. 1947, cols. 10911 and 10915.
[3] H of A, 21 Jan. 1947, col. 10923.

Close and intimate links were retained with the Commonwealth and with Britain in particular. Added to the important economic relationships were ties of blood and history which had been reactivated by the sense of comradeship developed during the war. There was also in South Africa a government firmly committed to maintaining close relations with Britain and led by a man whom the British greatly respected. There was criticism of South Africa in Britain, but the links were not under direct challenge. If a challenge had come within the Commonwealth at that time it would have come from India, but Nehru refused to raise the dispute because he said 'the Commonwealth might have been considered as some kind of a superior body which sometimes acts as a tribunal, or judge, or in a sense supervises the activities of its member nations'.[1]

Relations with Britain were easier and more relaxed in this immediate post-war period than at any subsequent time. Britain remained a major colonial power, and although differences on racial issues were emerging, race relations had not yet become an all-pervasive issue for South Africa. Although Smuts's hopes for Britain and the Commonwealth as a third super power were quickly dispelled, he retained considerable, if not uncritical, faith in the organization. In September 1946 he said of the Commonwealth that: 'On the paths of freedom and peace there is no more inspiring example to follow in the whole range of human affairs today.'[2] In the following year, when he was already disillusioned with the United Nations, he said that he was confident that Britain could recover from the economically crippling blow of the war. 'I go so far', he went on, 'as to say that I look upon Britain as a safer guarantee of peace in the world than the United Nations itself.'[3] Smuts was always trying to prod Britain into seizing the initiative in international affairs, and in Western Europe in particular. He saw the introduction of Marshall Aid in 1947 as 'a glorious opportunity for Britain to put herself at the head of this great movement and put her weight behind Winston's vision of a European union. It is no use her wallowing in her own misery and frustration. Proudly she should once more resume her glorious role in world affairs and in action find her solution.'[4]

[1] Mansergh, *Documents . . . 1931–1952*, vol. I, p. 851.
[2] *The Times*, 30 Sept. 1946
[3] *The Times*, 28 May 1947.   [4] Hancock, *Smuts*, vol. II, p. 449.

With gratitude for past efforts, and hopes that an economically revived Britain would play a major role in international affairs, South Africa gave substantial financial help. In October 1947 Hugh Dalton, the Chancellor of the Exchequer, announced that South Africa would make a gold loan of £80 million to Britain, and that if South Africa called on her sterling reserves during the period of the loan she would replace the reserves with gold. In return, Britain agreed to purchase £12 million of South African agricultural produce each year for the next three years. 'The Government of the Union,' said Dalton, 'under its great leader Field-Marshal Smuts, stands at the side of the mother country in peace and in war.' There was similar gratitude from Clement Attlee, the British Prime Minister, after receiving a gift of more than £1 million from the people of South Africa;[1] and Harold Wilson, who was then the President of the Board of Trade, publicly emphasized the importance of Britain's economic links with South Africa.[2]

The continuation of the close and intimate link with Britain was symbolized by the visit of King George VI and the Royal Family to South Africa in 1947, their first post-war overseas tour. Nothing could have given Smuts greater pleasure. For him the monarchy had taken on an almost spiritual aura. It not only symbolized the indefinable links which bound together the Commonwealth as a whole and Britain and South Africa in particular, but was the symbol around which white South Africans could be united. It was on this rock that Smuts intended to build his united white South Africa.

For Smuts the royal visit fulfilled his greatest hopes. He thought that the links between the two countries had been strengthened and the task of reconciling Afrikaner and English-speakers advanced. Near the end of his tour, the King, as monarch of all the Commonwealth countries, asked white South Africans: 'Are we not one brotherhood—the greatest brotherhood in the history of man, a brotherhood that has been strengthened not weakened by past differences?'[3] And when he returned to London he struck a note of firm confidence. He said that the 'faith of South Africa in Britain is not only unimpaired but has become stronger on account of her unflagging effort in war and peace. . . . South

---

[1] *Documents relating to the South African Aid to Britain Fund* (HMSO, 1947).
[2] *The Times*, 20 Jan. 1948.   [3] *The Times*, 31 Mar. 1947.

Africans are convinced that the mission of Britain in the world is not ended but is only entering upon a new phase.'[1]

This was music to Smuts's ears. Yet while for him and his closest followers the tour had been an unqualified success, there is another memory which still holds firm even among some United Party supporters and certainly among their opponents. This memory is of Smuts overplaying his hand, fawning on the royal party so that he made himself look ridiculous. In this picture, Smuts humbled himself too much, and in humbling himself humbled his country. Both sets of memories are firm today, suggesting that the royal tour did little to heal the divisions among white South Africans, and little if anything to enhance Smuts's personal prestige.

The royal tour may also have helped to mask the fact that despite continuing contacts Britain and South Africa were in some important respects drifting apart. At the time of the United Party government the drift was very slow, but it was there. It is partly explained by changes in the international climate, but also partly by internal developments in each country. The first signs came in 1945 when Churchill was defeated in the British general election and a Labour government came to power. Churchill's defeat came like a hammer-blow to Smuts. He saw it as a betrayal of a great leader by the British people.[2] He was also fearful of the new government. J. C. Smuts wrote: 'My father mourned not only the eclipse of one of his closest friends, but was appalled at the implications for the future. He had seen British Labour in action before.'[3]

Relations with the Labour government were not, in the event, as difficult as Smuts first feared, but they were never as intimate as the old relationship with Churchill. Heaton Nicholls, who was then High Commissioner in London, wrote: 'During the Churchill regime, Smuts' advice was always given grave consideration and more often than not accepted. With the Labour Party, of course, his advice was not always so welcome. He was regarded as being in the non-socialist camp, a friend of Churchill and therefore

---

[1] *The Times*, 16 May 1947.

[2] Douglas Mitchell, a close colleague of Smuts, told me that the news of Churchill's defeat was the start of the deep gloom which often overtook Smuts in his last years.

[3] J. C. Smuts, *Jan Christian Smuts*, p. 486.

one of the "old gang". Nevertheless his advice always carried
weight.'[1]

In the eyes of many white South Africans, the Labour Party
was suspect; full of men with ideas of equality and fraternity, who
in the past had criticized South Africa's racial policies and identified themselves as 'Kaffir Boeties'. For the United Party there was
the further doubt that the Labour Party was less committed to the
imperial tie than their Conservative rivals. These doubts were
reinforced when the Attlee government decided to give independence to India and Pakistan, and allied this with a general acceptance that the aim of imperial policy was to direct the colonies
towards self-government. By 1947, with India, Pakistan, and Ceylon
independent, with Britain still economically weak and uncertain of
her international role, a new Commonwealth was emerging, very
unlike the one Smuts had foreseen. The Commonwealth of 'like-
mindedness' was giving way to the Commonwealth of diversity.
Publicly, Smuts accepted what was happening with good grace,
and Hancock says that gradually he came to realize that the British
withdrawal had some creative elements, and he respected the
British realism.[2] But he never liked it. He thought the decision to
quit India was an 'awful mistake'[3] and when Ceylon was granted
independence he wrote: 'Ceylon a Dominion this year? Am I mad
or is the world mad?'[4] What would he have said of Ghana's
independence ten years later?

The Commonwealth changes reflected broader changes in the
pattern of ideas and relationships within the international community. The white man's order was rapidly dying. As the great
Western Empires broke up into independent states, at first in
Asia and then later in Africa, a great emotional drive for racial
equality gained momentum. Often it was a vague, unrealized ideal,
even in those new states which shouted loudest, but for South
Africa it had an unambiguous message of opposition to the
existing racial structure of the society.

Inside the Commonwealth the clash between the Asian members
and South Africa created an invidious position for Britain. Mrs.
Pandit, in a brilliant, emotional speech at the United Nations in
December 1946 (a speech in which she attacked South Africa so

---

[1] Nicholls, *South Africa in My Time*, p. 387.
[2] Hancock, *Smuts*, vol. II, pp. 447–8.
[3] J. C. Smuts, op. cit., p. 507.   [4] Hancock, *Smuts*, vol. II, p. 447.

fiercely and successfully that Smuts is reported to have told her: 'Young woman, you do not realize what harm you have done to me'), appealed to Britain to make a stand against racial discrimination. 'This', she said, 'was a "test case" which would decide whether the charter of the United Nations would be or would not be a scrap of paper.'[1]

Britain, at this stage, avoided an open commitment. Attlee, in one of his clipped, clear statements, refused to be drawn. He said: 'The position of Indians in the Union of South Africa is not one in which it would be proper for His Majesty's Government in the United Kingdom to intervene.'[2] But the Indian appeal marked the starting point of a conflict of loyalty between the increasing demands of the newly independent states for support on racial equality and the demands of loyalty to one of the old Dominions who had stood by Britain during the two wars. It also raised the question of how to interpret the Commonwealth principle of non-interference in each other's affairs. In 1948 Malan questioned Smuts about this. Malan said that the entry of Asian states into the Commonwealth would mean that increasing pressure would be put on South Africa to grant racial equality. Smuts replied that the question of equality had been raised at previous Imperial Conferences, but that South Africa had always stood firm on her right to decide her own policies and would do so in the future. Smuts said that as early as the Imperial Conference of 1921, when under attack from India, he had made clear his policy towards racial equality: 'Namely, that we in South Africa did not recognize equal rights ... that we did not recognize such a thing [equality] and had never recognized it and would never recognize it and the Imperial Conference left it at that.' He accepted that with Asian states gaining full membership of the Commonwealth the matter would probably be raised again, but he asserted:

The position of South Africa remains unchanged. We are a sovereign state and our future and status will not be decided by another body. We appear at the Imperial Conference as one of its members to consult about mutual interests, but we are not going to prejudice our position thereby. Our standpoint remains what it was and as it has been maintained hitherto—namely that we have special conditions in our country and we will not allow any interference with our internal affairs.

[1] *The Times,* 9 Dec. 1946. [2] *Hansard,* 12 Dec. 1946, vol. 431, col. 256.

On further questioning from Malan, Smuts said that he was prepared to take account of international opinion but: 'We have developed a white community here and I can visualize no future government which will ever dare to touch the basis on which South Africa has been developed. I can see no government in this country which will risk that.'[1]

A bitter experience for Smuts was that his Nationalist opponents were able to use his international difficulties as a rod with which to beat him. In the past the attacks on Smuts had been that he spent too much of his time and energy on international affairs. Now the opposition were able to add that he spent this time and energy unsuccessfully. They attacked him on general issues like his acceptance of 'Great Power' status in the United Nations, and they accused him of being weak in the face of communism, of giving way to the Russians in Europe, and allowing Germany, a bulwark of anti-communism, to be devastated.[2] But naturally, the strongest and bitterest of the Nationalists' attacks concerned the international criticism of South Africa's internal policies. Why, the Nationalists asked, had he responded so lamely to India's attacks? Why had he taken the South West Africa case to the United Nations? Strijdom, a future Prime Minister, asked Smuts whether he realized that in accepting the United Nations Charter he had accepted the principle of equality for all men, and left open the door for other states to interfere in South Africa's affairs. Smuts would be 'responsible should we be bound, irrespective of colour or race, to extend political and economic rights as well as rights in every other sphere. And then the Prime Minister will be recorded in the history of South Africa as the man who has accomplished the downfall of white civilization in South Africa.'[3]

In attacking the government's policies the National Party underlined the close association between internal and foreign policies. While criticizing Smuts for his 'maladroit' performance at the United Nations, Malan stated that Indians should not be given representation in either the provincial or national assemblies. Instead, Malan wanted mass deportation, because he said the Indians were infiltrating the European areas, and because they

[1] H of A, 5 Feb. 1948, cols. 1007 and 1008.
[2] Vandenbosch, *South Africa and the World*, p. 128.
[3] H of A, 2 Feb. 1946, col. 1224.

had shown their disloyalty to South Africa by complaining to a foreign power and by supporting a movement which was antagonistic to South Africa. He said that the National Party policy towards the Indians was based on the priority of 'South Africa first'. This could not be said of Smuts. 'The Prime Minister's action gives the impression that he is first a United Nations man and then he is a South African. I put it the other way around. I am in the first instance a South African man and then if it can do any good work I am in the second place a United Nations man.'[1]

Smuts's reply, in which he confessed that the past few months had been the gloomiest of his life, has already been noted. It is not the details of the reply that are so important but its mood, its spirit. This was the speech of a sad, disillusioned man: a man who could not understand or sympathize with the new international climate in which he found himself. One of Smuts's great past strengths, his ability to become larger than himself or his country in handling international affairs, had deserted him, or been denied to him. This rebounded on his party within the Union. Although the external attacks tended to rally white South Africans together in a sense of common indignation, and although there was sympathy for Smuts in his attempts to defend his country, there was no longer the confidence in his ability to understand or to handle foreign affairs. In that sense foreign affairs played some part in the 1948 election. While the election was primarily fought on internal issues—with the National Party parading the slogan 'the Kaffir in his place, the coolie out of the country'—on many questions, including race relations, foreign and domestic affairs overlapped. In its electioneering the government was unable to counter discontent over domestic policies and the call of the National Party for tougher racial discrimination by parading a successful record in foreign policy.

The years between 1945 and 1948 plainly mark the start of a new era in South Africa's foreign policy. The issues that were raised, the attacks which were directed against the Union and her response to these attacks, mark a break with the past. They also mark the end of Smuts's long years in office. His admirers will remember the days when he was a dominant, international and Commonwealth figure, when he had vitality and certainty of

[1] H of A, 21 Jan. 1947, col. 10899.

touch which is captured in his London statue—the lithe, stretched body, the confident forward thrust of the head. His detractors will remember the final years when that certainty had gone, when he had become the heavy, seated, brooding figure of the Cape Town statue.

PART TWO

THE 1950s—
THE EARLY YEARS OF
NATIONAL PARTY RULE
(1948–1959)

4

THE NATIONALISTS
ESTABLISH THEIR RULE

The period between 1948 and 1959, which for convenience will be referred to as 'the 1950s', saw major developments in international affairs. The Cold War was at its height, and in Africa the colonial powers (with the exception of Portugal) started to shift their policies towards eventual withdrawal. It was a time of reassessment and growing uncertainty in the continent, but from the South African viewpoint the period had a coherence as a new government established itself in power. The change in government came with the election victory of the National Party. This was a close and, even for many Nationalists, a surprising victory. In the years which immediately followed the election there was an atmosphere of uncertainty and tension in the Union as the new government sought to establish itself. But by the mid 1950s, and even more by the late 1950s, all this had changed. The Nationalists, with two further substantial election victories in 1953 and 1958, had established themselves as *the* ruling party in South Africa.[1]

In opposition the Nationalists had criticized Smuts for concentrating too much of his attention on international affairs, and when they came to power their main concern was internal affairs—the introduction of National Party policies within the Union and

---

[1] Seats won at elections:

	1943
United Party	89
National Party	43
Labour Party	9
Dominion Party	—
Independents	—

	1948
National Party	70
United Party	65
Afrikaner Party	9
Labour Party	6

(The National and Afrikaner Parties formed an alliance.)

	1953
National Party	94
United Party	57
Labour Party	4

	1958
National Party	103
United Party	53

securing the party's hold on the government. Partly because of these internal commitments, and partly because the international options open to South Africa were increasingly circumscribed, the objectives of foreign policy became less expansive and more closely tied to domestic policies.

The personal interests of Dr. D. F. Malan and Mr. Johannes Strijdom, the first two post-war Nationalist Prime Ministers, reflected the change of emphasis. As characters they were very different—Malan quiet and charming, Strijdom forthright and aggressive—but in both cases their major interests were in internal affairs. Yet, because of their office and the constant interaction between domestic and foreign policies, they had a significant role in foreign affairs. In 1955 Strijdom took the important step of separating the offices of Prime Minister and Minister of External Affairs. Mr. Eric Louw was appointed the Minister of External Affairs.[1] Louw came to his office with considerable diplomatic experience, including a period at the United Nations. He was a fiery, determined man, a wholehearted advocate of his government's policies who was always spoiling for a fight.[2] Whether his militant, aggressive style, and especially his eagerness to tell others what was wrong with them, helped South Africa's cause is questioned even by some Nationalists. One of his old colleagues told me that 'he won every battle but lost every campaign'. Against these doubts must be set Louw's great debating skill and the respect he gained within the Department of External Affairs. He breathed a fire and enthusiasm into a department which could easily have suffered a loss of morale and confidence under persistent international pressure.

On Strijdom's death, Dr. Hendrik Verwoerd became South Africa's Prime Minister. Outside South Africa, each step in the chain of succession to the Premiership was interpreted as a further move to 'the right'—from Malan the father of modern Nationalism, to Strijdom the advocate of 'baaskap', to Verwoerd the architect of 'apartheid'. Verwoerd retained a separate Foreign Minister, keeping Louw until his retirement in 1964 and then

[1] For an account of the development of the ministry see John Barratt, 'The Department of Foreign Affairs', in Denis Worrall (ed.), *South Africa: Government and Politics* (Pretoria, J. L. van Schaik, 1971). The ministry became the 'Ministry of Foreign Affairs' in 1961.

[2] This is a view which was confirmed in private conversations with Louw's ex-colleagues.

appointing Dr. Hilgard Muller. But the new Prime Minister was a man of immense energy and self-conviction, who played a dominant and central part in foreign affairs, as in all other spheres of government. Verwoerd's period of office overlaps the late 1950s and the early 1960s and his policies will be examined more fully in the next section of the book.

While the different personalities of the Nationalist leaders played a part in shaping policy, their main concern, like that of the United Party government before them, was concentrated on the defence of the white society. There was, therefore, much common ground in South Africa's foreign policy, whether it was being made by the United Party or the Nationalists, by Smuts or by Louw. Because of this the exaggerated claim is sometimes made that there was no change when the National Party government first came to power. The argument is that Malan took little interest in foreign affairs, he made no dramatic gesture like leaving the Commonwealth, and he retained senior officials, like D. D. Forsyth, who had served Smuts, and so, it is said, there was no change in foreign policy. But while the changes may not have been spectacular, they could be detected, and detected early. They were changes which stemmed not only from the increasingly hostile international environment, but from the aims and ideals of the National Party which were being realized inside the Union.

In examining the aims and ideals of a political party there is always the danger of oversimplification. It is tempting to speak of the National Party as if it were a monolith, its members having uniform beliefs and patterns of behaviour. The National Party, like all political parties, contains a range of views and attitudes. It suffers, like other parties, from internal rivalry and conflict. Accepting, however, the dangers of generalization, there are characteristics of the National Party and its Afrikaner followers which help to explain the policies pursued by the government.

The National Party has always claimed for itself a coherent set of beliefs and values. This gives it an ideological base which can be contrasted with the more pragmatic approach of the United Party.[1] As well as preaching an absolute division between white and non-white, it has, as a predominantly Afrikaner party, com-

---

[1] Denis Worrall examines the ideological base of the National Party in *South Africa: Government and Politics*, ch. 5.

mitted itself to advancing the cause of Afrikanerdom in South Africa. At a National Party Congress of 1941 a resolution was passed which demanded: 'The recreation of South Africa into a free independent republic, based on a Christian-National foundation, and incorporating in its nature and character the best which the Boer Nation in the past devised in this sphere, in accordance with its own national nature and traditions.'[1]

For many National Party supporters, the 1948 election victory was more than a simple change of government: it was a people inheriting their right. For most Nationalists the Afrikaners are the 'core' element of South African society. All the other groups and peoples are something less than 'true' South Africans—the non-whites because South Africa is a white, Western state; the English speakers because their loyalties have been divided between Britain and South Africa. The Afrikaners have formed themselves into a tight, exclusive people with an infrastructure of social groups underpinning this exclusiveness.[2] Their faith in themselves is bolstered by the Dutch Reformed Churches, which preach a special role for the Afrikaners, and, by selection and interpretation, give a scriptural base for their racial policies. There have always been Afrikaners who do not support the National Party (between 15 and 20 per cent according to de Villiers), but they are often dismissed as traitors to their own heritage.[3]

Ironically the tradition of Afrikaner leadership continued in the United Party. On Smuts's death in 1950, he was succeeded by Mr. J. G. Strauss, who led the party until 1955, and then Sir de Villiers Graaff, who retained the leadership into the 1970s. The early days of opposition were especially galling for the United Party. White South African politics has often been bitter. It was particularly so during the late 1940s and early 1950s. War-time memories were still sharp, and the rivalry between the parties intensified as the Nationalist government implemented its apartheid policies and fought to win even more of the Afrikaner

[1] Quoted by Carter, *The Politics of Inequality*, pp. 218–19.

[2] There is a wide range of Afrikaner groups, stretching from the 'Broederbond', a secret élite body which has been accused of dictating government policy, to separate Afrikaner organizations of the Boy Scouts, Red Cross, and university students.

[3] For an account of Afrikaner Nationalism see the chapter by René de Villiers in the *Oxford History of South Africa*, vol. II, pp. 365–423.

majority away from the United Party.[1] There were fierce clashes when the United Party accused the government of exercising nepotism in appointing Afrikaner supporters to government posts, and even fiercer ones over the implementation of some aspects of apartheid. This culminated in a major parliamentary-cum-legal battle over the decision to remove the coloured voters of the Cape Province from the Common Voters' Roll.[2]

The Nationalists have been resilient against internal and external criticisms through a firm conviction of right—a certainty of purpose which has been built on their strong religious faith and an interpretation of history which sees the Afrikaners struggling to preserve their culture, their freedom, and their identity against the twin foes of British imperialism and the African masses. All historical memory is selective. While Smuts and his followers in tracing the relations with Britain would emphasize events like Campbell-Bannerman's decision to trust the white people of South Africa,[3] the Nationalists would remember Lord Milner with his ambitions to establish a permanent British majority in South Africa and to make the English language and culture predominant.[4] With this keen sense of the past the Nationalists nursed their fears for their language, their culture, and their identity.

The general attitudes were reflected in particular policies, as the government sought to remove the symbols of subordination and divided loyalty. In 1957 it was enacted that the Union Jack would no longer be flown at official ceremonies. 'God Save the King' was abandoned and 'Die Stem' became South Africa's sole national anthem. Appeals to the Privy Council were suspended. These steps were principally of importance in South Africa's internal politics and as such were deeply felt by both major parties, but they also mirrored a clear change of attitude towards relations with Britain.

Another issue which overlapped the borders of internal and

---

[1] According to the *Union Year Book No. 24*, 1948, 57 per cent of the white population spoke Afrikaans as a home language and 39 per cent English.

[2] See Carter, *The Politics of Inequality*, pp. 119–45. The anger of the United Party over the constitutional and race relations issues was no doubt intensified by the fact that the Coloureds had traditionally supported the United Party.

[3] See Mansergh, *South Africa, 1906–1961*.

[4] For Milner's views, see L. M. Thompson, *The Unification of South Africa 1902–1910* (Oxford, Clarendon Press, 1960), p. 7.

external policies and which also saw a clear change was immigration. Permanent immigration into South Africa, as opposed to migration of temporary labour, is confined to white people. The United Party government had introduced a rigorous immigration scheme and had concentrated its main efforts on attracting immigrants from Britain. Of the immigrants, Smuts had said: 'Let them come, the good and the bad, let them come in their thousands, their tens of thousands, their hundreds of thousands, we shall absorb them all.'[1] The immigrants did come, in their tens of thousands at least. In 1946 there were 11,256; in 1947, 28,839; and in 1948, 35,631, and of these a large majority came from Britain. As well as strengthening British and Commonwealth links, Smuts argued that increasing numbers of whites were required to help South Africa's expanding economy and to strengthen the white population. He laid particular emphasis on attracting professional men and skilled workers, both to help economic development and to retain skilled jobs exclusively in white hands. 'We want', he said, 'to make hay while the sun shines. . . . As we are on the Black Continent we want good Europeans.'[2]

Even if the United Party had remained in power, it would have been forced to put a temporary brake on immigration because the very success of the policy had produced serious housing and employment problems, but there was more at stake for the National Party than these temporary problems. The new government faced a dilemma which no National Party government has been able to resolve satisfactorily. On the one hand the Nationalists want to strengthen the white population and help economic development but on the other they want to retain the exclusiveness of the Afrikaners and their control of government. During the 1950s the National Party gave its main priority to ensuring its hold on government and to defending Afrikaner values. It spoke of the need for a gradual and slow process of absorbing immigrants into South African society and its values. It placed a lower priority on economic development than the United Party and continued to accuse its opponents of being driven along by big business with its insatiable appetite for labour. Beneath these reactions was the old Afrikaner fear of being swamped. Strijdom accused the United

---

[1] Quoted by Gail Cockram, *Vorster's Foreign Policy* (Pretoria and Cape Town, Academica, 1970), p. 89.
[2] J. C. Smuts, *Jan Christian Smuts*, p. 494.

Party of pursuing a policy whereby 'through immigration Afrikanerdom was to be ploughed under in South Africa'.[1] As the National Party government struggled to draw the support of the Afrikaner majority behind it, it was not prepared to see that majority dwindled away by a mass of immigrants and particularly British immigrants. While the government did not stop immigration entirely, and continued to accept British immigrants, there was a conscious policy decision to cut down the overall numbers and to reduce the proportion of Britons. The figures make this very clear and bring out the contrast with the United Party's policy.

Year	Total of White Immigrants	Immigrants from United Kingdom
1946	11,256	7,470
1947	28,839	20,603
1948	35,631	25,513
1949	14,780	9,655
1950	12,803	5,097
1951	15,234	5,903
1952	16,473	6,941
1953	16,257	5,416
1954	16,416	4,629
1955	16,199	4,444
1956	14,917	4,476
1957	14,615	4,723
1958	14,673	4,450
1959	12,563	3,782

Another decision which reflected a similar determination to counter the political impact of immigration was the introduction of the strongly contested South African Citizenship Act of 1949.[2] Before the passage of this Act, a person with the status of a British subject (i.e. citizens of the United Kingdom, Canada, Australia, and New Zealand) automatically acquired South African citizenship, with the right to vote, after two years' residence. The new Act extended the period to five years, and citizenship was no longer automatic but was at the discretion of the Minister of the Interior who could withdraw it by executive action.

[1] H of A, 27 Jan. 1957, col. 28.
[2] See Carter, *The Politics of Inequality*, pp. 51–60. Non-British immigrants continued to have a six-year period before being granted citizenship.

The government's suspicion of immigrants extended to fears about the importation of 'liberalistic' views—of opening up South Africa to those who did not understand or sympathize with existing racial policies. Also, with their strong Calvinistic Protestant traditions, the Nationalists were suspicious of Roman Catholics, and this suspicion often reinforced a distrust of Mediterranean Europeans, with their swarthy skins and their alien cultural backgrounds. The ideal immigrants as seen by the Nationalists were Protestant Dutch and German, the stock from which the Afrikaner community had largely been built, but for all its efforts the government had little success in attracting these immigrants.

While the government's policies as they affected relations between the white communities created bitter disputes within the Union, the main focus of international attention was concentrated on South Africa's racial structure. Unlike Smuts, the National Party was never accused of hypocrisy, of paying lip service to racial co-operation while practising discrimination and segregation. There were no doubts about its aims and principles. But this refusal to compromise and the lack of flexibility did make the task of gaining any international friends that much more difficult. Apartheid became part of the international political vocabulary as the Union's racial problems were played out on a world stage. Government actions, such as drawing up population registers based on race, the provision of separate, but certainly not always equal, facilities,[1] the implementation of legislation such as the Group Areas Act of 1950 and the Bantu Education Act of 1953, were widely reported. Even more attention was given to the opponents of the government's policies. Individuals like Chief Albert Luthuli and the Anglican clergymen Trevor Huddleston and Michael Scott gained international fame. There was also widespread sympathy for the African National Congress as it organized a passive resistance campaign in 1952, and a school boycott in 1955 to protest against the Bantu Education Act.[2]

[1] Even in legislation it was recognized that facilities need not be equal. (See Edgar H. Brookes, *Apartheid*, London, Routledge and Kegan Paul, 1968—section dealing with 'Separate Amenities Act No. 49 of 1953', pp. 87–90.)

[2] For an account of the African National Congress see Edward Feit, *South Africa: the Dynamics of the African National Congress* (London, Oxford University Press for the Institute of Race Relations, 1962) and *African Opposition in South Africa* (Hoover Institute Publication, 1967).

There was further sympathy for the whites and non-whites against whom the government took action as it tried to suppress opposition by use of such measures as 'banning' and the Suppression of Communism Act. Particular attention was paid to the notorious Treason Trial which started in December 1956 with the arrest of 156 people and was not completed until March 1961 when the last of the accused were acquitted.[1]

The hostile international reactions incensed the South African ministers—none more so than Eric Louw. He accused foreign journalists and broadcasters of giving false and distorted images of South Africa. In 1958 he announced the results of a survey which had been conducted by the Information Department, analysing coverage of South African affairs in foreign newspapers. The individual items were divided into 'positive', which, Louw said, was 'not slanted one way or the other; news which is not only bad news'; and 'negative', which he said was selected or distorted to give a bad impression. According to the survey, only 11 per cent of the items were 'positive', while 75 per cent were 'negative'.[2] (The remaining 14 per cent were unclassifiable.) The government tried to counter the adverse image through its own information services, and in 1955 the State Information Office was transferred from the Ministry of the Interior to the Department of External Affairs.

The government asserted that South Africa was being used as an international butt. It refused to believe that the hostility and opposition could be based on deeply held principles, and explained it away in terms of expediency. It accused the new Afro-Asian states of attacking South Africa to draw attention away from their own faults and weaknesses. It accused the older states of going along with these criticisms, not because they believed them but because it suited their interests to woo the new countries.

The National Party government was inclined to generalize about its opponents, to group them together as 'communists' or fellow travellers. As soon as it came into office the government set up a committee to investigate communism in the Union. Commenting on the committee's findings, C. R. Swart, the Minister

---

[1] IRR 1961, pp. 62–3. In this case the prosecution failed to gain even one conviction despite a vast expenditure of time, money, and effort by the state.
[2] *Southern Africa*, 20 Sept. 1958; H of A, 19 Aug. 1958, cols. 2509–10.

of Justice, said that communism was 'a national danger', which was 'undermining our national life, our democratic institutions and our Western philosophy'.[1] The committee's report was followed by the Suppression of Communism Act of 1950. By this Act, the Communist Party or any other organization which was found to be promoting communist activities was declared unlawful. Wide definitions were given to 'communism' and 'communists', including what became known in the courts as 'statutory Communism'.[2] This associated communism with any doctrine or act 'which aims at bringing about any political, industrial, social or economic change within the Union by the promotion of disturbances or disorders, by unlawful acts or omissions or by the threat of such acts or omissions or by means which include the promotion of disturbances or disorders, or such acts or omissions or threats'.[3]

The view of an all-pervasive communism can be a reassuring one for white South Africans and is accepted by many members of the United Party as well as the Nationalists. If it is possible to believe that there is an evil force working to undermine the country—a force which brings together the country's internal opponents, the communist states, the Afro-Asian bloc, and the 'leftists' and 'liberals' of the Western states—then the strength and range of hostility to South Africa can be explained away. Even more reassuring, if non-white opposition within South Africa can be associated with communism, the need for a radical re-examination of South African society is removed. The view has helped to rationalize and reinforce the whites' determination, giving them a belief that difficulties inside South Africa are not of their own creation but stem from external subversive forces. 'Non-Europeans in this country', said Malan, 'are being incited and deliberately incited and this is not being done by communists alone but by liberalists and is being done from overseas.'[4]

The South Africans have also hoped that their strong anti-communist stand would attract support from the Western states. At best this has been only partly successful. Even during the 1950s internal developments in South Africa were strongly criticized

[1] Quoted in Carter, *The Politics of Inequality*, p. 63.
[2] It was charges under the 'statutory communism' clauses that were faced by the defendants at the Treason Trial.
[3] Carter, op. cit., p. 65. See also the chapter by G. Nande in Christopher R. Hill's *Rights and Wrongs* (Harmondsworth, Penguin, 1969).
[4] H of A, 25 Jan. 1952, col. 227.

1. Smuts with Queen Elizabeth (then Princess Elizabeth) at a
military review to honour her 21st birthday during the Royal tour
of South Africa in 1947. *Cape Times*

2. Malan addressing a public meeting, *c.* 1950.   *Cape Times*

and Western states became increasingly reluctant to be too closely associated with the Union.

Internally the National Party government claimed that apartheid was a unique solution for South Africa's racial dilemmas, but when defending itself against international attacks, it would shift the emphasis to claim that apartheid was not a new policy, that it simply rationalized and regulated racial distinctions that had previously been accepted both inside the Union and by other states. South Africa had not changed. Why then, asked the Nationalists, should they be condemned for pursuing previously accepted policies?

The United Party contested this interpretation. They drew what for them were clear distinctions between their policies and those which were being followed by the Nationalists. They were more pragmatic, less committed to a doctrinaire stance, and more anxious to gain international acceptance than the Nationalists.[1] Because of this they argued that they could have succeeded in halting South Africa's increasing international isolation. Perhaps because of its greater flexibility the United Party would have offered concessions on racial issues which would have softened the criticism of some Western powers. Perhaps because of the importance it placed on the British and Commonwealth links it would have been prepared to make some shifts in internal policies to retain these links. Also, the party's strong ties with international business and commercial interests might have given it a more sympathetic audience in the West and have prompted it to seek greater international co-operation. But even recognizing this, any concession acceptable to the United Party would have fallen short of even moderate international demands and have only temporarily delayed diplomatic hostility.

The distinctions which the United Party drew between itself and the National Party government were irrelevant to the demands of their principal international critics. Both the parties were committed to white minority rule. What was demanded was not an amendment here and a modification of policy there, but a root and branch change in South African society.

The National Party government realized the weakness of their

---

[1] For an account of the United Party at that time see Carter, op. cit., pp. 282–301.

opponents' case. In May 1957 when de Villiers Graaff attacked the government for leading South Africa into isolation by following rigid, ideological policies, Strijdom thrust back by saying:

The ideological policy to which the outside world objects is that we will not allow political equality between white and non-white. That is what they demand of us. They demand that we should not differentiate by legislation or otherwise between white and non-white. Our policy is that to protect the white man these discriminatory laws with regard to the franchise for example are necessary to place the power to govern in the country in the hands of the white man so that he can retain or maintain his supremacy or 'baaskap'.

Then he asked the United Party:

Are they opposed to this discriminatory legislation which I say has the effect of retaining in the hands of the white men power to govern the country—because that is discriminatory legislation? . . . Are they for example going to repeal the 1936 legislation and restore the Natives to the Common Roll? And if they say they are not prepared to do that I ask what then is the difference between that party and us. If we are unfair to the non-whites in this respect are they not then just as unfair?[1]

[1] H of A, 7 May 1957, cols. 5554 and 5556.

5

A DIVIDED WORLD

With its strong opposition to communism, the South African Government was prone to interpret international politics as a simplistic power-cum-ideological struggle between communism and anti-communism. While this was a widely held interpretation of international politics during this period of the cold war, a particular set of beliefs was required to apply it to the specific case of South Africa. Few other governments shared such beliefs. Yet the South Africans persisted in their claims, appealing for Western support and sympathy. Among other things they claimed that the hostility of Afro-Asian states to the Union was a direct reflection of communist influence, and argued that colonial territories were so vulnerable to communist infiltration that the greatest caution should be exercised in granting them independence.

The government's fears of communist subversion led to a break in diplomatic relations with the Soviet Union in 1956. The Russians were told to close their embassy and the South African representatives were recalled from Moscow. In a statement to the House of Assembly, Louw accused the Russians of encouraging subversion and discontent within the Union and of flouting its laws. The specific complaints ranged from contacting subversive groups to holding drinks parties for mixed racial groups.[1] A couple of months later, Louw spoke of the spread of Russian activities throughout Africa. He said that they had already infiltrated into North Africa and Ethiopia, they had made overtures to Ghana, stirred up trouble in Nigeria, and were generally extending their activities through their embassies and radio propaganda.[2] The

[1] H of A, 1 Feb. 1956, cols. 733–4. Other embassies including the British and American have been criticized from time to time by the South African Government for holding mixed parties.

[2] H of A, 26 Apr. 1956, col. 4401.

great fear was that this would spread to South Africa's non-whites. 'Communism', said Malan, 'is a double danger to South Africa. . . . Communism can be more destructive in South Africa than elsewhere not merely because of its ideology, but because of the fact that it makes a special appeal to the country's non-European population, and if the communists achieve in South Africa what they want to achieve as far as the non-European population of the country is concerned, the death knell will have been sounded for white civilization in South Africa.'[1]

South Africa's relations with the communist states were hostile and unambiguous. The communists replied to South African accusations by calling the Union the 'homeland of neo-fascism' and its government 'Nazis'.[2] Neither side expected nor received co-operation or sympathy from the other. After breaking off relations with Russia, South Africa had no direct diplomatic contact with communist states, other than at the United Nations, where the communist states were among the Union's leading critics.

White South African attitudes towards the loosely defined Afro-Asian group, which at that time consisted mainly of Asian and Arab states, were coloured by fears rooted in their own society. The new states mirrored in the international community the chronic fear of a non-white challenge to continued white supremacy inside the Union. The South African Government persistently rejected the accusation that there was an essentially colonial situation in South Africa and complained about the inexperience and immaturity of the new states. Malan once said the Afro-Asian states were like children in a household. 'What', he asked, 'would be the position in any household today if the children in that house and adults in the house were in all respects treated on an equal footing?'[3] As the South Africans saw it, the result in the international household was that the new inexperienced states, 'the children', were able to keep up a continuous campaign to encourage non-white discontent inside the Union. According to the government the message which was continuously being transmitted to the non-whites of South Africa was that they were

---

[1] H of A, 25 Jan. 1951, col. 180.
[2] Quoted by Carter, *The Politics of Inequality*, p. 401.
[3] H of A, 3 May 1954, col. 4419.

oppressed and denied their rights, that they should resist and organize themselves against continued white minority rule.[1]

When Eric Louw arrived at the Commonwealth Economic Conference in London in November 1952 he asserted that all the non-white disturbances in Africa were of one piece, and associated together Mau Mau in Kenya and recent disturbances in Northern Rhodesia. He said that the main causes of these troubles were the encouragement the Africans had received from the United Nations, from the 'liberals' of Europe and the United States, and from British socialists and misguided clerics. All these people, he said, had been influenced by communists or communist propaganda. He completed the catalogue of evil international forces by asserting that South Africa's critics in England and the United States 'are being used as tools by India in her vendetta against South Africa and for the furtherance of her aim to secure *lebensraum* in Africa for her wretched, starving millions.'[2]

It was impossible to be consistent with such simplistic arguments and on occasions the Nationalist ministers would distinguish between the international groups who opposed their racial policies. When racial policies were not uppermost in their minds the ministers could argue strongly for trying to attract Afro-Asian states into the non-communist camp. Even in India's case, Malan gave as one of his reasons for supporting her continued membership of the Commonwealth in 1949 the need to retain her friendship for the West. There were particular circumstances to explain Malan's enthusiasm for India's continued membership,[3] but nevertheless he publicly stated that in the struggle between East and West 'it is important to retain the confidence of the Indians'.[4] Later he went even further to say: 'India, like the rest of the world, is today taking her stand with the anti-Communist countries. She regards Communism in Asia or Communism which is trying to gain a foothold in India also, as a danger, just as we regard it as a danger.'[5]

As the South Africans usually saw the communists and Afro-Asian states as natural opponents, so they saw the Western states

[1] For example, see Malan's statement, H of A, 3 May 1954, col. 4493.
[2] *The Times*, 25 Nov. 1952.
[3] See ch. 7, p. 92. India's application came after the declaration of a republic.
[4] H of A, 16 Apr. 1951, col. 6893.
[5] Mansergh, *Documents . . . 1931–1952*, vol. II, p. 868.

as natural allies.[1] These states were anti-communist; many had colonial possessions; and it was from Western Europe that white South Africa drew its roots. In 1951, when there were discussions about closer co-operation between the states of Western Europe, Malan was asked whether South Africa had been invited to attend or send observers. He said that South Africa had not been invited but if an invitation were received he would take it up because 'we are a country which shares Western European civilization and we want to protect this'. He said that the interests and dangers faced by Western Europe and South Africa were identical and so they were bound to work together as close friends.[2]

The South Africans never faltered in their claim to a Western identity. In part this was recognized. The Union was deeply integrated into the Western economic system, she was a firm if somewhat peripheral ally during the cold-war days, there were ties of blood and culture accepted by some Western Europeans, and there was some sympathy and understanding among the colonial powers for South Africa's problems in governing diverse races. But South Africa was never fully integrated into the Western camp. She was at best on the fringe—geographically remote, consumed by unique racial problems, an alien and little understood country for many Western states. While in some ways she was certainly a valuable ally, especially to a country like Britain that had interests in southern Africa and the surrounding oceans, in other ways she was undeniably an embarrassing one.

Even for themselves the South African identification with the West was cautiously selective. For example, they had no sympathy with the socialist movements, nor with 'liberalism' or some of the cultural developments of Western society, especially its permissiveness and its changing attitudes towards race. 'The nations of Europe', declared Malan, 'are becoming decadent.'[3]

It was again South Africa's internal racial policies that were responsible for the embarrassment and increasing alienation from the West. The Nazis' racial theories had left behind a distaste for ideas and policies based on claims to racial superiority. The South Africans might try to persuade other Western states that their

---

[1] The South Africans would see themselves as part of the group of 'white' states made up of Western Europe, North America, and their offshoots in Australia and New Zealand. Their main interest was usually focused on a few of these states, notably the United Kingdom and the USA.

[2] H of A, 16 Apr. 1951, col. 7017.   [3] H of A, 3 Apr. 1954, col. 4496.

circumstances were very different from those in Europe, that it was wrong to judge South Africa without fully understanding her unique situation, but the judgements *were* made and they became progressively more critical. The anger and frustration this could cause was captured by Malan in 1954 when he said: 'One finds in the world today and especially in England that there is a sickly sentiment in regard to the black man. . . . They venerate a black skin.'[1]

South Africa's militant critics never allowed the Western states to forget South Africa and her racial politics. The case against South Africa was presented as a clear-cut moral issue. Each state had to stand up and be counted. Compromise was impossible, for he who was not against apartheid was for it. In 1951 the Indian delegate at the United Nations said: 'If the discriminatory policies of South Africa were permitted to flourish free from censure by the Western democracies, the Asian and African peoples could give little credence to the avowed desire of the West to unite for peace and to achieve collective security based on respect for human rights and fundamental freedoms.'[2]

Right from the beginning of the post-war period the Western powers were caught in this dilemma and it only increased with time. For them and particularly the United Kingdom there was the persistent problem of balancing an increasing sense of moral indignation at the Union's racial policies against existing tangible interests, and especially economic interests. There was an inextricable interplay of values, attitudes, and interests.

For many of South Africa's opponents the reluctance of the Western states to commit themselves to action against the Union was explained almost entirely by economic interests.[3] On their side the Western states often expressed sympathy with the 'moral grounds' on which South Africa's policies were attacked, but to their ears the attacks were often made in emotive, extreme terms, and were translated into unpractical suggestions for action. Also, the Western powers shared South Africa's legalistic approach to international affairs, with its emphasis upon the *status quo*. They stressed that the procedures, as well as the substance, of a dispute were of importance. They tried to balance their moral indignation with their desire for order, stability, and accepted modes of

---

[1] H of A, 3 Apr. 1954, col. 4496.   [2] *UN Year Book 1951*, p. 350.
[3] For an outline of attempts at international action see ch. 6.

conduct. And they carried into international affairs the characteristic of searching for compromise and consensus. While on one hand they tried to temper the attacks upon South Africa, on the other they sought to persuade South Africa to modify her policies. In a situation which was essentially polarized, the policy of the Western states gave an impression of ambivalence and uncertainty, breeding resentment and distrust both from the South Africans and their more militant opponents.

Among the Western states, South Africa's relationship with the United Kingdom remained the most important. For the Nationalists it was a confused, complex, love–hate affair in which attitudes from the past were freely mixed with judgements of the present. The traditional Nationalist suspicion and hostility towards Britain was tempered by the fact that Britain was the devil they knew, who still played an important part in South Africa's economic and cultural life. Also in the 1950s Britain was not a physically remote power. British colonies were scattered across southern Africa—in the High Commission Territories, and in the Rhodesias and Nyasaland which were formed into the Central African Federation in 1953. The British Imperial factor was still a firm reality in southern Africa.

Despite the suspicion and resentment which was shown by both sides, Britain was probably South Africa's most reliable diplomatic ally during the 1950s. The British consistently supported South Africa at the United Nations on clause 2(7), against interference in internal affairs, and usually urged moderation on the Union's militant opponents. Yet the Nationalists never threw off their past suspicions. 'South Africa', said Malan, 'has during her history come to know . . . two Englands. The one is England at her worst. The other is England at her best. South Africans this side of the house and the Afrikaner-speaking sections of our people know them both.'[1] The Nationalist government continued to measure the disadvantages of the relationship as carefully as it measured the advantages.

Diplomatic relations between the two governments remained reasonably good but were cooler and more formal than in Smuts's day. According to Heaton Nicholls, who had been the United Party's High Commissioner, the family atmosphere largely disappeared, and 'instead of the friendly standing from which the

[1] H of A, 27 Jan. 1950, col. 242.

High Commissioner could call on and talk to any minister in London without notice in the Press, such friendly visits now began to assume the appearance of visits between representatives of foreign states. . . . The pushing-at-arms-length policy has ministered to our Republican pride, but it has lost us our Commonwealth comradeship.'[1] This situation was aggravated by important policy differences which were emerging during the 1950s, especially over colonial developments.

The government was particularly resentful of the volume of public criticism of South Africa which was heard in Britain. There was an expectation that the British, with their colonial and southern African experience, would have a greater understanding of the Union's problems. When this failed to appear, the South Africans were aggrieved and resentful. To draw the contrast sharply—the South Africans never expected anything but criticism and opposition from Russia and so they accepted it without surprise, but the British knew South Africa, and were a Western colonial power. They *should* understand.

Characteristically, Eric Louw was incensed more than most. One of his outbursts was in a letter to *The Times* on 7 January 1957. The letter was written when Louw heard that Mr. Gerald Gardiner Q.C. had been sent to South Africa to witness the Treason Trial on behalf of Christian Action, the Bar Council, and *Justice* (which was said to have members from the three major British political parties). Gardiner was to report on the conduct of the trial, and to act as a watchdog of civil liberties. Louw protested against 'this calculated insult to our magistrates and judges'. He claimed that standards of justice and equity in the South African courts were as high as any in the world, 'as high as in any British court of law', and much higher than in 'some countries that pose as the guardian of civil liberties and of fundamental human rights'. Speaking of the three organizations that had sponsored Gardiner's visit, Louw wondered why the communists had not also been included. He asked 'what business is it of these bodies to concern themselves with the internal affairs of a sovereign independent state? . . . If this impudent interference in our internal affairs is sought to be justified (as has been suggested) by the fact that South Africa is a member of the Commonwealth, then the sooner we get out of the Commonwealth, the better!' He said that the attitude

[1] Nicholls, *South Africa in My Time*, p. 405.

of certain organizations, newspapers, and individuals in the United Kingdom was not based on concern for civil liberties but was a 'manifestation of the campaign of hate that has been conducted against South Africa for the past eight years by a section of the British Press, by the Communists and Socialists, and also by individuals like Canon Collins, Father Huddleston and the Rev. Michael Scott'. This criticism, he said, came despite the fact that South Africa was Britain's second-best customer and despite the great help that South Africa had given to Britain which had been publicly acknowledged by 'Mr. R. A. Butler, the present Chancellor, and Mr. Hugh Gaitskell, the Labour Party Leader'.[1]

Louw's letter did not represent a considered South African view for it was obviously written in a rage and caused the South African Government some embarrassment,[2] but it shows one streak that was always there for the National Party ministers in their complex relationship with Britain.

Another regular irritation for the Nationalist government was the attitude of the Labour Party in opposition.[3] Even in office several members of the Labour government had been openly critical of South Africa's racial policies. In opposition, this criticism became sharper and louder. At the 1956 Party Conference a proposal was put that the next Labour government should expel South Africa from the Commonwealth. Although the motion was rejected the reasons for rejection given by James Griffiths, the Shadow Minister, were no consolation for the South Africans. After speaking against apartheid, he argued that the best way to bring about change was to retain contact. 'Let us', he said, 'mobilize moral opinion behind us within the Commonwealth and the United Nations. Let us give all our support to those in South Africa who keep on fighting this policy.'[4] The South African Government, strongly resentful of the criticism, questioned whether it would be possible to co-operate with any future Labour government.

In their search for a Western friendship the South Africans recognized the importance of the United States. Yet, as in Britain's case, the United States raised confused and conflicting attitudes.

[1] *The Times*, 7 Jan. 1957.
[2] See the attack made by Mr. Sydney Waterson of the United Party in H of A, 4 Feb. 1957, cols. 566–7.
[3] The Conservatives were returned in 1951 and stayed in office until 1964.
[4] *The Times*, 5 Oct. 1956.

As one of the super powers, and as the leader of the Western world and its economic system, America was of obvious importance to South Africa. But while the South Africans respected the United States' strength and economic power, and hoped for co-operation against communism, relations were never smooth. The United States remained a somewhat remote and unknown quantity. Also, while both states faced the problems of racially mixed populations, their differences of circumstances and approach to these problems tended to drive them apart rather than bring them together. For internal as well as international political considerations no government in the United States could afford to be seen as a close friend of South Africa. Allied to this was the traditional American suspicion of Western European colonialism, which became associated during the 1950s and on into the 1960s with the drive to win the allegiance of the new non-committed states.

The ambivalent South African attitude towards the United States is captured in a speech by Louw in 1957. He started by criticizing those who were exerting pressure on the colonial powers to withdraw, and although he did not mention the United States, it was obvious where the criticism was directed. Then he turned specifically to American interests in Africa. He welcomed American attempts to counter communism, including the Eisenhower Plan for the Middle East. He also welcomed American economic activity in Africa, which, he said, was prompted by the search for a mass market and for raw materials. However, an activity he did not welcome was the writing of critical reports by visiting Americans. He cited a report by Senator Green, who, after a fleeting visit to the Union, had written a critical report saying that the United States would have to choose between continued friendship with South Africa and upholding human rights, dignity, and freedom. Despite such criticism, Louw finished by asserting that, in general, relations with the United States were good and that South Africa would continue to encourage the friendship.[1]

He was still claiming good relations in 1959 after an important adverse American vote in the United Nations. Louw argued unconvincingly that the vote did not represent a change of American policy. He tried to explain it away by referring to the internal and external pressures on the American Government, by mentioning the moderating influence the United States had had on the

[1] H of A, 10 June 1957, col. 7632.

wording of the resolution, and by noting the unfortunate chance that the leader of the United States delegation happened to be a prominent labour leader well known for his dislike of South Africa.[1] The implication of Louw's statement was that whatever the public face of its policy the United States, as a leading Western state, would not pursue policies antagonistic to the Union. Yet the frustrations as well as the hopes of gaining support were never far from the surface. Speaking of the Western states in 1957 Louw said that they could not continue to push South Africans 'around today as they have been doing in the last eleven years and tomorrow expect us to support them on some issue'.[2]

It was economic contacts which provided the strongest base for relations with the Western states. The foundation of South Africa's economic growth has been her immense mineral wealth. The mining industry, 'truly a colossus' in the South African economy,[3] continued to flourish throughout the 1950s and 1960s. South Africa has mineral wealth out of all proportion to her size and is the world's main exporter of mineral products. She has the world's largest deposits of gold, chromium, platinum group metals, manganese, vanadium, asbestos, and vermiculite; Africa's largest deposits of iron, coal, and uranium; as well as being rich in diamonds and copper.[4] This mineral wealth has helped to overcome a serious trade imbalance in other commodities, and has been of central importance in foreign relations, as many countries are dependent on South Africa for vital minerals.

While throughout the post-war years gold continued to be the single most important mineral, other minerals increased in importance. In 1945 gold accounted for 82 per cent of the value of all metals. Twenty years later it had fallen to 62 per cent. Among the developments in the industry was the mining of prescribed atomic minerals. By 1960 they were worth R98.5 million,[5] and added to South Africa's strategic importance as well as her wealth. While minerals continued to be a major factor in South Africa's economic growth, manufacturing industries, which had received a stimulus in the war, continued to expand rapidly during the

---

[1] H of A, 11 May 1959, col. 5520.   [2] H of A, 10 June 1957, col. 7600.
[3] Houghton, *The South African Economy*, p. 97.
[4] A. A. von Maltitz, 'South African Minerals and their Importance to World Industry', *South Africa International*, vol. 1, no. 4, April 1971.
[5] Houghton, op. cit., p. 252.

VALUE OF MINING OUTPUT 1945–1969[1]
(IN MILLION RAND)

Year	Gold	Other	Total
1945	211	44	255
1950	290	104	394
1955	365	217	582
1960	536	321	857
1965	767	386	1153
1969	779	708	1487

post-war years. The Nationalist victory in 1948 did not change the situation. 'On the contrary,' wrote Horwitz, 'the year 1948 was, if anything, an even more critical date in the history of forced industrialization. Not only was "Made in South Africa" identified in the Nationalist Party credo as sound nationalism but the balance of payments crisis attendant on its accession to power gave it a new imperative.'[2]

VALUE OF GROSS INDUSTRIAL OUTPUT[3]
(IN MILLION RAND)

Year	1944/5	1954/5	1962/3
Value of output	608	2,154	3,518

As well as the increase in the value of industrial output, manufacturing began to play a relatively more important role in the overall economic performance as indicated in the next table:

RELATIVE CONTRIBUTION OF MAJOR SECTORS
TO NATIONAL INCOME[4]
(SHOWN AS PERCENTAGES)

Year	Agriculture	Mining	Private Manufacturing	Commerce
1945	12	14	19	14
1950	13	14	22	15
1955	14	12	25	13
1959	12	13	25	12

[1] Based on Houghton, op. cit., p. 251.

[2] Horwitz, *The Political Economy of South Africa*, p. 283.

[3] Houghton, op. cit., p. 120.

[4] *Union Statistics for 50 years 1910–1960* (Pretoria, Bureau of Census and Statistics, 1960).

IMPORTS INTO SOUTH AFRICA 1946–1959
(IN MILLION RAND)[1]

	1946	1947	1948	1949	1950	1951	1952	1953	1954	1955	1956	1957	1958	1959
1. Total	430·2	600·7	707·0	630·2	613·7	938·3	836·3	850·9	887·2	962·0	989·8	1099·6	1110·9	977·3
2. Africa	32·4	34·3	36·6	41·9	60·8	79·2	80·4	78·2	92·2	73·3	80·9	75·4	75·3	69·6
3. United Kingdom	148·3	187·7	236·3	262·8	252·7	330·6	288·2	318·3	305·2	333·2	313·0	358·4	374·9	303·2
4. European Economic Community[2]	16·9	35·2	37·0	30·0	46·9	116·7	94·4	112·8	110·5	126·4	142·0	177·0	201·7	178·6
5. United States of America	113·6	210·4	245·4	162·6	98·1	182·3	175·2	156·9	175·1	200·9	198·4	215·1	194·7	167·1

[1] Taken from *Union Statistics for 50 years 1910–1960*.
[2] The European Economic Community did not come into existence until 1957 but it is a useful way of grouping together an important market for South Africa.

EXPORTS FROM SOUTH AFRICA 1946–1959
(IN MILLION RAND) EXCLUDING GOLD[1]

	1946	1947	1948	1949	1950	1951	1952	1953	1954	1955	1956	1957	1958	1959
1. Total	179·9	184·8	242·0	279·5	457·6	626·7	579·4	599·0	560·9	663·2	740·1	803·4	715·2	789·0
2. Africa	40·1	46·1	60·0	71·9	93·4	127·4	119·6	130·8	144·4	129·9	144·6	155·6	135·6	147·9
3. United Kingdom	35·4	54·8	66·4	70·8	120·0	152·1	144·7	156·0	160·8	204·7	216·9	220·2	213·2	219·4
4. European Economic Community	39·0	34·2	54·3	67·8	129·6	183·5	195·0	187·7	122·0	140·8	162·7	164·6	122·4	130·6
5. United States of America	34·5	21·1	17·4	20·9	39·7	67·0	38·7	37·9	41·7	53·3	57·6	50·6	51·0	70·3

[1] Taken from *Union Statistics for 50 years 1910–1960.*

The development of manufacturing industries extended existing international contacts, and in other cases created a new pattern of relationships as South African industries sought new markets, resources, and machinery. This economic expansion was of major importance in South Africa's international relations over the post-war years. The economy had its problems, especially in balance of payments and inflationary crises, but Houghton saw these as 'the direct consequence of the rapid expansion'.[1] With the Gross National Product increasing at an average of more than 5 per cent per annum, South Africa's contacts with other states were strengthened, so that the economic interests of these states were increasingly served by a stable and prosperous South Africa.

This economic expansion could not mask major socio-economic defects within the society. Economic development was uneven, with large tracts of subsistence farming and general under-development among non-whites coexisting with prosperous and expanding sections of the white economy, especially in the urban industrial complexes of the Witwatersrand, Durban, and the Cape. The distribution of wealth and income was equally uneven, with a great gap separating the whites from the other racial groups, and in terms of economic growth *per capita* South Africa's performance was not particularly impressive. With her expanding population, the figure of 5 per cent annual growth was converted into 2 per cent *per capita* growth. These socio-economic issues captured considerable international attention, but they always had to be balanced against South Africa's success in strengthening and expanding her economic contacts. South Africa had moved on to a different economic plane from all other African countries to join the world's major trading states.

The figures for foreign investment and foreign trade reveal both South Africa's strong international contacts and her reliance on the West. The years between 1947 and 1954 were especially successful in attracting external capital investment with an annual inflow of R176 million. The year 1947 was outstanding, bringing in R357 million, much of it to finance new goldfields in the Orange Free State. The inflow fell in the following four years and between 1957 and 1959 there was a small capital outflow.[2]

---

[1] Houghton, 'Economic Development 1865–1965', in *Oxford History of South Africa*, vol. II, p. 38.

[2] Houghton, *The South African Economy*, p. 175.

Within South Africa the government was criticized by the United Party for pursuing policies which stifled economic growth. It was asserted that the National Party had never understood the needs of the mining and manufacturing industries, and this was apparent in the restrictive white immigration policy and the limitations imposed on non-white labour by apartheid. The critics claimed that it was despite the government's policies that South Africa enjoyed continued economic expansion. Such criticisms are difficult to evaluate because of the complex issues and questions that are involved—such questions as: How far can a government consciously shape economic development? In what sense is a government obliged to follow certain policies because of economic circumstances? The Nationalist government, like all other governments, sought to achieve both economic and political objectives. It had to pursue its political aims within a framework of economic constraints, but the United Party had a point in that as far as it was able the Nationalist government gave precedence to its political objectives. Its first priority was not to create conditions for profit maximization. The economic history of South Africa 'is more than an account of state interference into private enterprise. It is a record of the interaction of a political economy in which the political factor, Afrikanerdom in and out of Government, has always had an ultimate—a way of life to preserve and to promote. . . . The network of economic development had to follow accordingly.'[1] In conflict situations the political objective took precedence, but usually the government attempted to channel economic development to support its apartheid policies, so that economy and polity worked hand in hand.

In external relations economic contacts were very advantageous to South Africa. For all their criticisms and diplomatic coolness, many Western states had such strong economic links with the Union that they had an inbuilt stake in retaining a strong, stable, and ordered South Africa. A situation which became increasingly plain during the 1960s already firmly existed during the 1950s. South Africa had to endure increasing diplomatic isolation, but her position within the Western economic framework was never seriously challenged. Undoubtedly the South Africans bitterly resented the diplomatic and verbal hostility directed at them. They hoped to generate love as well as profit, but the profit was a great consolation.

[1] Horwitz, *The Political Economy of South Africa*, p. 12.

6

APARTHEID UNDER ATTACK AT THE UNITED NATIONS

While Smuts had been torn between his initial enthusiasm for the United Nations and the hostility he had met there, the Nationalists faced no such dilemma. Their narrower, 'South Africa first', approach made them suspicious and wary of international organizations in general and the United Nations in particular. Also they had the advantage of a post-war period in opposition, when they were able to take stock of the international situation without immediately being involved in it. They came to office prepared for international hostility. This hostility was not as strong as it became in the 1960s but it grew steadily over the period. The implementation of apartheid was widely interpreted as a rejection of the principles upon which a multiracial international community was to be built. At the United Nations there were persistent and bitter accusations and counter-accusations, with a stream of votes and speeches critical of South Africa's policies, and complex wrangles over legal points. In 1952 the pretence was dropped that the attacks were concerned only with specific issues such as South West Africa and the treatment of Indians. The whole structure of the Union's racial policy came under open attack. Apartheid was placed on the General Assembly's agenda at the request of fourteen Arab and Asian states who declared that 'the race conflict in the Union of South Africa, resulting from the policy of apartheid, is creating a dangerous and explosive situation which contributes both a threat to international peace and a flagrant violation of basic principles of human rights and fundamental freedoms which are enshrined in the Charter of the United Nations'.[1]

Like Smuts, the Nationalist government attempted to counter the attacks by emphasizing South Africa's rights under Article 2(7) of the Charter. Her strongest critics continued to contest this, at

[1] IRR 1951–2, p. 10.

first by claiming that the dispute over the treatment of Indians threatened good relations between two United Nations members and therefore was a matter of international concern, and later, as the attacks were extended to include apartheid, that racial discrimination was not confined by state boundaries, that it involved all men and was a threat to world peace.

From the beginning the Nationalist government was strongly critical of the United Nations. Two examples from the hundreds of complaints they made will illustrate the point. In October 1953, at the Annual Conference of the National Party of the Orange Free State, a setting in which he would have felt no inhibitions, Malan said that the United Nations was 'a failure, a cancer eating at the peace and tranquillity of the world, and unless radically reformed, it should disappear from the face of the earth'.[1] Four years later, in the less heady atmosphere of the House of Assembly, Louw said the United Nations was 'in decline' and 'at the crossroads'. He attacked it yet again for interfering in South Africa's domestic affairs and for breaking its own Charter, and thought that the organization might soon destroy itself.[2]

The Nationalist ministers frequently called for reform of the organization, but their unspecific hopes never seemed likely to succeed. What appeared more likely was that South Africa would decide to withdraw her membership. The Nationalist government seriously and frequently considered this step. In the first months of office Louw told the General Assembly: 'There is a growing volume of opinion in South Africa that if the United Nations continues on the road it has followed during the past two years, the question will later have to be faced whether consideration of our own national interests is compatible with continued membership.'[3]

Threats of withdrawal continued over the years, and in 1955 were carried out in the case of a United Nations agency, the United Nations Educational, Scientific and Cultural Organization (UNESCO). In explaining the decision, Louw described UNESCO as a 'futile' organization, staffed by woolly-headed academics, which instead of concentrating on its real tasks had become a sounding board for anti-South African agitation.[4] The possibility of leaving the parent organization also continued to be

---

[1] *The Times*, 22 Oct. 1953.
[3] *The Times*, 25 Sept. 1948.
[2] H of A, 10 June 1957, col. 7604.
[4] H of A, 5 May 1955.

discussed. In April 1956 Louw said that South Africa would not withdraw unless the position was made 'impossible for us'. But he added that the position could become intolerable in terms of national pride and prestige if, as in the past ten years, the United Nations continued 'to regard the Union practically as a criminal and to treat the Union delegate practically as an accused person in the dock, as someone to be attacked'.[1]

A few months later the South African Government came as near as it ever has to withdrawal. It was on the recurring issue of the inclusion in the General Assembly's agenda of items which were unacceptable to South Africa. The South African Government announced that it would withdraw from active participation in United Nations affairs. Louw told Parliament that South Africa would remain a member but until Article 2(7) of the Charter was respected she would retain only token representation. South Africa would not participate in Assembly debates and would only vote when Article 2(7) was at issue, or in other exceptional circumstances.[2] Later Louw said that this situation could not continue indefinitely and the government would have to consider whether to retain any form of membership.[3]

The United Party urged the government to stay and fight its case, and this was the conclusion which the government finally reached for itself in 1958. Louw explained this by saying that 'in view of the more reasonable and conciliatory attitude towards South Africa shown by a fairly large number of delegations, the Cabinet has agreed that the policy of "token representation" has achieved its purpose, and that in the circumstances the Union could now return to full participation in the work of the United Nations.'[4] He stated that South Africa would in fact play a more active part in future United Nations discussions, although it would never compromise on the issue of Article 2(7). Louw announced that he would himself attend the opening of the next session of the General Assembly and that a permanent representative with the rank of Minister Plenipotentiary would be appointed.

The contrasting decisions of 1956 and 1958 plainly reflect the delicate balance for the South African Government between withdrawal, which might have avoided some humiliation and the constant hostility and criticism, and retaining membership, which

---

[1] H of A, 26 Apr. 1956, col. 4437.　　[2] H of A, 10 June 1957, col. 7598.
[3] IRR 1956–7, p. 234.　　[4] H of A, 15 July 1958, col. 351.

gave them an opportunity to fight back against the critics and retain some useful international links. Louw's claim that there was a 'more reasonable and conciliatory attitude' in 1958 is very questionable for the South Africans were soon under the old pressures and attacks. Perhaps they returned hoping that their dramatic gesture had had a sobering effect on the critics, but the initial defiant gesture may also have come from a desire to impress the white electorate at home with the government's toughness and determination. The gesture having been made, the government could explain to the South African audience that firmness had paid its way, that South Africa had shown that it would not be bullied.

Occasionally the South Africans had moments of optimism at the United Nations—for example in 1958 when they decided to resume full representation, and in 1959 when Eric Louw was elected Vice-President of the General Assembly as the Commonwealth candidate.[1] But more usually they came to expect little but hostility from most of the members, and faint embarrassed smiles from the rest. The South Africans were always having to defend a position. They were never able to relax, and certainly never able to seize diplomatic initiatives.

Opposition to South Africa at the United Nations divided itself very broadly into two main streams. One consisted of 'the militants'—the Afro-Asian and the communist states. They shared a 'revisionist' view of international politics, and in South Africa's case not only criticized but called for direct international action to change her racial policies. Although they buttressed their claims with legal arguments, their chief emphasis was on questions of principle, of human rights and dignity, and the dangers that South Africa's policies created for the whole international community.

The other main stream, 'the moderates', largely comprised the Western states and their associates, who adopted a more cautious legalistic approach. They were inclined to support a *status quo* position in international relations. Some of these states were colonial powers, and some had strong ties with South Africa. They were critical, but searched for compromises and put their trust in bringing change by diplomatic pressure and discussion.

[1] John Barratt, *South Africa and the United Nations* (Johannesburg, South African Institute of International Affairs, Newsletter No. 1, Feb. 1969).

While the Nationalist government could put up a blank refusal to discuss South Africa's internal racial policies, and base this refusal on a clause in the Charter, the circumstances surrounding South West Africa were more complex and difficult to handle. There continued to be legal uncertainty about the exact status of the territory and the responsibilities inherited from the old mandate. This was an important constraint on the South African Government because of its legalistic approach to international affairs. This approach may partly be explained by South Africa's internal political evolution, in which constitutional-cum-legal questions about relations between the various provinces, between the provinces and the central government, and between the central government and the United Kingdom, have played a prominent part.[1] But in international relations more than a traditional, legal style has been involved. As in Smuts's time, recourse to legal argument was the natural reaction of a state forced on to the defensive. Yet in the case of South West Africa the legal position has constantly been in dispute.

The debate about South West Africa continued throughout the 1950s. The militant critics argued that South Africa could claim no rights to the territory because of her refusal to accept United Nations rulings, and because the racial policies she had extended to South West Africa contravened the Charter's Declaration of Rights. There were frequent calls for removal of South Africa's administration from the territory.

Naturally the South Africans were more prepared to work with the moderates, who, when there was sharp conflict, favoured setting up an investigating committee or making reference to the International Court of Justice. On occasions the South Africans themselves made compromise proposals. The most important of these came in 1950, following an advisory decision on South West Africa by the International Court of Justice. The South Africans had emphasized from the beginning that they would not feel bound by the judgement. The Court unanimously found that the mandate was a treaty still in force and that attempts to modify the status of the territory by South Africa must have the consent of the

---

[1] For the issues involved in the formation of the Union see Thompson, *The Unification of South Africa 1902–1910*. The suggestion that a legalistic style in internal politics has been carried over to international affairs was suggested by a senior South African official.

United Nations. By majority votes the Court advised that the General Assembly had supervisory functions over the mandate, but that the supervision should be limited to that applied under the mandate system. Finally, by eight votes to six, the Court found that there was no obligation on the Union to place the territory under the trusteeship system. These findings met little enthusiasm from the South African Government. While the government was relieved that the Court had advised, albeit by a narrow majority, that it was under no obligation to conclude a trusteeship agreement, it disliked the other findings and in particular the finding that the United Nations had a supervisory role.

The South African Government re-emphasized that the Union was under no obligation to comply with the findings, and that while the government would continue to search for a mutually agreeable solution, it refused to recognize a United Nations right of supervision. As an alternative it proposed a resumption of international obligations under the League of Nations mandate by negotiating a new agreement with the three remaining Principal Allied and Associated Powers from the First World War settlement—Britain, America, and France. Under these proposals, the South Africans, although not admitting that the United Nations inherited the League's powers, suggested that the agreement should be confirmed by the United Nations and supervised by the International Court of Justice. This was a clear admission that South Africa could not act unilaterally, but the precise form of the proposed supervision was vague, with no right of the three powers to receive reports. The proposal came to nothing as an Ad Hoc Committee of the United Nations, established to report on the territory, found it unacceptable because it did not implement the Court's advice.

The attempt to reach a compromise was renewed in 1957 and 1958 with the appointment of a Good Offices Committee of the United Nations, which was to find 'a basis for an agreement which would continue to accord to the territory of South West Africa an international significance'.[1] The Committee, in its membership (Britain, America, and Brazil) and its terms of reference, with no mention of United Nations supervision, was very much the creature of 'the moderates'. For some time it seemed that progress

---

[1] Quoted by Imishue, *South West Africa*, p. 51.

might be made on a novel proposal by the Committee. This was to consider the possibility of dividing South West Africa between the north, where the bulk of the African population lives, and the south, where there is a much greater mixture of races. The detailed terms of administration would have to be negotiated, but a much stronger 'international' role would be exercised in the north. The Committee had only recommended that consideration should be given to the proposal, but even this tentative step found no support at the United Nations. Equally, there was no response in South Africa to renewed pleas to accept United Nations supervision for the whole territory.

While these attempts at compromise were made, and while there may have been some genuine desire on each side to reach agreement, there was never a strong chance of success. Although the United Nations resolutions were usually compromises between moderate and militant views, they were never acceptable to the South Africans. Nor were South African proposals acceptable to 'the militants' who were active on bodies like the Committee on South West Africa, which was created in 1954 and submitted its annual reports despite opposition and refusal to co-operate by the South African Government.

If the South Africans could complain that there were few signs of acceptable compromises coming from the United Nations, their critics could equally complain about South African attitudes. The South Africans did not take the final formal step of declaring South West Africa an integral part of South Africa, but otherwise they drew few distinctions. The government worked on the belief— a belief shared by the great majority of whites—that it had every right to regard South West Africa as an integral part of the Union without responsibility to the United Nations or anybody else. In 1948 Malan said the government was preparing steps, including legislation, 'from which it will be clearer than ever before that we regard South West Africa as an integral part of the Union'. As a result of this closer association 'there will be practically no difference between what is usually described as formal incorporation and the position that will be created'.[1] For his part Louw said that the Nationalist government was resolved to keep control of South West Africa in the hands of 'representatives of European

---

[1] H of A, 31 Aug. 1948, col. 1288.

culture' lest it fall into the hands of a 'black proletariat with strong communist backing'.[1]

The legislative steps were taken as Malan had promised. In 1949 the South West Africa Amendment Act gave the whites of the territory their first direct representation in the central legislative bodies of the Union, with six members in the House of Assembly and two in the Senate.[2] In 1954, under the South West Africa Native Affairs Administration Act, native affairs were transferred from the Administrator in the territory to the Union Minister of Native Affairs, and all Native Reserves in South West Africa were placed under the South African Native Trust. Like the Union itself, South West Africa was to remain white-dominated. 'We will never', said Malan, 'throw the whites of South West Africa "to the wolves".'[3]

Following the anti-apartheid resolution of 1952, the Union faced a stream of resolutions and votes against general racial policies. They came up every session and usually involved considerable debate and activity inside the United Nations to reach a form of agreement between the militants and the moderates. There was a common stamp about them so that one example captures their overall spirit and intention. At the end of January 1957 the General Assembly resolved by 56 votes to 5, with 12 abstentions, to deplore South Africa's failure to observe her obligations under the Charter, and her extension of discriminatory measures which would make future observance of these obligations even more difficult. In the light of the Charter the Assembly called on South Africa to reconsider her apartheid policies and to co-operate in a constructive approach to the question.[4]

In such resolutions the South African Government was repeatedly 'condemned' and its policies 'deplored'. It was 'urged' and 'called upon' to take action, but no resolution calling for direct United Nations action ever gained sufficient support to be effective. The moderates were opposed to it. Also South Africa's geographical remoteness from the main East–West conflict areas meant that she was not naturally drawn into the arena of Great

[1] Walker, *History of South Africa*, p. 790.
[2] Non-whites were not given the franchise.
[3] Quoted by Carter, *The Politics of Inequality*, p. 386.
[4] IRR 1956–7, p. 235.

Power confrontation. It required a clear international initiative to take direct action against the Union. In the event those who could have taken the initiative were not prepared to do so.

What then did the criticism mean in terms of threats or pressure which might make the South African Government change its policies? In specific terms the answer appears to be very little. Other than the blanket fear of communism, which the South Africans assumed could only be met by major Western alliances, there was no direct military danger perceived by the South Africans. And while there were calls for sanctions and boycotts during the 1950s, international economic co-operation with the Union continued to flourish. This need not imply that South African resentment and indignation at United Nations resolutions was a sham. No government enjoys being bitterly criticized. Also they resented and feared isolation from the Western states whom they regarded as their natural allies. The South Africans wanted 'to belong', to have friends and allies in case of future needs and dangers. Certainly they could see that friends were becoming more difficult to find. But there is little evidence to suggest that the pressure did anything to divert the South African Government from its apartheid policies. It may have made the government more cautious in its application of certain aspects of the policy, but by the end of the 1950s the South Africans had already given a remarkable demonstration of determination and inflexibility in the face of sustained international pressure. They had shown that they were not prepared to change their policies because of international hostility which was not backed by direct action.

THE SEARCH FOR ALLIANCES

During the 1950s the Nationalist government was often accused by its critics inside and outside the Union of pursuing isolationist policies. This accusation requires considerable qualification. If isolationism implies a refusal to change internal policies in response to criticism and thereby forgo international support and co-operation, then the South African Government was isolationist. But it was not isolationist in the sense that it purposefully withdrew South Africa into itself and attempted to cut off or restrict contacts with other states. During the 1950s the South African Government searched for agreements with the Western states, especially those directly involved in Africa. The situation, therefore, contained a direct contradiction. The South Africans wanted international co-operation, but were not prepared to abandon the internal policies which frustrated the prospects of this co-operation.

Like others, the South Africans were eager to have a sense of identity in the international community. This partly explains the government's repeated emphasis upon its place among the Western states, but added to this was another objective—the search for security. A central objective of the South African Government during the 1950s was to gain membership of a Western defence alliance. The search for alliances was conditioned first by the South Africans' view of a world divided between communists and anti-communists, second by their particular interests in the African continent, and third by their continued membership of the Commonwealth.

Communism was seen as the major military threat. Within the borders of the Union the fear was of communist subversion and the promotion of internal disorders among the non-whites. Elsewhere—in Europe, in the Middle East, and in Asia—the

South Africans saw communism as an expanding military danger, as yet far from South Africa's own borders but constantly on the move threatening new areas. To help counter this threat the National Party government was forced to reassess its traditional view of South Africa's defence strategy. Previously the party's distaste of ties with Britain had led it to argue against defence alliances and against committing South African forces outside the borders of the Union. When it came to power these old inhibitions were suppressed. Small but symbolic forces were sent on anti-communist missions, to Korea and to help with the Berlin airlift.[1]

The South African Government's main military ambitions were in Africa. 'South Africa's aim', said Malan in 1951, 'is to take responsibility, in so far as agreement can be reached with other countries, for territories to the north of South Africa. We want to help in the protection of our neighbours.'[2] Yet while the South Africans wanted to play a military role in the continent, they saw South Africa as a 'small power' and assumed that the main burden of defending Africa and the surrounding oceans must fall on the leading Western states. Elsewhere in this cold-war period the Western states organized alliances to counter communist expansion, and the South Africans wanted a similar alliance covering Africa. They would especially have liked the North Atlantic Treaty Organization (NATO) to extend its cover into the South Atlantic. In 1952 Malan, writing for a French newspaper, stated that while NATO was confined to the area north of the Tropic of Cancer, any future war could not be confined by such geographical limits. He also emphasized that as many of the Treaty's signatories had territories in Africa they had direct interests in the defence of the continent.[3]

Similarly the South Africans welcomed other Western defence agreements such as the South East Asia Treaty Organization (SEATO) and the agreement between Australia, New Zealand, and the United States (ANZUS). The government ministers spoke wistfully of the possibility of extending these alliances to cover

---

[1] South Africa sent sixty airmen to help with the Berlin airlift, and in the Korean War a squadron of South African Mustangs and Sabres flew with the United Nations force. (*South African Panorama*, vol. 15, no. 5, May 1970, p. 8—published by South African Department of Information.)

[2] H of A, 16 May 1951, col. 7021.   [3] *La Revue Française*, Nov. 1952.

southern Africa and sometimes referred to the Union as 'an auxiliary of the NATO alliance'.[1]

Based on the assumption that it was primarily geographical remoteness that preluded South Africa from existing arrangements, the government set out to help create new alliances which would cover the African continent and the southern oceans. The concern with African defence extended to the Middle East, 'the gateway to Africa'. In the early 1950s when Britain was trying to form the Middle East Defence Organization (MEDO), South Africa agreed to join and bought additional tanks and aircraft specifically to make her contribution to the alliance. A government statement said that 'in accordance with its declared policy of assisting in the defence of the Middle East and the African continent against Communist aggression, the Government has undertaken in time of war to send ground and air forces to the Middle East. . . . In pursuance of this undertaking, the Union has accepted membership of the Middle East Command.'[2] This enthusiasm for a Middle East alliance was not matched by other Commonwealth countries so MEDO was abandoned, leaving South Africa with no direct role in the Middle East.[3] From the British point of view part of the task envisaged for the alliance was covered when the southern flank of NATO was extended to cover Greece and Turkey, but this was no consolation for the South Africans.[4]

The failure in the Middle East did not deter the South Africans from continuing their search for a broader African alliance. Together with the British Government they took the initiative in sponsoring a defence conference at Nairobi in 1951. This was

[1] See G. R. Lawrie, 'The Simonstown Agreement: South Africa, Britain and the Commonwealth', *South African Law Journal*, vol. LXXXV, part 2, May 1968, pp. 157–77. Lawrie optimistically assumed that close ties with NATO were still possible in 1968. He wrote: 'South Africa's relations with the West in general are now the important factor in her role and it should be recognized that this factor today requires ties with all the NATO powers and not a special tie with Britain alone.'

[2] Quoted by Lawrie, op. cit., p. 161.

[3] See M. A. Fitzsimons, *The Foreign Policy of the British Labour Government 1945–51* (Indiana, University of Notre Dame Press, 1953), p. 165. See also J. E. Spence, *The Strategic Significance of Southern Africa* (London, Royal United Service Institution, Whitehall, 1970), p. 11.

[4] CENTO, the Middle East alliance in which Britain became involved, originated as the Baghdad Pact—a bilateral treaty between Turkey and Iraq to which Britain, Pakistan, and Iran subsequently adhered. I have found no reference to possible South African membership.

attended by the colonial powers with interests in East and Central Africa (Britain, France, Portugal, Belgium, and Italy), by South Africa and Southern Rhodesia, and the United States Government sent observers. The British Government announced that the conference would discuss ways and means of facilitating communications and the movement of military forces in East and Central Africa. It was not, said Lord Ogmore, the chief British representative, to concern itself with planning, but was to ensure a flow of men, machines, and equipment in the event of a conflict. In particular, the conference would discuss the movement of troops and supplies from southern Africa to the north and east, ensuring that territorial boundaries did not hamper movements.[1] Mr. Sauer, the South African representative, interpreted this as a consideration of 'what facilities they can give on a mutual basis to help one another in the unfortunate event of a war to check communist aggression'.[2]

The eagerness of the South Africans to see progress was demonstrated by their friendship and co-operation. They modestly declined the offer of co-chairmanship, and Sauer stated: 'We shall seek no facilities in the territory of another that we are not prepared to grant to that other in our own country in return. Let us take the big view throughout.'[3] Within the terms of this 'big view' the South Africans saw the Nairobi Conference not as an end in itself but as the seed from which an important alliance could grow. But Ogmore warned that the conference was limited, first because it did not aim at strategic planning, and second because it could make recommendations but not decisions. At the end of the conference, the Portuguese delegate reminded members that his country had made no commitments and had undertaken no obligations.

During the Nairobi Conference the French delegate suggested that its scope should be extended to cover the whole of Africa, but Ogmore replied that if West Africa were also to be covered further preparations would be required, and perhaps invitations sent to additional countries. He suggested that a separate conference should be organized. This was done, although not with the urgency that the South Africans had hoped. The second conference—attended by France, Britain, Belgium, Portugal, and South Africa—assembled at Dakar in 1954. Its results, except that

[1] *The Times*, 21 Aug. 1951.   [2] ibid., 23 Aug. 1951.   [3] ibid.

it was concerned with the west rather than the east, were very similar to those of the Nairobi Conference.

After the two conferences Erasmus, the Minister of Defence, claimed that South Africa had undertaken substantial commitments in the event of communist aggression in Africa and had become closely associated with other governments in African defence.[1] But if the South Africans thought they were 'committed' the other governments did not. No African alliance emerged. Even then the South Africans did not lose heart, and it is partly in terms of this search for alliances that the Simonstown Agreement should be seen.[2]

The Simonstown Agreement consists of an exchange of correspondence and memoranda between Selwyn Lloyd on behalf of the British Government and Erasmus on behalf of South Africa. One memorandum which was concerned with 'The need for international discussions with regard to regional defence' reflected most closely South Africa's aims at Nairobi and Dakar. The memorandum states that 'South Africa and the sea routes round Southern Africa must be secured against aggression from without', while the internal security of the territories was a matter for individual countries. 'The defence of Southern Africa against external aggression lies not only in Africa but also in the gateways to Africa, namely the Middle East.' The United Kingdom would therefore contribute forces for the defence of Africa, including southern Africa and the Middle East, and South Africa would 'contribute forces in order to keep the potential enemy as far as possible from the borders of South Africa, in other words for the defence of Southern Africa, Africa and the Middle East gateways to Africa'.

The two governments resolved to sponsor a conference to forward 'the planning already begun at the Nairobi Conference' and to 'endeavour, at this conference, to secure the setting up of suitable machinery to pursue the aims of the conference on a continuing basis'.[3] Even though this held out hopes for an alliance, the British did not feel that they were committed to one.

[1] *The Times*, 9 Apr. 1954.
[2] Cmd. 9520 (London, HMSO, 1955). Also see Lawrie, op cit., and C. J. R. Dugard's article, 'The Simonstown Agreements: South Africa, Britain and the United Nations' in the same number of *South African Law Journal*, May 1968, pp. 142–56. I have drawn heavily on the articles for this section.
[3] Quoted by Lawrie, op. cit., pp. 161–2.

When they came to register the correspondence as a Treaty at the United Nations they attached a reservation to Part 1 stating that it 'does not contain any substantive obligations, but is registered in order to facilitate understanding of the other two Agreements'.

At their most optimistic the South Africans hoped that two types of alliance might develop from the Simonstown Agreement. One would be an African alliance, similar to the one they had tried to nurture at the two conferences. The other would be primarily a maritime alliance based on the oceans and coastlines around the Cape. In April 1956 Strijdom said that Britain and South Africa hoped that other Western powers interested in Africa and in the coastline of southern Africa would become parties to the Agreement. He specifically mentioned France, Portugal, and the United States.[1] In the following year, after a meeting between Erasmus and Lord Mancroft, the British Minister Without Portfolio, the aim of promoting a conference was reasserted.[2] Nothing came of it.

The South Africans continued to hope and take comfort where they could. In July 1958 Erasmus declared that the stationing of a British strategic reserve in Kenya and the building by the Belgians of a large new military base at Kamina in the Congo created major bulwarks against the advance of communism south through Africa. He also announced that a conference of naval officers had been held at Cape Town, attended by Britain, France, Belgium, Portugal, and South Africa,[3] but this was certainly not the major conference envisaged in the Simonstown Agreement. By 1959 Erasmus finally gave up in despair. He spoke of 'the tragedy' of the Western powers having no plans for the defence of South Africa, with its vital strategic importance, its mineral wealth, and its control of the sea routes around the Cape—the 'Gibraltar of Southern Africa'.[4] He declared that one day the maintenance of Western civilization might well depend on these regions.[5]

Why did the South Africans fail to persuade the Western powers with interests in Africa to form an alliance? One suggested explanation is that the South African refusal to agree to black men bearing arms destroyed any hope of co-operation with the

---

[1] H of A, 23 Apr. 1956, col. 4106.   [2] Lawrie, op. cit., p. 174.
[3] H of A, 24 July 1958, cols. 941–2.   [4] *Southern Africa*, 3 Jan. 1959.
[5] ibid.

3. Strijdom (centre, with hat) leaving the House of Assembly, Cape Town, in 1956. In the background are ladies of the 'Black Sash' movement who have frequently protested against National Party policies and legislation. In this case their protest was against the South Africa Act Amendment Bill.

Cape Times

4. Eric Louw speaking at the United Nations in November 1961.
United Press International

colonial powers who were forced to rely on black troops.[1] The inference which is drawn is that if the South Africans allowed this to stand in the way they were not as keen on an agreement as they had suggested. No doubt this question of arming black men was important, but it was only one of the issues which undermined the chance of co-operation. Examining the broad range of dangers perceived by the South Africans and the Western powers, there was some common ground but also some distinct differences. They could all agree about a communist threat to the Middle East but the colonial powers did not share South Africa's strong fears of imminent communist penetration in the rest of the continent. There were also important differences of views about future political developments concerning black men in Africa, and it was in this context that South Africa's refusal to arm Africans is best explained. The South African Government has always feared an armed African uprising, and therefore has an instinctive reaction against arming black men. This same fear helps to account for the South African Government's attempts to retain the colonial *status quo*. But even the colonial powers had growing doubts about the possibility or desirability of retaining the colonial structure. In the 1950s these were usually no more than doubts and certainly the colonial powers had not yet decided on the rapid withdrawal that came early in the 1960s. But the uncertainty was there, and on the west coast, in 1957, Britain took the first steps in the colonial withdrawal by granting independence to Ghana.

The colonial uncertainty added to the Western states' doubts about becoming too closely associated with the Union. An alliance with the Union would be diplomatically unpopular, while the contribution which the South Africans were able to make to any such alliance was unlikely to counterbalance this unpopularity. The limited military contribution that South Africa was prepared to make brings into doubt the South Africans' public anxieties and their enthusiasm for an alliance. In 1955, of a total government revenue account expenditure of R501·6 million, only R39·4 million, or 8 per cent, went on defence. In 1960 the proportion had fallen to 7 per cent (R39·2 million from R602·8 million).[2]

[1] See W. C. B. Tunstall, *The Commonwealth and Regional Defence*, Commonwealth Paper No. VI (London, Athlone Press, 1959), pp. 12 and 47; J. E. Spence, *The Strategic Significance of Southern Africa*, p. 11; and *Oxford History of South Africa*, vol. II, p. 479.

[2] *Union Statistics for 50 years 1910–60.*

The South Africans, both in the case of MEDO and the Simonstown Agreement, had shown that they were prepared to expand their forces to meet new obligations, but South Africa remained a 'small' power and the main burden of providing men and equipment would have had to fall elsewhere. Britain, with her possessions in southern Africa, accepted a continuing military role, but the other Western powers did not. For them it would have meant new obligations in a continent with an uncertain future, and an alliance with an unpopular ally. At this time there were also serious doubts about the standards of efficiency and morale in the South African forces. The United Party accused the Nationalist government of 'playing politics' by giving preference to Afrikaans-speaking officers with National Party sympathies over those who had fought in the war and had proved their ability. Erasmus was also criticized for his lack of administrative and planning skills.[1]

The conclusion must be that despite their professed anxiety for membership of an alliance, the South Africans' sense of an immediate military threat was not as strong as their public statements suggested, and certainly not as strong as it became in the early 1960s when large resources were diverted to expanding the armed forces.

In the absence of a formal alliance, co-operation with Britain, based on the Commonwealth link, continued to provide South Africa's main external military support. Training and defence exercises were shared, military information was exchanged, and Britain was the major source of South African arms. The Simonstown Agreement can be interpreted as a direct continuation of the old Commonwealth link. As C. J. R. Dugard has pointed out, it follows very closely the ground covered in a 1921 agreement between Smuts and Churchill.[2] The new emphasis given in the 1955 agreement was that South Africa would make a greater naval contribution to the defence of the Cape route, and specifically undertook to purchase six anti-submarine frigates, ten coastal minesweepers, and four seaward defence boats from Britain. Also

[1] Walker, *History of South Africa*, ch. 17 outlines some of the criticism. Also, appraisal of the situation by the government in 1960, which was followed by a major reorganization of the armed forces, indicates that there was substance in some of the accusations. (See South African Government White Paper WP BB 1964 on Defence—Annexure to Proceedings of House of Assembly.)

[2] Dugard, 'The Simonstown Agreements', pp. 142–5.

South Africa took over responsibility from Britain for the naval base at Simonstown although the British retained rights to use it at all times. The agreement could only be terminated by mutual consent.

It is ironic that the only defence agreement achieved by the Nationalist government was with the old imperial enemy, and the overall balance of the agreement favoured Britain. She continued to have facilities in South Africa, which could be used even if Britain and not South Africa was at war, while the South Africans made a greater contribution to joint defence, and had signed away their right to break the arrangements unilaterally. The doubt about the agreement for Britain lay in the future. It formally tied her to South Africa and by doing so laid her open to criticism as an ally of apartheid.

While the Simonstown Agreement demonstrated continued Anglo-South African co-operation, the cooler, less committed attitude of the Nationalist government towards Britain asserted itself during the Suez crisis of 1956. In many ways Suez seemed an ideal situation for South African involvement—it concerned 'the gateway to Africa', there were rumours of communist activity, and it saw combined action by the two principal Western colonial powers. Within South Africa the arguments for involvement were pressed on the government by the United Party. Mr. J. G. N. Strauss, the United Party leader, asserted that it was not a local issue, and 'it should also be clear to South Africans that events in Egypt are connected with the expansionist policies of the Communist States'. South Africa should shoulder her responsibilities as the leading African State.[1]

Even the accusation of communist involvement was not enough to tempt the South African Government. The government's general stand was that South Africa was keenly interested in Middle East developments, she respected the rights of Britain and France to look after their own interests, but the dispute over the nationalization of the canal did not directly concern South Africa. The Union had not been a signatory of the Canal Users' Agreement and her ships did not use the canal. Louw further argued that as the Canal Company was registered in Egypt the dispute was an internal Egyptian affair, and that South Africa had always

[1] Quoted in James Eayrs, *The Commonwealth and Suez: A Documentary Survey* (London, Oxford University Press, 1964), pp. 65–6.

emphasized her respect for non-interference in internal affairs.[1] Ministerial statements emphasized that South Africa hoped for a peaceful solution, with continued friendship with all sides.[2]

The chief direct impact of the crisis on South Africa was to increase the number of ships using the Cape route and so calling at South African ports. In this sense the closure of the canal served South Africa's interests, but this was probably a marginal factor in shaping the South African Government's attitude. What does explain its aloofness? The suspicion must be that in addition to the reasons given by Louw and Strijdom, and the lingering doubts about 'fighting Britain's wars', it was the inept handling of the affair by the British Government that alerted the South Africans to keep out. At the beginning Strijdom said: 'It is best to keep our heads out of the beehive'[3]—the beehive image captures well the furious diplomatic activity and subterfuge that surrounded the Suez crisis. Also, despite the activity, there was a breakdown of communication and Commonwealth consultation, which embarrassed the British High Commissioner, Sir Percivale Liesching,[4] infuriated Louw, and blunted the edge of United Party criticism. Even if the South African Government had wanted to give military support, it would have been impossible to do so because, like other Commonwealth governments, it was not informed of the Anglo-French plans, nor invited to participate. There was then no choice in terms of giving direct military assistance. There was, however, a choice in terms of diplomatic activity, of votes at the United Nations, and public statements. In this, much to the anger of the United Party, the South Africans remained neutral to the point of abstaining on a United Nations vote condemning the Anglo-French invasion.[5]

To the end of the immediate crisis the South Africans remained aloof and uncommitted, but this did not indicate any respect for the Egyptian Government, especially as it increased its contacts with Russia and its support for the black African Nationalist movements. In Egypt's conflict with Israel the South African Government, despite an old National Party strain of anti-semitism, generally sympathized with the Israelis. Egypt was

[1] The fullest statement by Louw was to the House of Assembly, 11 Feb. 1957, cols. 923–6.
[2] Eayrs, op. cit., p. 62.   [3] ibid.
[4] Information given in private conversation, and see Eayrs, op. cit., pp. 190–1.
[5] Eayrs, op. cit., p. 246.

usually numbered among the irresponsible and hostile Afro-Asian states. Even in the aftermath of the Suez crisis Louw was back in the fray, the cool, aloof approach forgotten. In December 1956 he said that the problems of the canal 'will not be solved by a thoroughly divided United Nations, in which the Bandung countries, generally acting with the Communist states, are playing so important a role under the leadership of India'. He said that in resisting communism 'the Western Nations run the risk of being sadly disillusioned if in this matter they are relying on support from the East, either in their own national interest or for the purpose of resisting communist expansion. Nehru, Chou En-Lai and their Bandung associates have other fish to fry.' He feared that the Western powers might try to buy off the Asian states by abandoning Africa.[1] In January 1957 he became even more belligerent when he said that with the Suez Canal blocked South Africa was now in a position to retaliate against the sanctions previously applied by India. When in reaction to this the Indian shipping lines instructed their vessels to by-pass South African ports Louw retorted: 'My "ballon d'essai" succeeded admirably. Few South Africans will regret the fact that the Indians have now inconvenienced themselves.'[2]

Some years later Verwoerd said that Britain's mistake at Suez had been to draw back. 'If Britain', he said, 'had been prepared to execute the policy which she had believed to be the correct one and had not allowed herself to be dissuaded, I am sure there would be less unrest in the world and especially in Africa today.'[3] This regret at Western failure to impose their will reflects more accurately South Africa's long-term attitude to the Middle East than the cool, aloof pose of 1956.

Suez was the classic example of a breakdown of Commonwealth co-operation. It was also a clear reflection of something that had been apparent long before Suez, that the Commonwealth no longer functioned as a unit in military matters. With Britain's relatively declining world power, some Commonwealth countries had opted for regional alliances rather than relying on the old, loosely defined, Commonwealth links. Also, with the expansion of the Commonwealth and its greater diversity, it was plain that some members did not want to become involved in defence ties.

[1] ibid., pp. 448–9.   [2] ibid., p. 396.
[3] ibid., p. 394 (statement of 29 Mar. 1962).

For those who wanted it, including South Africa, Commonwealth defence co-operation in such matters as training, exchange of information, the supply of arms, and the unwritten guarantee of British support remained very useful, but it was no longer a comprehensive guarantee.

The defence link was only one of the advantages offered by the Commonwealth and it was these advantages, plus the domestic political consideration of avoiding a major controversy among the white population, that persuaded the Nationalist government to retain membership during the 1950s. The Ministers were, however, always careful to stress that there was a choice for South Africa, that membership was retained not because of ties of tradition, emotion, or sympathy, but because there were immediate advantages. The option of leaving was always stressed.[1] The ambivalence never disappeared, for there were so many facets to the Commonwealth that an advantage for South Africa in one direction could easily be countered by a disadvantage in another. In the broadest terms, South Africa's failure to gain admission to a Western alliance, and the increasing hostility of the United Nations, made the Commonwealth link that much more attractive, but against this the character of the Commonwealth was continuing to change in ways which did not suit South Africa.

The South Africans primarily saw the Commonwealth as a relationship with Britain, and the debate about retaining links with Britain continued to raise some of the emotive tones of the past, but they became tempered with time. The United Party gradually became less pro-British, especially as the changing colonial policy was unfolded. On the other hand the Nationalist government, without ever losing its suspicions, saw advantages in a continuing connection—the trading preferences, British diplomatic support, some military co-operation, and the hope of an alliance in Africa.

For the Nationalists one major obstacle that appeared to have been removed was the acceptance of republican status within the Commonwealth. In 1949 the Commonwealth leaders agreed to this for India. The decision was greeted with an outburst of enthusiasm from the South African Government, which can only be explained in terms of internal South African policies. The

---

[1] See, for example, Strijdom, H of A, 23 Apr. 1956, col. 4129, and Verwoerd, H of A, 18 Sept. 1958, cols. 4161–2.

persistent theme of the United Party had been that South Africa could not have it both ways, that it could not retain Commonwealth membership and abandon the monarchy. This case was swept aside by the Indian decision, and while the Nationalists did not immediately force the republican issue, the future path appeared to have been cleared. Malan could afford to enthuse, if only briefly, about the Commonwealth as an international organization.[1] In May 1949 he said that provided it 'remained faithful to its character' and did not impose on 'the freedom and independence of its members South Africa would remain a member'. He argued that it was wrong to think that the Commonwealth

is no longer a powerful force in a world in which we are facing a dangerous situation, in which there is the possible threat of war in the future, and the threat of aggression from Russia, from Communist countries. . . . The trend of events in recent times has revealed a feeling of solidarity amongst the various members of the Commonwealth that was probably not expected in the world outside and that probably surprised even members of the Commonwealth itself. . . . The only explanation I can give is that in the first place there are common interests between the various members of the Commonwealth, and it is in that light that they can see the position. Furthermore they have a common or general outlook on life. There are some members who are closer to each other than others, but politically they have a common outlook; even in the case of India which is otherwise perhaps furthest removed from the other members of the Commonwealth, she has decided to model her constitution on the lines of the British constitution and our constitution in this country. . . . Moreover, as I have stated here before, India, like the rest of the world, is today taking her stand with the anti-communist countries.[2]

The Commonwealth also gave South Africa an *entrée* into international circles and access to a valuable information service provided by the British Government[3] which would otherwise have been closed to her. Membership meant that despite her widespread unpopularity she was an 'insider' in a major international group. The Nationalist government appreciated this. Strijdom, arriving at the 1956 Commonwealth Conference, said

[1] I was told in conversation that Malan had a long private interview with King George VI during the King's 1947 visit to South Africa and that Malan's warmth towards the Commonwealth grew as a result.

[2] Mansergh, *Documents . . . 1931–1952*, vol. II, pp. 861–8.

[3] Malan acknowledged this (H of A, 7 July 1953, col. 55).

that 'there is a need in these days of danger and uncertainty in the international field for maintaining ties of friendship and for the promotion of co-operation between all States who hold the same views or similar views as we do',[1] and he repeated the importance of being involved in consultation and receiving information as a member of a major international group.[2]

These were the advantages which the South African Government saw in Commonwealth membership, but even among these apparent advantages there were misperceptions which were to lead to disillusionment and discontent. The South Africans wanted an essentially anti-communist Commonwealth, with each member having broadly similar attitudes and forms of government, and respecting the rule of non-interference in each other's internal affairs: the right, as Malan put it, for each member 'to determine its own destiny'.[3]

Developments within the Commonwealth challenged these assumptions. The old Commonwealth members stood firmly in the anti-communist camp, but the new Asian, and later the African, members set out to avoid commitment to either bloc. With their clear 'he who is not for me is against me' attitude to communism, the South Africans found this impossible to accept. They were to renounce completely Malan's 1949 view of India as an anti-communist state and instead accused her of close co-operation with the communists.

As more states, and particularly the first African states, moved to independence within the Commonwealth, further gloom spread through the South African Government. As seen by the South Africans, the Commonwealth was in danger of being swamped by new, immature, and irresponsible members, and moreover members who were hostile to South Africa and prepared to interfere in her internal affairs. The South Africans pointed out to the British that the common bonds which had held the Commonwealth together were rapidly disappearing. They advised against granting independence hastily. They also had the point confirmed that membership of the Commonwealth was not an automatic right for ex-colonies, that general approval and not just British approval was required for membership.

In 1951 Malan made a statement which provides a striking

[1] *The Times*, 25 June 1956.   [2] H of A, 7 July 1953, col. 55.
[3] Mansergh, *Documents . . . 1931–1952*, vol. II, p. 861.

contrast to the enthusiastic response he had given to the Indian republican decision two years previously. He accused Britain of 'killing the Commonwealth' by the recent announcement that African and West Indian colonies would be led to independence within the Commonwealth and put on the same footing as old members. He said that British policy in West Africa would lead to ferment in the continent and to attempts to expel the white man, and he accused Britain of unilaterally admitting India, Pakistan, and Ceylon without the consent of other members. 'The Commonwealth', he said, 'can, and could in the past, exist only as a result of a feeling of solidarity between its members. This feeling of solidarity could and does exist only as the basis of two things, namely specific common interest and sufficient homogeneity of cultural and political outlook.' When there had been only five members the position was simple 'because the conditions for solidarity were still present—namely common interest and the necessary homogeneity. . . . But now as a result of latest events and a declaration of policy, the question necessarily arises—what greater solidarity or common interest or homogeneity does there exist, for example, between South Africa and India than exists between South Africa and Holland, or Belgium, or France, or Germany, or, for example, between Australia and the Negro States in West Africa than between Australia and the United States? To this question there can only be one answer.'[1]

To add to the feeling of alienation from the new members, there was South African indignation at those Commonwealth countries which, although respecting the Commonwealth's tradition of not discussing each other's internal affairs at their own meetings, were among South Africa's chief critics outside. India was seen as the main offender, but from the mid 1950s Ghana also became a much resented critic. Occasionally, South African ministers still had their moments of optimism when they would claim that relations with these Commonwealth countries were good. In May 1959 Louw claimed that South Africa had shown how it was possible to establish good and friendly relations with new Commonwealth countries in Africa like Ghana and Nigeria.[2] Also, the opportuni-

---

[1] *The Times*, 24 Feb. 1951. Strijdom made similar statements when he became Prime Minister. See, for example, his speech in the House of Assembly, 2 May 1957.

[2] H of A, 20 Mar. 1959, col. 2940. (Nigeria had not then attained independence, but it was in prospect.)

ties at Commonwealth meetings for personal contacts with leading critics like Jawaharlal Nehru and Kwame Nkrumah may momentarily have eased relations. But the usual South African reaction was anger and resentment at finding themselves the target of attacks. Closer to the prevailing South African reaction than the occasional expression of friendship and conciliation, were Malan's statement in 1953 that India was a danger to the Union and the colonial powers and was breaking up the Commonwealth by her attacks upon South Africa;[1] and Louw's statement in 1958 that it was unbelievable that a man in as responsible a position as Mr. K. A. Gbedemah, the Ghanaian Finance Minister, could suggest that colonialism would be dead in five years and that African States would not tolerate the continued subjection of the black majority of South Africa by the white minority.[2]

[1] H of A, 11 Aug. 1953, cols. 1324 and 1327.
[2] *Southern Africa*, 5 July 1958.

8

FRUSTRATED HOPES IN AFRICA

In Smuts's time the retreat of Western colonialism had been confined to Asia, and even in the earliest years of Nationalist rule there were few indications of the rapid changes that were to come to black Africa. By the mid 1950s the situation had changed. There were unmistakable signs that independent black states would emerge from the old empires, but the pace and pattern of change was uncertain, nor was it clear how extensive the decolonization would be. In retrospect it is easy to identify the misconception and misunderstanding of all those involved in a rapidly changing situation, whether they be the colonial governments, the African nationalists or the South African Government. There was a natural temptation on all sides to let judgement be dictated by desire. The South Africans opposed the colonial withdrawal, and publicly declared that if it was to come it must be spread over generations.

At that time all the territories in southern Africa, other than the Union, were under colonial control. The Portuguese ruled the two large territories of Angola and Mozambique while the remainder were British possessions. In 1953 the British brought together the two Rhodesias and Nyasaland to form the Central African Federation, with a locally based white government responsible for internal affairs. Britain also controlled the three High Commission Territories of Bechuanaland, Basutoland, and Swaziland. The British presence, bringing with it the contacts and pretensions of a major power, remained an important factor in calculating southern Africa's future.

Although South Africa was interested in the entire continent, it naturally paid most attention to its immediate neighbours to whom it was tied by long-established economic and communication links. As South Africa's economic expansion continued, making

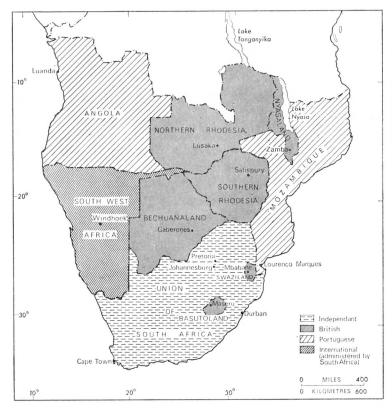

Southern Africa—1950

(Between 1953 and 1963 Northern Rhodesia, Southern Rhodesia, and Nyasaland were brought together into the Central African Federation.)

her 'the most highly industrialized nation on the continent',[1] the links grew stronger. For example, the growing South African manufacturing industries found an important outlet for their goods in the Rhodesias.

When the South Africans speculated about their continental contacts they emphasized the material links of trade, technical co-operation, and defence. In 1956 Louw announced that a roving Trade Commissioner had been appointed to cover all sub-Saharan Africa, that new permanent trade representatives were being posted to African countries, and that a government subsidy was being given to a shipping line which would forge direct contacts between South Africa and the west coast.[2] The interest in trade was matched by an interest in technological co-operation covering such fields as pest control and the development of power and water resources. The South Africans, who were founder members of the CCTA (Commission for Technical Co-operation in Africa South of the Sahara), saw co-operation in these fields as the firmest foundation for international friendship in the continent. It was in these economic-cum-technological fields, not in any political-cum-ideological understanding, that the South Africans hoped to see advances in continental co-operation. They still retained this view even in the late 1950s when the political scene was changing rapidly and they were reluctantly coming to accept the emergence of black states.

A further, compelling reason for the white South Africans' close attention to the remainder of the continent, and their hopes for influence there, was the realization that developments in other territories had a direct impact on the Union's own internal development. There was no way of sealing off the Union's non-white population from knowledge of changes elsewhere in the continent.

The National Party government acknowledged its continental interests from the beginning. Shortly after the 1948 election victory Malan said:

We, as South Africans, as one of the countries of Africa, cannot dissociate ourselves from the destinies of those countries. We are a part of Africa. We are the only country in Southern Africa with a white civilization, or at any rate a permanently established and fairly large white population, and our actions here in South Africa are largely influenced by what takes place in the rest of Africa. Not only do we wish to be on

[1] Houghton, *The South African Economy*, 2nd ed., p. 170.
[2] H of A, 26 Apr. 1956.

friendly terms with the territories of Africa for that reason, but we also
have a growing trade with these territories. It is inevitable that by trade,
by the attempt to control disease, that South Africa is integrated with
these [territories]. . . . South Africa also has the right by virtue of its
position as a white man's country and its experience during the course
of years in connection with the native problem and the coloured problem to aspire to leadership in this matter and to act as adviser to the
peoples of the Northern territories.[1]

He followed this up by appointing Mr. Charles te Water as roving
ambassador. In 1949 te Water travelled widely in Africa and in
Europe, where he visited the colonial capitals and spoke of South
Africa offering friendship and co-operation.

Te Water's visits[2] were the first of a handful of South African
initiatives during the 1950s, but they brought no returns because
they ran into the same difficulties as the search for defence alliances.
The Western colonial powers did not share South Africa's views
about continental development, and they were increasingly reluctant to be associated with the Union. At a time when most of them
were starting to question their past policies and their old attitudes
towards race relations, the white South Africans were as firmly
wedded as ever to continuing white supremacy.

The white South Africans faced an enormously difficult intellectual task in absorbing and understanding the changes which
were taking place around them. Strijdom once appealed for time
so that white South Africans could adjust to the new situation.
He said that given time they would accept it, but they did need the
time.[3] South African society had been so firmly based on the
assumptions of white supremacy and the perpetual subordination
of non-whites that the whites had the greatest difficulty in accepting that these assumptions could or should be challenged elsewhere. In the early 1950s, many South Africans, including Malan,
thought it inconceivable that the colonial authorities would withdraw to hand over power to independent black states.

Malan's broad views were set out in his 'African Charter'. The
Charter was not a formal document but a set of ideas and aims which
he hoped would be supported by the Western colonial powers and

---

[1] H of A, 1 Sept. 1948, cols. 1323–4.
[2] *The Times*, 20 May 1949. For a brief outline of te Water's visits, see Walker,
History of S. Africa, p. 785, and Vandenbosch, *S. Africa and the World*, pp.
158–9.
[3] H of A, 2 May 1957, col. 5214.

the United States. Nothing came of it and the Charter is now largely forgotten in South Africa, but it was not just an impromptu idea. Malan first spoke about it in 1945 while in opposition,[1] and was still talking about it in 1953. At the time, his followers praised him for his foresight and imagination. *Die Burger* saw him 'standing on Kilimanjaro' surveying all Africa.[2]

The Charter set out five aims: first, to protect Africa against Asian domination; second, to preserve Africa for the Africans; third, to ensure that Africa developed on Western Christian lines; fourth, to keep communism out of the continent; and, finally, to make Africa 'non-militarized'.

The first of these aims, the protection of Africa against Asian infiltration and domination, reflected a strong white South African fear of the time. Malan may have emphasized the fear more than most, but he was expressing a general and not just a personal fear, which was found in the United Party as well as among the National-ists.[3] In 1953 Malan said that the aim should be to 'protect the peoples, the indigenous population of Africa against penetration by the peoples of Asia'.[4] He showed a particular suspicion of India, and accused Nehru of trying to drive the white man out of Africa by fostering disloyalty in the Union. 'India', Malan said, 'already had a firm footing in parts of Africa and with its population of over 400 million people is seeking a place where it can unload its super-fluous population and the most obvious place to unload them is Africa.' These baseless fears prompted Malan to offer help to Australia if ever she were threatened by India's attempts to domin-ate the lands around the Indian Ocean. He told Sir Robert Menzies, the Australian Prime Minister, that 'if ever India knocks on the door of Australia we will prove that we are a friend of Australia'.[5]

(Looking forward for a moment, both Strijdom and Louw continued to show concern about Asian expansion after Malan's retirement. For example, Louw warned against underestimating the importance of the first Afro-Asian Conference at Bandung in 1955. He stressed that it had been called an *Afro*-Asian Con-ference although the great majority of independent states attending it had come from Asia. He said this revealed what was going on in

---

[1] Vandenbosch, op. cit., p. 157.
[2] Quoted by A. G. Barlow (H of A, 2 Sept. 1948, col. 1421).
[3] For example, Sydney Waterson (H of A, 12 May 1949, col. 5666).
[4] H of A, 11 Aug. 1953, col. 1327.   [5] ibid.

the minds of Eastern states, and suggested, in an oddly inappropriate metaphor, that the white man was being 'frozen out of the East'.[1] Strijdom, like Malan, offered help to Australia and shared a deep hostility towards Nehru.[2])

The catchphrase for the second aim of the Charter—'Africa for the Africans'—had an odd ring coming from a South African Prime Minister, but among 'Africans' Malan included the permanent European population. He said: 'Africa should be safeguarded for the European in so far as he is settled here permanently because he has borne civilization on his shoulders and is still necessary here.' But then he added that 'for the rest Africa should be there for the benefit of the natives'.[3] The major proviso that must be added is that Malan was convinced that the 'benefit of the natives' involved continued European leadership.

This leadership would achieve the third aim of the Charter—to guide black Africans along 'the road of European civilization'. In 1949 he said his aim was to gain an understanding between Western states with interests in Africa, to 'see if we can retain Africa as a reserve, if I may call it that, for the further development of the West European Christian civilization'.[4] This led him to the ironic assertion that British imperial control, which the Nationalists had always argued, and argued bitterly, was detrimental for the whites, was beneficial for the non-whites. 'England in Africa', said Malan, 'is indispensable as a civilizing influence. England's leadership and guardianship cannot, in the interests of the natives themselves, be spared.'[5] The same conviction reinforced the white South Africans' view of themselves as potential leaders in the continent. Their claim was based not only on their technical and economic achievements, their political independence, and their experience of African conditions, but on their conviction that, as a Western European people, they had a natural predominant position. It was the assertion of a superior culture.

The fourth aim of the Charter was to keep Africa free from communism, 'the curse of the undeveloped and backward peoples', as Malan described it. The anti-communist legislation

[1] H of A, 5 May 1955, col. 5129.
[2] H of A, 18 Apr. 1955, col. 4024. By the late 1950s the talk of Indian expansion had disappeared.
[3] ibid., col. 1327.   [4] H of A, 11 May 1949, col. 5662.
[5] H of A, 16 May 1951, col. 6819.

and the search for defence alliances which have already been described were part of the attempts to achieve this.

The fifth and final aim of the Charter was to prevent Africa from becoming militarized. This aim requires considerable explanation, for at the very time that Malan was proclaiming his Charter South Africa was taking the initiative in negotiations for Western military alliances in Africa. There was some ambiguity in Malan's statement, but what he appears to have meant was that 'the natives' should not be armed. 'Do not allow', he said, 'the natives of Africa to become militarized. One does not hand a rifle to a child.'[1] The 'white' governments, including the colonial governments, would continue to have military forces, but black men in these forces would not be given arms. This had always been South Africa's own policy, but it had never been followed by any of the colonial powers, and it was as impracticable for them in the 1950s as it had always been.

The Charter gained no support outside South Africa. It is of no importance in terms of its achievements, but it does reveal views and assumptions which were shared at that time by many white South Africans. To the Western states Malan's ideas and principles must have appeared curiously inappropriate and unpractical. Was Africa really threatened by Asian hordes? What was meant by preserving Africa as a reserve for Western European civilization, and what did those demilitarization proposals imply? At a time when the African continent was on the edge of enormous changes it appeared that Malan was trying to fossilize it.

The agony of reappraisal involved for white South Africans as the black states moved to independence can be traced in government reactions to developments in the Gold Coast (the future Ghana). Malan viewed developments there with considerable disbelief and undeniable opposition. He criticized Britain for 'forcing' political change on a people who were unprepared for it, and claimed that 90 per cent of the Gold Coast's population was illiterate. He said that he was not opposed to black African states in principle, but Britain had taken a 'thoughtless action' and a 'disastrous step' which would have repercussions throughout Africa.[2] The British had raised hopes and aspirations where they never should have been raised. On another occasion he said:

[1] H of A, 11 Aug. 1953, col. 1328.
[2] H of A, 7 July 1953, col. 1312.

I assume that in the greater part of Africa south of the Sahara, until we get to the Rhodesias, the natives are still at a very low level of civilization. If we apply the democratic system in such a country there can only be one of two results or both results may flow from such a position. The one is that the people will sink back into barbarism or such a condition of chaos may develop that the only salvation for such a territory is dictatorship.[1]

The prospect so appalled Malan that when he first spoke of constitutional changes in the Gold Coast he still believed, or at least said he believed, that it would take generations for that territory to reach self-government and independence. This was plainly wishful thinking and by the mid 1950s Malan came to realize it, but he never faltered in his opposition to British policy.

The developments on the West Coast brought an important statement from Malan in 1951 on the government's policy towards 'natives' inside South Africa. This came when the United Party accused Malan of criticizing British policy in the Gold Coast while allowing the Minister of Native Affairs, Dr. Hendrik Verwoerd, to pursue similar policies in the 'native' areas of the Union. The opposition asserted that Verwoerd's Bantustan policy would lead to independent African states in their own midst. Malan denied this. While he accepted that Africans would gradually acquire more powers within their own areas, he added: 'In their own areas they will always have to stand under the guardianship and the domination of the white man in South Africa. Call it "baaskap", call it what you like. We have always used the expression that we are their guardians and we remain their guardians.'[2]

Of even greater significance in terms of the change of government attitudes in later years was Verwoerd's own statement in 1951. Speaking in the Senate he said:

Now a Senator wants to know whether the series of self-governing areas would be sovereign. The answer is obvious. It stands to reason that White South Africa must remain their guardian. How could small scattered states arise? The areas will be economically dependent on the Union. It stands to reason that when we talk of the Natives' right to self-government in these areas we cannot mean that we intend to cut large slices of South Africa and turn them into independent states.[3]

---

[1] H of A, 16 May 1951, col. 6820.   [2] ibid.
[3] Quoted by U. O. Umozurike, 'International Law and Namibia', *Journal of Modern African Studies*, vol. 8, no. 4 (Dec. 1970), p. 596.

In the mid 1950s there was a clear change of attitude towards the emergence of black states. Chronologically this roughly co-incides with Malan's retirement in 1954, but the change is best explained in terms of circumstances and not of personalities. When he took office Strijdom, like Malan before him, was arguing for close co-operation with the colonial powers to ensure continued white supremacy in Africa.[1] He changed his attitude because it became clear that despite his wishes he had no choice but to accept that territories like Ghana were moving towards self-government. Having accepted this, the South African Government's attitude became more flexible, and attempts were even made to establish contacts with the new states, but this does not imply that the South Africans liked what was happening. They were simply making the best of a bad job, and in doing so revealed ambivalent and often conflicting attitudes towards the new states.

For the white South Africans there was the constant difficulty of reconciling what was happening with what they thought *should* happen. The difficulty increased as the pace of development accelerated. While the South Africans continued to persuade themselves that only a handful of territories would gain independence under black governments and that none of these would be near South Africa's borders or contain white settler populations, they made some attempts to gain contact with the black states. 'Extending the hand of friendship to emergent African States' was first announced by Strijdom when he spoke to the Natal Party Convention in 1955.[2] After that the Prime Minister made frequent references to the need to win the friendship of Africa's black millions. In 1956 he told the House of Assembly that:

As far as the non-white States with their millions of inhabitants are concerned, our attitude towards them as co-interested parties in Africa will have to be such that we do not regard each other as enemies, but as Nations and Governments acknowledging and respecting each other's right to exist. The aim of the Nationalist Government is to do every-thing in its power to give guidance and direction as far as these matters are concerned.[3]

[1] Vandenbosch, *S. Africa and the World*, p. 162.
[2] Colin De B. Webb, 'The Foreign Policy of the Union of South Africa' in J. E. Black and Kenneth Thompson (eds.), *Foreign Policies in a World of Change* (New York, Harper and Row, 1963), p. 440.
[3] H of A, 23 Apr. 1956, col. 4104.

These offers of friendship and co-operation must be matched against the continued determination to support white rule and the outbursts of frustration and resentment at the colonial withdrawal. In contrast to the offer of friendship to black states, Strijdom said in January 1955 that there must be the greatest possible co-operation between the white communities in southern Africa to ensure their survival. 'That is what we generally mean when we talk about an African policy.'[1] In March 1959 Louw said: 'We in South Africa see no danger in states attaining their independence. Of course not, we cannot stop it.' But then he went on to say that independence should not be given too rapidly. He listed criteria which he said should be used in evaluating whether states were ready for independence. They should, he argued, be capable of administering and governing themselves, and they should be economically mature. He did not say how to measure his standards, but certainly he thought that many of the new states and their leaders did not match up to them. He told the House of Assembly: 'Some of these leaders are not yet one generation removed from the primitive conditions of their forefathers. There are many of them whose fathers and mothers were completely primitive, barbaric people.'[2]

An important step in the changing pattern of attitudes towards black Africa was taken by Louw in March 1957, when he spoke at the University of Pretoria. He asserted that South Africa must 'accept its future role in Africa as a vocation and must in all respects play its full part as an African power'. By making its scientific and technical assistance available to the black states Louw argued that the Union would be able to demonstrate the value of a society that has preserved its white identity and its Western culture, while establishing mutual trust and understanding. The Union could become 'a permanent link between the Western nations on the one hand and the population of Africa south of the Sahara on the other'. The African states would come to realize that apartheid was no threat to them and they could all combine to counter external interferences.[3] This speech, with its emphasis on technical co-operation and South Africa's involve-

---

[1] Vandenbosch, op. cit., p. 163.
[2] H of A, 20 Mar. 1959, cols. 2940–1.
[3] The speech is outlined in Webb, op. cit., pp. 440–1 and contained in Fact Paper 33 (April 1957) published by the South African Information Service.

ment in the continent, pointed the path which the South Africans continued to see for themselves throughout the 1960s and into the 1970s.

As well as the assertions of good faith in the mid and late 1950s, the South Africans made some attempts at direct contact. The main activity was directed towards offering technical assistance and attending conferences and committees concerned with technical and economic matters.[1] Also the Union was represented at Ghana's Independence celebrations and a telegram of congratulation was sent to the Sudan on its Independence. South Africa became one of the founder members of FAMA (the Foundation for Mutual Assistance in Africa South of the Sahara), and her representatives attended the inaugural meeting at Accra in Ghana during February 1958.[2] When a Ghanaian representative came to South Africa for a CCTA conference he was, much to the ire of the United Party, treated in the same way as the white delegates. The South Africans drew encouragement from President Nkrumah's statement that while he deplored apartheid Ghana would continue to trade with South Africa and was prepared to receive technical aid from her. 'We cannot', he said, 'interfere in the internal affairs of another country, and we shall have to be very careful what we do. If public opinion throughout the world can bring pressure to bear on South Africa, it would be a different matter.'[3]

The changed tone towards Ghana at the time of her Independence had become so marked that Louw stated that good relations with Ghana were fundamental to South Africa's policy;[4] and as early as 1956, long before there were any whispers of an 'outward policy', Louw said that South Africa was considering organizing an area where non-European international representatives could stay. He admitted that this was a difficult problem as was South Africa's representation in non-white states, which would have to be left for a future decision.[5]

[1] In April 1960 Louw told the House of Assembly that during the past few years 112 technical officers had been sent to African states to give assistance, and 444 had attended meetings of such bodies as CCTA, the Air Transport Council, and the African Meteorological Organization. (H of A, 20 Apr. 1960, col. 5666.)

[2] IRR 1957–8, p. 234. (FAMA was under the aegis of CCTA, and the first meeting was attended by Britain, Belgium, France, Portugal, the Federation of Rhodesia and Nyasaland, Ghana, and South Africa.)

[3] The Times, 8 Mar. 1957.   [4] The Times, 7 Jan. 1957.

[5] H of A, 27 Apr. 1956, col. 4508.

Despite these moments of optimism and despite the attempts to make contact, co-operation with the black states never flourished. By the end of the 1950s it had become clear to the South African leaders that the new states, far from welcoming South Africa's guidance and friendship, were busily allying themselves with the Union's chief international critics. In 1959 when Verwoerd was pressed by the opposition to establish closer contacts with the new states, he replied by asking how it was possible when they refused to be friendly.[1] Yet even in the late 1950s the situation was not quite as polarized and difficult as it became later. On at least one occasion the South Africans failed to respond to an opportunity that would never have been offered a few years later. In 1957 the Ghanaian Government, in the first flush of independence, invited all the independent states of Africa, including the Union, to a conference at Addis Ababa. This placed the South Africans in a dilemma. They had accepted the existence of some black states, but they still placed great hopes on persuading the colonial powers to remain in Africa. Based on these hopes, the government refused Ghana's invitation. Strijdom wrote to Dr. Nkrumah to say that South Africa favoured a conference of 'all Governments with direct responsibilities in Africa including the colonial powers'.[2]

Relations with the three British High Commission Territories of Basutoland (now Lesotho), Bechuanaland (now Botswana), and Swaziland, sometimes referred to collectively as 'the Protectorates', provide a set-piece in South Africa's policy.[3] Their geographical position gave these territories an importance for South Africa out of all proportion to their wealth or the size of their populations, and raised questions which overlapped internal and external policies. Lesotho is entirely surrounded by South Africa, a black island within the white state, while the other two territories are bounded by South Africa on three sides. The geographical proximity had led to close economic integration, with the Protectorates leaning heavily on South Africa. They were, and are, linked by communication and monetary systems, by a common customs union, and by the constant flow of labour and goods over their

---

[1] H of A, 4 May 1959.   [2] The Times, 30 Apr. 1957.
[3] See Lord Hailey, The Republic of South Africa and the High Commission Territories (London, Oxford University Press, 1963), and Richard P. Stevens, Lesotho, Botswana and Swaziland (London, Pall Mall Press, 1967). Basutoland was not, in fact, a Protectorate but an annexed territory.

borders. The geographical proximity also gave the Territories an importance in terms of the defence of the Union. The Nationalist government asserted that the Territories were South Africa's by right. It argued that they were internal and integral parts of the country, that there was an indisputable constitutional claim based on the Act of Union of 1910 which envisaged the transfer of the Territories from Britain to South Africa,[1] and that to avoid friction and misunderstanding with Africans inside South Africa the Union's 'native' policy should be extended to the Territories. Malan promised that the existing rights of the inhabitants would be respected. He said, with some justification, that the British had introduced so little economic and technical development that materially the inhabitants would be better off under the Union. When the Tomlinson Commission Report on separate development was published in 1956, all three territories were theoretically included in the proposed Bantustan system.

In the early years of their rule the Nationalists, quick to take offence and anxious to be seen to uphold their own and their country's dignity, were convinced that national prestige was involved in asserting their rights to the Protectorates. As the British continued to refuse the transfer so the South African frustration increased, and behind the frustration was the suspicion that the British still distrusted the Afrikaners. Malan took up the challenge immediately he came to office. He used private negotiations, public appeals, and threats of retaliation to try to gain his point. There were even whispers in the National Party that South Africa should act unilaterally and seize the Territories.[2] The full strength of South Africa's feeling was made clear by Malan in February 1951 at a dinner for Mr. Patrick Gordon Walker, the British Colonial Secretary. Malan said:

Whether the delay is due to the fact that we are not trusted with the protection or promotion of Native interests you will best be able to judge. . . . But apart from the question of grievous mistrust there is another aspect of this outstanding question which as a member of the Commonwealth we cannot ignore. It affects our equal status and place among the other members of the Commonwealth as well as our self-respect as a nation. . . . Constitutionally [the Union] stands on a footing of equality with the other members of the Commonwealth. . . . But in

[1] Thompson, *The Unification of S. Africa 1902–1910*, pp. 271–8.
[2] Hailey, op. cit., p. 93.

one vital respect she differs from them all, and that is, that within her embrace, and even actually within her borders, she is compelled to harbour territories, entirely dependent on her economically and largely also for their defence, but belonging to and governed by another country. Such a condition . . . will not for a single moment be tolerated in their case, either by Canada or Australia or New Zealand, not to speak of India or Pakistan or Ceylon or Britain herself. And so long as this is tolerated by South Africa, there can be no real equality nor even full independence for her. . . . And no one can blame her if under such circumstances she feels herself relegated to a position of inferiority and in fact to the position of a semi-independent and third-class country.[1]

There was the further problem for the South Africans of envisaging what future there could be for the Protectorates if they were not incorporated into the Union. One possibility was that the British would stay on indefinitely, a prospect no Nationalist government could accept with equanimity. Yet the alternative, that the Territories would become independent black states, seemed even more unattractive, and even ludicrous, to the South Africans at that time. Was it practical, they asked, for territories which had such small populations, which were so economically underdeveloped and socially backward, to become independent states? In any case, would South Africa be prepared to permit such a dangerous step? Malan said of the British:

They do not want to let it go out of their hands. What are they going to do about it? They can do what they did on the Gold Coast. They can do what was done in Nigeria. But can they make any of these Protectorates a free and independent country? Can we in South Africa, who are a free and independent State, permit Negro States, Bantu States, to arise within our borders—States which are free and independent and which can lay down their own policies in every respect? We cannot possibly do so.[2]

During the 1950s the British themselves were confused and uncertain about the future of the Protectorates, which had always had exceptional treatment because of their peculiar constitutional position in relation to South Africa.[3] Added to the constitutional issue was the question of their poverty and small populations. British colonial rethinking had not reached a stage where it was

---

[1] Mansergh, *Documents . . . 1931–1952*, vol. II, pp. 928–9.
[2] H of A, 11 Aug. 1953, col. 1328.
[3] Stevens, op. cit., p. 4.

accepted that territories as small and poor as the High Commission Territories could gain independence.[1] But although British policy was uncertain, it was plain that she was not prepared to transfer the Protectorates to South Africa. With Britain involved in a radical reappraisal of her colonial policies and South Africa continuing to implement apartheid, it was neither desirable nor practicable for a British government, whether Labour or Conservative, to agree to the transfer. Although they always tried to avoid direct friction, the British, throughout all the South African pressure, emphasized that no change could take place without consultation with the inhabitants of the Territories and without the agreement of Parliament. The South Africans never had a chance of overcoming either of these hurdles. While the South African Government claimed that the Africans in the Territories would benefit by being under South African rule, and that if they knew the true situation they would agree to the transfer, all the sounding of African opinion by the British Government indicated the reverse.[2]

The conflicting views on the reactions of the inhabitants of the Territories leads directly to the other central issue in the dispute. This was how developments within the Territories would affect native policies in South Africa, and conversely how South African views influenced the British Government's policy inside the Territories. The South Africans disliked having different, more 'liberal', native policies on their borders. They had always feared the unsettling effect this could have on Africans in the Union. These fears about differences in 'native policies' gradually gave way to even greater fears that if the Territories were granted autonomy they could become centres of subversion against South Africa—Trojan horses in their midst. Basutoland, said a Nationalist newspaper, had become 'a breeding ground for Communists'.[3]

The British also had a difficult path to tread. At that time, with the Union still under the Crown and a member of the Commonwealth, they had no wish to offend the South Africans, and yet the Protectorates could not be entirely divorced from the general

---

[1] See J. M. Lee, *Colonial Development and Good Government* (Oxford, Clarendon Press, 1968). For example, Lee mentions Attlee's doubts about the future of small territories (p. 128).

[2] See, for example, *The Times*, 11 Oct. 1950, reporting the reaction of the Basuto Native Council; also *The Times*, 2 and 24 Feb. 1951, reporting opposition in Bechuanaland and Swaziland.

[3] Quoted by Hailey, op. cit., p. 93.

stream of post-war colonial policy. There was never any real thought of transfer, but the dominating presence of South Africa inhibited the British. Stevens has written that the failure to develop Legislative Councils, as in other British colonial territories, was to avoid the impression that Africans in the Territories were 'enjoying political rights which African people in the Union have been denied'.[1]

The British dilemma was revealed in the dramatic incidents surrounding Seretse Khama, the designated Chief of the Bamangwato of Bechuanaland. While at Oxford, Seretse, without following tribal custom, married an English girl. The tribe was divided on the issue and this created one of the problems for the British administration. But the whole affair was quickly caught up in the wider question of relations with South Africa. Miscegenation brought out the deepest racial fears and antagonisms of white South Africans. The Nationalist government had set out to secure 'racial purity' by formal legislation. In 1949 it introduced the Mixed Marriages Act, which forbade marriages between whites and non-whites, and in the following year came the Immorality Act, which made sexual intercourse between white and non-white a criminal offence. It was while the South Africans were taking these steps to defend their racial purity that the Seretse Khama marriage came to flout these deeply held prejudices.

Obviously the South Africans disapproved of the marriage, but there is dispute about whether they made representations to the British Government. The South African press reported a speech by Malan in which he condemned the marriage and said that a telegram had been sent to the British Government unequivocally stating the Union's attitude.[2] The British denied that any official representation had been made, and even if representation was made it is uncertain how far the British allowed South African reactions to influence their decision to prevent Seretse Khama from returning to Bechuanaland. The case was so caught up in administrative muddle, with half-broken pledges and a judicial inquiry which the British Government refused to publish, that there must have been confusion, even in the minds of the British ministers and officials, over whether their decisions were based on

[1] Stevens, op. cit., p. 137.
[2] Mary Benson, *Tshekedi Khama* (London, Faber and Faber, 1960), p. 193.

fears of trouble among the Bamangwato, trying to save their own faces, or concern about South African reactions.[1]

Although the British Government may have been correct in stating that no formal representation had been received from the Governments of South Africa or Southern Rhodesia, white southern African views were expressed very clearly and openly. As well as Malan's statement, Sir Godfrey Huggins, the Southern Rhodesian Prime Minister, was reported as saying that it would be a 'disastrous' decision if Seretse were allowed back and that he had already written to the British High Commissioner in South Africa to say how gravely the Southern Rhodesian Legislative Assembly viewed it.[2] Mary Benson suggests that the reason for Seretse's exclusion by the British may be explained by a warning which came from Smuts. He feared that if Seretse and his wife returned, the Nationalist government would demand incorporation of Bechuanaland and perhaps even threaten to blockade the territory. Smuts said that his United Party 'would be unable to oppose such a move because of the emotions aroused, for white South Africans were hardly sane on the subject of miscegenation'.[3]

The Seretse Khama affair underlined for the white South Africans the dangers of having different native policies on their borders. It presented them with a perfect example of the situation they feared, challenging and undermining the principles on which they had built their racial policies. But times change and the personal fortunes of Seretse Khama directly reflect the shifting pattern of inter-state relations in southern Africa. In 1956, after agreeing to surrender all claims to the chieftaincy for himself and his family, Seretse was allowed to return to Bechuanaland, with no protest from South Africa. Later he entered politics and became the first Prime Minister of independent Botswana. Today, as leader of a neighbouring independent State, the South Africans make friendly overtures to him.

In the early years of Nationalist rule, some ministers felt that there was a real chance of the High Commission Territories being

---

[1] For example, in a parliamentary debate, Mr. Amery accused the Government of being 'anxious to avoid giving offence to South Africa and the Rhodesians' (*Hansard*, vol. 489, 26 June 1951, col. 1262).

[2] *The Times*, 8 July 1949.

[3] Mary Benson, op. cit., pp. 200–1. Hailey, op. cit., p. 89, says that the letters of Smuts which have been preserved bear out only part of this version.

transferred to the Union, but hope faded during the 1950s.[1] At the beginning of his premiership Strijdom reaffirmed the government's intention of incorporating the Territories,[2] but he never threatened direct action as Malan had done. He and Louw continued to make public claims and kept up negotiations with Britain, but there was a suspicion that they did this more to satisfy demands within the National Party than with any real hope of persuading the British Government.

By the mid 1950s there appeared to be no clear South African view about the future of the Protectorates, other than the lingering but unlikely hope of a British change of heart. It was less of an issue than it had been in Malan's time, and it was probably assumed that the Protectorates would continue to be administered by Britain and that the problems of different 'native policies' would still have to be accepted. But what if these policies, instead of running counter to each other, were running in parallel? What if Britain's policies in the Protectorates were similar to South Africa's in her Bantustans? With some justification the United Party had already suggested that Verwoerd's policies were pointing this way. When he became Prime Minister Verwoerd made the usual claims to the Territories and advanced the old arguments about the interests of the inhabitants being best served by incorporation in the Union. In one sense he reinterpreted previous claims by stating that the Territories had two guardians—Britain, who was their constitutional and governmental guardian, and South Africa the economic guardian. He argued that of these two the economic was the more important and that this should be recognized by transferring the constitutional guardianship to the Union so that the overall development of the Territories could be co-ordinated.[3] Verwoerd must have realized that the chances of incorporation were very small, for increasingly he compared developments in the Protectorates with those in the Bantustans. He never withdrew the Union's claims, but the absorption of the Territories was no longer essential for South Africa. Verwoerd's claim was that the government was leading the Bantu of South Africa to full realization and the Africans in the Protectorates could benefit in the same way.[4] The message was repeated by other members of the government.

[1] Personal interviews.   [2] H of A, 18 Apr. 1955.
[3] H of A, 4 May 1959, cols. 5254–7.
[4] H of A, 27 Jan. 1959, col. 64.

Mr. de Wet Nel, the Minister of Bantu Development and Administration, spoke of 'the natural South Africa' in which almost half (i.e. including the Protectorates) belonged to the Bantu, and he foresaw the day of a 'greater Basutoland' and a 'greater Swaziland' incorporating both the areas that were within the Protectorates and those parts of South Africa which were occupied by the Sotho and Swazi.[1]

While there was an acceptance of similar policies and developments, the limits of such developments, as seen by the South African Government at that time, must also be noted. These were made clear in an article written by Dr. W. W. M. Eiselen, the Secretary of Bantu Development and Administration.[2] Eiselen said that South Africa aimed at a Commonwealth of black and white States, with South Africa as the 'mother country'. He referred to a statement made by Sir Percivale Liesching, the retiring British High Commissioner, in which Sir Percivale had said that while the High Commission Territories were advancing towards a greater degree of self-government, this did not imply that they would ever advance as far as Ghana (i.e. to full independence within the Commonwealth). Eiselen confirmed that South Africa still claimed the Protectorates, but even setting the claim aside, he said that policy in the Bantustans mirrored Sir Percivale's statement about the Protectorates. The Union Government was prepared to give the Bantustans greater autonomy, but would stop short of full independence. There would be no surrender of European trusteeship. Continued white supremacy was the *sine qua non* of racial peace and harmony.

The late 1950s, the end of a decade of change and challenge within Africa, had revealed clear signs that even greater changes lay ahead. It was even reflected in the political vocabulary of white South Africa. The 'natives' were disappearing, but they were not to be replaced by 'Africans'. That could have implied that Afrikaners were not 'Africans', that they had abandoned their identity with the soil in which they had grown, suffered, triumphed, and been shaped into a distinctive people. In the new vocabulary the 'natives' gave way to the 'Bantu'.

---

[1] H of A, 30 Jan. 1959, cols. 244–5.
[2] *Optima* (Johannesburg), Mar. 1959.

PART THREE

THE EARLY 1960s—THE YEARS OF CRISIS AND DOUBT
(1960–1966)

9

DANGERS WITHIN AND THE
GRANITE RESPONSE

In the early 1960s white South Africa felt threatened and endangered. Some of the dangers were new, stemming from a changing international order and the rising expectations of black men in Africa; others were rooted in the past but gained a new intensity. The period began with an acute crisis in 1960, when there was a cumulative sense of dangers building up on each other and threatening to overwhelm the white society. Then gradually the tension eased, as the internal and international threats were balanced by an increasing confidence among white South Africans that they were capable of withstanding the dangers. Doubts and uncertainties remained, but the sense of acute crisis had disappeared.

Because the threats against South Africa were soon matched by counter responses from the white society much of the evidence for the early 1960s is contradictory. It is easy to select evidence to support conflicting views. For example the South African Government always chose to emphasize the strength and stability of the country, while its opponents highlighted its weaknesses and internal conflicts, and both had good grounds for their claims. Certainly at the time the future pattern was far from clear. For the South African Government it was a period of great pressure and tension as it surmounted the early crises, then plotted a course through the years of uncertainty and doubt.

For the purpose of this study it is convenient to break up the dangers and the government's responses into broad areas, although in many cases they overlap. In this chapter the main concentration will be on the internal setting. In the following two chapters the challenges from international organizations and from developments within the African continent will be examined. Finally, the white South African acceptance of isolation and their military and economic strength will be discussed.

At the beginning of 1960 Verwoerd announced that there would be a referendum in October to decide whether South Africa would become a republic. The referendum was very much Verwoerd's decision. He went ahead with it despite the doubts of many white South Africans including some of his government colleagues. The doubters argued that white South Africa was under such pressure that it was unifying themes and not divisive issues that were needed. Verwoerd countered these arguments by claiming that it was only when a republic was established and when the final ties of imperial sentiment were severed that white South Africa would be united as one people. He also dismissed the genuine fear of some National Party members that the referendum would go against the government. During the 1950s the National Party had gained an increasing number of parliamentary seats, but had never gained an overall majority of votes cast in an election.[1] The United Party opposed a republic, and, if the division of votes fell out as in past elections, the government would be defeated. Verwoerd went his own confident way, saying that a republic would be declared if there were only a majority of one, and suggesting that other ways would be found if there was an adverse vote at the referendum.

There were a few white voices complaining that the non-whites should be given an opportunity to express their views on this major issue. But the United Party, with its strong attachment to the monarchy and its fears that the declaration of a republic could drive South Africa into deeper isolation by endangering its position in the Commonwealth, provided the main opposition to the proposal. In an attempt to counter these fears Louw tried to gain prior approval for South Africa's continued membership of the Commonwealth at the conference of May 1960, but the other leaders refused to be drawn on a hypothetical question which had important implications for South Africa's internal politics. Instead, they persuaded Louw to have informal talks about South Africa's racial policies, an ominous indication for the South Africans of the real issue that would be at stake in their application for continued membership.

[1] In the 1958 election, the Nationalists gained 48·9 per cent against the United Party's 50·36 per cent (Carter, *Politics of Inequality*, p. 494). The peculiarities of the constituencies and the distribution of white population account for the discrepancy. There is weighting in favour of the rural constituencies which are predominantly Afrikaner, while the English-speakers tend to be concentrated in urban constituencies which give UP candidates large majority votes.

At the referendum Verwoerd secured considerably more than his one vote majority, but the split among white South Africans was clear—850,458 for the Republic and 775,878 against it.[1] For Verwoerd the referendum was a personal triumph. He had succeeded against the opposition of the United Party and the doubts of some colleagues in reaching the great Nationalist Afrikaner goal.

In itself the republican issue would have made 1960 a period of high drama for South Africa, but in the few months between Verwoerd's announcement and the holding of the referendum there was a series of events which were to shake the foundations of white South Africa and make the republican issue only one among a series of crises and dramas.

Events within South Africa must be seen in the context of a continent undergoing dramatic changes. In the early 1960s the colonial empires in the 'middle belt' of Africa were transformed into independent black states, and, despite the determination of the white governments in southern Africa to hold on to their power, the impact of the changes spilt over into the subcontinent. In South Africa itself these developments produced a variety of responses, from fear, anxiety, and antagonism among most whites, to inspiration and hope for many Africans. The violence in the newly independent Congo, and the sight of the refugees who fled through South Africa, reinforced white fears about giving way to black nationalism. The South Africans determined never to let it happen to them. Their determination was increased by developments in the British 'white settler' colonies, where, as seen by the South Africans, white men were subordinated to black.

The first sharp impact to follow the announcement of the republican referendum came in Harold Macmillan's 'wind of change' speech. The speech has been given so much publicity that there is an instinct to distrust its importance, to suspect that only in retrospect has its significance become clear. In examining the content of the speech, the suspicion is reinforced, for although Macmillan went against the grain of white South African opinion there was nothing he said that had not been said elsewhere by other Western leaders, and he himself had made similar points in earlier speeches during the tour of Africa which had finally led him to the Union.

[1] IRR 1959–60, p. 7.

Yet, despite the suspicion, the 'wind of change' speech did have an immediate and sharp impact inside South Africa. The evidence is there—in newspaper articles, in parliamentary speeches, and in the memories of South Africans. The reason lies partly in Britain's position as the major Western power directly involved in southern Africa, and in her leadership of the Commonwealth. Macmillan was seen to speak not only for Britain but for all the Western states with whom South Africa had contacts. The reason is also to be found in the setting of the speech—where it was said, as well as what was said. Had Macmillan made the same speeech outside South Africa, the South Africans would have explained it away as another example of the attempt to curry black men's favours. But there was no explaining away a speech made directly to their faces in their own Parliament. A final reason is that Macmillan unearthed and exposed the white South Africans' own fears; fears about Western attitudes, about decolonization, about the growing strength of African nationalism, and about the dangers and un-certainties that lay ahead in a continent in revolution. Previously, these fears had been mixed with, and partly submerged by, hopes which were built on a selective interpretation of Western attitudes, that old South African mixture of optimism laced with exaspera-tion. Macmillan stripped away the illusions and was bitterly re-sented for doing so. Mr. Fred Barnard, who was Verwoerd's private secretary, wrote that Macmillan's speech 'was to come as a surprise attack, a move calculated to drive Dr. Verwoerd into a corner and to embarrass him in the eyes of his own Parliament, of his country and of the world . . . the speech occupied nearly ten pages; ten pages of silken, smooth-tongued, cold and calculated insult; of courteously phrased, remorseless condemnation of the country whose guest he was.'[1]

In the broadest terms Macmillan's message was that nationalism, which had swept through Europe and more recently through Asia, was now sweeping through Africa. Whether one liked this or not it was happening and policies had to be framed to take account of it. The interests of the Western states would best be served by recognizing and coming to terms with it. 'The great issue', said Macmillan, 'in the second half of the twentieth century is whether the uncommitted peoples of Africa will swing to the East or the

[1] Fred Barnard, *Thirteen years with Dr. H. F. Verwoerd* (Johannesburg, Voortrekkerpers Limited, 1967), p. 63.

West. The struggle is joined and it is a struggle for the minds of men.' He argued that British policy was not based upon opportunism, of accepting a situation they could not dictate, but was based on a conviction of right. He said that British policy in Africa, and here he aimed straight at the heart of white South Africa, was concerned not only to raise standards of living 'but to create a society which respects the rights of individuals—a society in which men are given the opportunity to grow to their full stature, and that must in our view include the opportunity of an increasing share in political power and responsibility; a society finally in which individual merit, and individual merit alone, is the criterion for a man's advancement, whether political or economic.'

Macmillan continued by saying that Britain's aims in her colonies were based on a policy of non-racialism. He accepted that it was impossible to isolate one part of the continent from another and that British policy might create difficulties for the South Africans, but he did not doubt that they would appreciate that the British had to do their duty as they saw it.

He tried to sugar the pill by stating that the British Government was opposed to boycotts or sanctions against South Africa, that the differences which existed now would disappear in time, and that meanwhile friendly co-operation would continue on a wide range of issues. But sugared or not, the pill was there. The British were coming to terms with African nationalism and the South Africans could expect no support if they chose to stand against it.[1]

It was the tone as well as the content of the speech that angered many white South Africans, and frightened others. Macmillan spoke on a grand historical scale. He started by stretching back to the Roman Empire and finished by reaching out to generations yet unborn. It was a speech hinting of historical inevitability, and suggesting that while the growth of an 'African national consciousness' took many forms it could not be stopped—'it is happening everywhere. The wind of change is blowing through the continent.' Macmillan admitted that Britain had made her mistakes, but for the South Africans there was a smugness in the speech,

---

[1] The bulk of the speech is in Mansergh's *Documents and Speeches on Commonwealth Affairs 1952–1962* (London, Oxford University Press, 1963), pp. 347–351.

an air of having backed a double winner—a just cause and an inevitable success.[1]

The dust had not settled from Macmillan's speech when South Africa was struck by the tragedy of Sharpeville. Had the speech so raised tension and fear on one side and expectation and confidence on the other that a violent incident was made more likely? Louw quoted an extract from the *Economist* to the House of Assembly which suggested as much.[2] But this seems very questionable. The most that could be said is that Macmillan had exacerbated an already extremely tense situation. He had certainly not created it. Against this, the South African Government would argue that the explosive situation had been created by a series of external influences, Macmillan's among them. It was seen as a cumulative process whereby external critics, by continuously telling the non-whites that they were unfairly treated, that they were held in subordination, that they should demand more rights, and that radical changes were on the way, had created a situation of frustration and discontent which had resulted in conflict and tragedy.

Sharpeville was the bloodiest of a series of confrontations between the South African police and demonstrators who had been called out by the Pan-African Congress (PAC)[3] to defy the pass laws—the system by which Africans have always to carry identification records. At Sharpeville 67 Africans were killed and 186 wounded.[4] (On the same day at Langa, an African township near

---

[1] There was a suspicion among some members of the South African Government that Sir John Maud, the British High Commissioner, had persuaded Macmillan to make the speech and perhaps had even written it. Maud, a man of great charm and ability, was distrusted in South Africa because of his known opposition to apartheid and because some regarded him as 'too clever by half'. For unfavourable comments on the speech and the circumstances surrounding it see Fred Barnard's book, loc. cit. Among other things, Barnard was annoyed that Macmillan did not hand over a copy of the speech before making it, as was normally done, and he suspected that Maud may have hoped that the speech would turn the referendum against a Republic.

[2] H of A, 29 Apr. 1960, col. 5671. The article from which Louw quoted was entitled 'Union's Moment of Truth', and stated: 'The crisis really began eight weeks ago, when Mr. Macmillan made his "wind of change" speech in Cape Town. This was followed by a period of shock and bewilderment which passed to self-analysis and anger and the violence of Sharpeville was the climax.'

[3] The PAC was formed in 1959 by a breakaway group from the African National Congress—see Richard Gibson, *African Liberation Movements* (London, Oxford University Press for the Institute of Race Relations, 1972), pp. 81–105.

[4] IRR 1959–60, p. 58.

Cape Town, three people were killed and about fifty wounded.) Because of the scale of the tragedy, Sharpeville would have stood out in South Africa's history whenever it had happened. But occurring when it did it gained a special importance. It was not the first or the last time that South African police have fired at and killed demonstrators, nor the first and last time that Africans have demonstrated against the pass laws. The others are forgotten; Sharpeville remains. It remains because it was not seen in isolation. In South Africa and in the outside world it was seen as part of the struggle in which the whole structure of South African society was challenged—a step, as Mr. Robert Sobukwe, the PAC President, said, to gaining 'freedom and independence' for Africans by 1963.[1] For the opponents of apartheid the demonstrators who were shot down were martyrs, symbolizing the oppression and ruthlessness of the South African Government— the final proof of the white government's inhumanity to the blacks.

Following Sharpeville the government and the African nationalists became locked in a fierce struggle. The two major rival African parties, the African National Congress (ANC)[2] and the PAC, organized strikes, demonstrations, and periods of mourning for the African dead. The enormous potential strength of the non-whites became imprinted on white South African minds. In Cape Town a mass march by thousands of Africans is as vivid in white public memory as Sharpeville itself. The marchers converged peacefully on central Cape Town to protest against the arrest under emergency regulations of some of their leaders. While the shootings in the African townships had been remote from the white urban areas, the march into Cape Town was a living witness that Africans were demanding political rights.

The government retaliated with repressive counter-measures. A state of emergency was declared, the African parties were banned, their leaders arrested, and those who escaped forced underground.

---

[1] IRR 1959–60, p. 55.

[2] For accounts of the ANC see Feit, *South Africa: the dynamics of the African National Congress* and *African Opposition in South Africa* (Stanford, Hoover Institute, 1967). See also Richard Gibson, op. cit., part 2. The two parties became strong rivals. They adopted different ideological stances: the ANC accepted a Charter which recognized a South Africa of mixed races, while the PAC placed more emphasis on African values and leadership.

For a time it seemed as though South Africa could be on the brink of civil war.[1]

After the banning of the African nationalist parties, the struggle between them and the government entered a new phase. Militant underground resistance movements, notably 'Umkhonto we Sizwe' (The Spear of the Nation) and Poqo, became active, aiming by the use of sabotage and violence to throw the white society into such fear and confusion that successful revolution could follow.[2] According to Richard Gibson, at Sharpeville 'the myth of the efficacy of peaceful, non-violent protest died in South Africa'.[3] The struggle between the government and the African nationalists was played out in a setting of secret meetings, night raids, bomb attacks, intimidation, police torture, informers, smuggled messages, imprisonment without trial, dramatic escapes, and arrests.

Leonard Thompson has identified three stages in the African opposition to white rule over the last fifty years. In the first of these stages the Africans were drawn from an élite group, were reformist in their objectives (i.e. prepared to work for change within the existing political structure), and non-violent in their approach. In the second period, which was roughly between 1948 and 1960, the movement remained non-violent but became national in its scope and revolutionary in its aims (i.e. it aimed to overthrow the existing structure). The third stage, which developed from 1960, was revolutionary and the Africans were prepared to use violent as well as non-violent means.[4] Thompson did not make the point, but the third stage is also characterized by increased external support for the resistance movements.[5] In the early 1960s many

[1] While the battle between the government and the African nationalists was developing, an unsuccessful attempt was made to assassinate Verwoerd. He was shot twice in the head, but miraculously escaped permanent injury. The attempt was made on 9 April 1960 by a white man, David Pratt, apparently unconnected with any of the resistance movements, but the act in itself both reflected and highlighted the air of tension and crisis in the country. When Pratt appeared before the courts he was found to be mentally disordered (IRR 1959–60, p. 89).

[2] 'Umkhonto we Sizwe' was backed by the ANC, and Poqo by the PAC.

[3] Gibson, op. cit., p. 90.

[4] Thompson, *Unification of S. Africa*, p. 165. See also E. Feit, 'Urban Revolt in South Africa', *Journal of Modern African Studies*, vol. 8, no. 1, Apr. 1970, pp. 55–72.

[5] Walshe, *The Rise of African Nationalism in South Africa*, emphasizes the importance of external influences and ideologies in the African nationalist movement since the First World War, but direct outside support was not anticipated until the 1960s.

African nationalists fled South Africa and set up exile organizations. These organizations aimed to influence international opinion
against the white government, to stimulate and retain contact with
the resistance movements inside the Republic, and to organize
for guerrilla war. London was the main centre for the attempts
to influence international opinion, while, after their independence,
Zambia and Tanzania became the main headquarters of the organizations and the holding grounds for the guerrilla fighters. They
were seen as the bases from which a revolution could be launched.
The training and equipping of the guerrillas were increasingly
undertaken by communist states, either in Africa or in the communist countries themselves. After the Sino-Soviet split the ANC
was backed by Russia, while the PAC had Chinese support.[1]

As well as the nationalists there was a substantial exodus of
other South Africans, whites and non-whites, from the Republic,
especially in 1960/1961. Some left because they abhorred what
was happening, some because they feared for their freedom or their
lives, some because they thought they could fight the government
more effectively from outside, others because they anticipated
revolution and did not want to be caught in it. The numbers of
those involved is impossible to estimate accurately, but it was
certainly many thousands of people. Amnesty International
reported that, between the 1960 emergency and late 1963, 1,200
refugees had passed through Bechuanaland alone.[2] In March
1964 Vorster stated that 562 people who had been charged with
sabotage had left the country, and estimates of those who had left
for guerrilla training varied between 900 and 5,000.[3] By 1970 Mr.
P. C. Pelser, the Minister of Justice, claimed that there was a
'manpower pool' of between 38,000 and 42,000 fully trained
guerrilla fighters ready to attack southern Africa, many of whom
had been recruited in South Africa, but just how many of these
were South Africans he did not say.[4]

For South Africa's external relations, the most important of
the refugees were those who organized themselves to fight apartheid from outside. Again there was considerable variety. Some
white exiles joined groups like the Anti-Apartheid Movement
which exerted persistent pressure on foreign governments and

---

[1] See Gibson, op. cit., part 2.   [2] IRR 1963, p. 58.   [3] IRR 1964, p. 75.
[4] *Today's News* (Director of Information, South African Embassy, London),
16 Sept. 1970.

international organizations, while, as already noted, some black South Africans chose direct action by joining the guerrilla fighters who were training in Africa and communist states. These active refugees created pools of organized opposition to the South African Government, whether the opposition emerged as a rally in Trafalgar Square or a guerrilla camp near the Zambesi. Their mere existence meant that foreign governments were never allowed to forget that there were South Africans of all races who were dedicated to overthrowing the existing political and social structure. For any foreign governments and organizations which were eager to challenge the South African Government, these pools of refugees provided ready-made allies. Yet for the refugees themselves exile was often a frustrating experience, as their hopes of rapid successes were not realized.

The South African Government denied that the internal troubles, and the growth of the resistance movements, came from the country's racial policies. Ministers persistently claimed that the troubles were initiated by subversive, communist, and liberal elements outside South Africa. Verwoerd said that Sharpeville and the events which followed must be seen against the background of developments in Africa, and 'when they were seen against that background it would be realized that they did not really have anything to do with any South African policy'.[1] In a BBC broadcast Louw said, 'What people overseas do not appreciate is that this is all the result of subversive activity which has been going on for some time with the aim of bringing black man's rule.' When he was asked if the African believed he had a grievance, Louw replied, 'He has been told he has one.'[2]

There was a great gulf between prevailing international attitudes towards African resistance leaders and the attitude of the South African Government. While to the South Africans these men were revolutionaries, sometimes murderers and assassins, bent on destroying a society which offered security and prosperity for all races, opinion outside South Africa was generally sympathetic to the radical reforms proposed by the African leaders. When ex-Chief Albert Luthuli,[3] President General of the banned ANC,

[1] *South Africa Digest*, vol. 7, no. 6, 18 Mar. 1960.
[2] *South Africa Digest*, vol. 7, no. 8, 16 Apr. 1960.
[3] See Albert Luthuli, *Let My People Go* (New York, McGraw Hill, and London, Collins, 1962) and Mary Benson, *Chief Albert Luthuli of South Africa* (London, Oxford University Press, 1963).

was awarded the Nobel Peace Prize for 1960, the awarding committee said that 'in spite of the unmerciful South African race
laws, Luthuli has always urged that violence should not be used.
To a high degree it is due to him that struggles in South Africa
have not taken the form of bloody conflicts.' At the time of the
award Luthuli, after years of trouble with the government, was
under a restriction order confining him to a small area near his
home in Natal, and banning him from attending meetings.
Reluctantly the government gave him a ten-day passport to receive
the prize in Oslo, but refused his application to extend his visit to
Tanganyika and the United States. The Minister of the Interior
said that the government could not understand or support the
award, which was regretted within South Africa. Luthuli, he said,
had not promoted peace and consequently the Nobel Prize would
lose much of its prestige in being awarded to him.[1]

Luthuli's was an individual case, and he personally had never
been accused of using direct violence. But international sympathy
was sometimes expressed in blanket terms for all those who
opposed apartheid, including those who had used violence. In
October 1963 the General Assembly passed a resolution by 106
votes to 1 which called on South Africa to release all political
prisoners immediately and unconditionally, and to end the trials
of those accused under the Sabotage Act and related legislation.
In December of the same year the Security Council unanimously
adopted a resolution calling on the Republic to liberate all the
people who were imprisoned or restricted in any way for opposing
apartheid. In March 1964 U Thant followed this up by appealing
to the South African Government to spare the lives of three men
who were to be executed for 'acts arising from their opposition to
the government's racial policies'. The South Africans, indignant
at what they saw as interference in their internal affairs and unjust
criticism of the legislative and judicial systems, replied that the
men had been convicted of deliberate murder and sabotage, and
no extenuating circumstances had been found. There was, they
said, no question of imposing the death penalty for opposing 'the
government's racial policies'; it was imposed for murder and
violence. They added that they resented this interference in
internal affairs and the degree of partiality shown by the Secretary General. After an unsuccessful appeal, the three men were

[1] IRR 1961, p. 29.

executed.[1] There were similar international protests at the trial in
1964 of a group of major ANC leaders who had been captured
while meeting at a secret headquarters at Rivonia, Johannesburg.[2]

By the end of 1963 the South African Government had, at least
temporarily, broken the resistance movements inside South Africa.
The African nationalist parties survived in exile and as small
underground cells within the country, but the immediate danger
of a major civil war had been averted. The African nationalist
leaders reluctantly came to realize that there would be no sudden,
mass uprising. Sobukwe's hopes of independence by 1963 were
seen to have been an illusion. The leaders came to recognize that
a protracted struggle lay ahead. 'The masses are ready for a long
Revolutionary war', said P. K. Leballo, who became National
Secretary of the PAC.[3] In accepting that a long struggle lay
ahead, the African nationalists also had to accept the problems
that came to exile groups which had no immediate prospect of
success—loss of morale, factional disputes, dissension among the
leadership, inefficiency, and corruption. But with their continued
training and planning for guerrilla war and internal revolution,
they remained a major threat to the white-dominated state. The
South African Government saw no reason to relax its vigilance.
If anything the legislation and police organization designed to
counter internal resistance movements and other internal dissension became stronger and more efficient. The greatest impact was
on the non-whites, but even white South Africans paid a heavy
price for their privileged position by accepting a great burden of
restrictive legislation and extensive government powers.

As the pressure increased during the early 1960s so the options
open to the South African foreign policy-makers became narrower
than ever. The government faced a hostile international environment in which policy became largely a response to external attacks.
Given that there were these severe limitations, Verwoerd played a
major role in shaping that response. Until his assassination in
1966 he dominated the government, concentrating much of the
responsibility for internal and external affairs in his own hands,
although he retained a separate Foreign Minister.[4]

[1] IRR 1964, pp. 107–8.   [2] IRR 1964, pp. 112–15.
[3] Quoted by Gibson, op. cit., p. 99.
[4] Louw until 1963, and then Dr. Hilgard Muller.

Munger has emphasized that policy-making in the South African Government is concentrated in relatively few hands, so that when an outstandingly powerful Prime Minister has emerged there has been a tendency to say 'leave it to Smuts' or 'leave it to Verwoerd'.[1] In Verwoerd's case this was reinforced by the strong sense of God-chosen leadership among the Nationalist Afrikaners. Verwoerd himself appears to have believed that he had been divinely chosen for his task. In a broadcast following his election as Prime Minister he said: 'We, as believing rulers of a religious country, will seek our strength and guidance in the future, as in the past, from Him who controls the destinies of Nations. . . . In accordance with His will, it was determined who should assume the leadership of the Government in this new period of the life of the people of South Africa.'[2]

Naturally such a powerful character attracted opponents as well as eager disciples. Even among his cabinet colleagues there were some who resented his domineering style, his inclination to interfere and make *ex cathedra* statements,[3] but Verwoerd's own convictions about the road to be followed and his role as the leader of white South Africa never faltered. In 1961 when he was under strong personal attack from the United Party he defended himself in the terms almost of a religious martyr. He said: 'I stay here only because my conscience tells me that I dare not run away from the task which my people have entrusted to me. . . . The fact is just that I am convinced that whoever sits here should be prepared to endure troubles for the sake of the future of his country. I am convinced that he will have to be prepared to suffer for his convictions.'[4]

In 1961 Verwoerd said that the Nationalists must stand by their racial policies 'like walls of granite',[5] and granite is the image that clings to Verwoerd—powerful, dominant, unswerving, supremely confident in his own ability and judgement.

---

[1] In 1965 Edwin Munger wrote that: 'If one were to list the most important people making foreign policy the names might well run: 1. Dr. Verwoerd. 2. Dr. Verwoerd. 3. Dr. Verwoerd. 4. Foreign Minister Muller. 5. The Cabinet and 6. Secretary G. P. Jooste, Brand Fourie, Donald Sale and one or two other professionals.' (The individuals listed under 6 are permanent officials.) Edwin S. Munger, *Notes on the Formation of South Africa's Foreign Policy* (California, Grant Dahlstrom/The Castle Press, 1965), p. 85.

[2] Alexander Hepple, *Verwoerd* (Penguin, 1967), p. 134.

[3] Personal communication.

[4] H of A, 10 Apr. 1961, col. 4196.   [5] IRR 1961, p. 10.

Some years later when he looked back to Macmillan's 1960 visit, Verwoerd outlined his ideas about how governments *should* behave. Macmillan had said that governments had to accept changes, even those they disliked. A primary aim of government, said Macmillan, was to remain in the midstream of public opinion, and to do this often involved trimming one's sails and abandoning previous policies and opinions. In saying this Verwoerd suspected that Macmillan was trying to deter him from going ahead with the republic and to persuade him to abandon apartheid. As Macmillan saw it, South Africa was heading against the stream of world opinion and 'history would take its course'. Macmillan's was essentially a consensus view of politics drawn from British experience, with its emphasis on compromise, pragmatism, and the search for the middle ground. The political experience of the Nationalists has been rooted in very different soil. They have struggled continually to preserve a particular culture and society against powerful opponents. They have survived as a distinctive people only by intransigence, by a refusal to compromise, by insisting on their particular rights, and by a dogmatic conviction of the justice of their cause.[1] Privately Verwoerd had found Macmillan's views about trimming the sails 'repulsive'.[2] Publicly he had replied: 'I said that I preferred to row upstream; that I preferred to set a course for myself rather than be carried along willy-nilly by the stream; that I believed that in that way I would be able to exercise some influence over the course of history and that I would then be in a position to ensure the fulfilment of the desire of that section of the Nation whose support I enjoy.'[3]

The strongest challenge to Verwoerd's conviction of right came in the crisis years of 1960 and 1961. In 1960, that year of fear and tragedy, there were many white South Africans calling for changes and modifications in apartheid. Even inside the National Party there was talk of the need for reform. To militant opponents of

[1] J. E. Spence has written: 'The more naive overseas critics . . . fail to realize the weakness, and—from the Afrikaner's point of view—the irrelevance of a pragmatic tradition of politics in a context where survival, measured in both physical and ideological terms, is conceived to be the first priority.' Spence, *Republic Under Pressure* (London, OUP, Chatham House Essays, 1965), p. 11.

[2] Barnard mentions this in his book. According to him, Macmillan's idea that 'one must trim one's sails to the wind and go with the current' was too much for Verwoerd who said in no uncertain terms that 'such a view was repulsive to him' (op. cit., p. 61).

[3] H of A, 5 Feb. 1965, col. 611.

apartheid these suggestions may have seemed peripheral to their main aim of removing all racial discrimination, but in the closed, inbred atmosphere of Afrikaner nationalism they had a sharp impact. The questioning and re-examination was widespread. At the South African Bureau of Racial Affairs (SABRA, an institution which had provided much of the intellectual backing for apartheid) a debate started about modifying apartheid by bringing the Coloureds closer to the white community. Coloured representatives were invited to discuss the issue. In July 1960 the political commentator of *Die Burger* suggested that Coloured voters should be permitted to elect Coloured members to Parliament. Within the Dutch Reformed Churches there were appeals from some theologians to go much further. In November 1960 eleven leading clerics published a denunciation of racial discrimination, and at a meeting of the World Council of Churches at Cottesloe some members of the Dutch Reformed Churches voted for a comprehensive resolution which denounced the government's policies.[1] The call for reform even spread into the government. At Humansdorp on 19 April Paul Sauer, the Minister of Lands, Forestry and Public Works, said that the 'old book' of South Africa's history had been closed a month before at Sharpeville, that the whole policy towards Africans must be reconsidered. For a time there was even speculation that there might be a split within the National Party with a group of M.P.s breaking away under Sauer.[2]

These were the voices calling for compromise and change, but they were not universal, and Verwoerd's was not among them. Within the party and SABRA he silenced, even if he never entirely eradicated, suggestions for modifying apartheid. For a time Sauer was kept in the background and sent on an official trip to Argentina. Talk of a break in the party quickly disappeared as Verwoerd rejected the 'dramatic ideas' of allowing Coloured representatives in Parliament, because he said it would be a springboard for the integration of the races, leading to biological assimilation. His distinctive reaction to the crisis of 1960 and 1961, and to the pressures applied on South Africa, was not to shy away from apartheid but to preach a more vigorous and thorough application.

[1] The various moves for reform are outlined in IRR 1961, pp. 9–10.
[2] Vernon McKay, 'A Day in the South African Parliament', *Africa Report*, Oct. 1968, p. 21.

He accepted that internal and external pressures were forcing changes on South Africa, but the changes Verwoerd was prepared to accept took him further along the road his opponents rejected. Far from deterring him from his self-conceived task, the crisis reinforced his resolution.

In a speech of May 1960, which had to be read for him as he was in hospital recovering from the assassination attempt, Verwoerd admitted that the recent disturbances had given cause for general reflection, but he saw no reason to depart from previous policy. After regretting the misinterpretation of this policy at home and abroad, he said that it was public opinion and not government policy that had been changed by recent developments. This change gave the government an excellent opportunity to push further ahead with the introduction of aspects of apartheid which previously had lacked popular support. As first steps towards this he announced more energetic efforts at economic development within the Bantustans, and a tighter control by the central government over the administration of Africans in urban areas, many of which were controlled by United Party local councils.[1]

As the immediate internal and external dangers faded so Verwoerd's prestige among white South Africans increased. His inflexibility and intransigence, which at first had been bitterly criticized by his opponents and had bred doubts among some of his supporters, drew increasing support. Eventually, most white South Africans were prepared to see the position in terms of the clear choice presented by the Prime Minister—to choose between 'international popularity and the destruction of the White nation in South Africa'.[2]

The importance of Verwoerd's leadership in the response to the dangers of the early 1960s must be set in the context of the Republic's economic and military strength (which will be described later). Without this strength the granite response would have counted for little. Nor did Verwoerd satisfy all his critics within South Africa. Some remained convinced that his inflexible stand greatly damaged the country's international position. Speaking in 1971 Marais Steyn, a leading member of the United Party, said: 'He did more to isolate South Africa than I think any other man. I think that as a psychologist he believed that if he could get the

---

[1] IRR 1959–60, pp. 103–5.
[2] Quoted by Vandenbosch, *South Africa and the World*, p. 243.

South African people to fear and hate the outside world, and he could project a "father figure" image, he would gain politically. I think he deliberately exploited this—to the long-term disadvantage of South Africa.'[1] But there were not many whites who shared Steyn's views in the early 1960s. The voices calling for compromise and flexibility grew weaker, as those supporting intransigence, the granite approach, became dominant.[2]

One important development in the government's response to the challenge of the early 1960s was to clarify and redefine nationalism within the context of apartheid. In terms of the white society, Verwoerd claimed that the success of the Republican referendum had made it possible to shift the emphasis away from exclusive Afrikaner nationalism towards an inclusive white nationalism. Afrikaner nationalism has been both 'an instrument of cultural defence against the English and of racial defence against the natives'.[3] It was the second of these that Verwoerd now chose to emphasize, and he could afford to do so because the National Party's grip within the white political system was secure.[4]

Like Smuts before him, Verwoerd began to argue for the reconciliation of all whites. But the two men started from very different bases. Smuts had tried to build upon the monarchy and the Commonwealth, using a party that was Afrikaner-led but largely English-speaking in its support. Verwoerd set out to build upon the new Republic and his instrument was an almost exclusively Afrikaner party. 'I see the National Party today . . .', he said in 1961, 'as a party which stands for the preservation of the white man, of the white government in South Africa.'[5]

Doubtless Verwoerd was right in suggesting that the declaration of the Republic was an important factor in the government's

[1] *New Nation* (Pretoria), Nov. 1971, vol. 5, no. 4, p. 5.
[2] For example, Muriel Howell in her 1961 report stated that: 'During the same period [i.e. the months after leaving the Commonwealth] the United Party moved discernibly to the right' (IRR 1961, p. 8).
[3] C. W. de Kiewiet, *The Anatomy of South African Misery* (London, Oxford University Press, 1956), p. 21.
[4] Stanley Trapido argues that the UP was no longer an alternative government. It has 'become the underlying assumption of the South African political system that the parliamentary opposition, whatever else its function, does not provide an alternative government' (*Journal of Commonwealth Political Studies*, vol. 4, 1966, p. 83).
[5] IRR 1961, p. 14.

resolve to foster white nationalism, but even more important was the general threat to white society perceived in the early 1960s. With an external environment largely hostile and the fear of non-white revolution within their borders, white South Africans drew together to defend their privileged position. The National Party could still appeal to the Afrikaners as Afrikaners, while appealing to the English-speakers as whites. The government constantly emphasized that white unity must be preserved at all costs. 'I want', said Verwoerd, 'to echo through the world, right into the forums of the United Nations Organization and right into the government bodies of the mightiest nations in the world, namely, that they will have to deal with a united South Africa should they try to force us off our course.'[1]

The divisions between the whites became relatively less important and this was reflected in foreign affairs. After the clash over the question of Commonwealth membership, Sir de Villiers Graaff, the leader of the United Party, could not remember any substantial difference between the government and the opposition on a major issue of foreign policy, although he thought there may have been a difference of emphasis following Rhodesia's UDI in 1965.[2]

Yet in the search for a new white nationalism there were important provisos. Verwoerd, even if he had wanted to, could not have opened his arms too widely to English-speakers because of the suspicion and opposition within his own party. There were strict terms on which the English-speakers could enter the Afrikaner stronghold. 'Their support was welcome, but not their ideas.'[3] Neither Verwoerd nor any of his followers had any intention of undermining the Afrikaner dominance of the party or the Afrikaner values for which it stood. The distinctiveness of Afrikaner culture and society was to be preserved; and there was to be no relaxation in education or language policies. The Afrikaners would remain the core element of the white society. This inbred cultural exclusiveness has continued to make it difficult for non-Afrikaners to establish a personal identity with the party, even when they have been strong supporters of the government's policies. Partly because of this the United Party has survived, still

---

[1] H of A, 24 Apr. 1964, col. 4914.   [2] Personal communication.
[3] Edwin S. Munger, *Afrikaner and African Nationalism* (London, Oxford University Press for the Institute of Race Relations, 1967), p. 79.

drawing considerable support although not threatening to oust the National Party from the control of the government.

One measurable sign of the Nationalist government's shift of emphasis from Afrikaner to white nationalism was revealed in its immigration policy. The year 1960 was a bad one for immigrants. Prospective settlers were frightened away and a substantial number of whites left the country. In that year there was a net loss of whites. From then onwards, however, the change in government policy to positive encouragement of white immigration ensured a sharp rise in numbers. The record figures for the last years of Smuts's administration were quickly left behind (see page 138). As late as January 1959 Verwoerd had still been riding the old hobby-horse by accusing the United Party of trying to swamp Afrikanerdom with large-scale immigration, and he had argued in favour of continuing the tight restrictions of the past decade. Explaining his reversal of policy, he claimed that Afrikaner values were now entrenched in the new Republic, and that the government's racial policies had been given a firm foundation. But more than these, the dramatic change serves to emphasize the change in white South Africa's circumstances and the strength of the perceived dangers. In a speech in 1965 in which he defended the change in immigration policy, Verwoerd said: 'Our motto is to maintain white supremacy for all time to come over our own people and our own country, by force if necessary.'[1]

Again the government's expanded immigration policy must be matched against Afrikaner fears. The National Party's suspicions and prejudices—against Roman Catholics, Jews, Mediterranean Europeans, and accepting too many English-speakers—did not disappear overnight. They became buried, but not extinguished, beneath the dangers that confronted white South Africa. The government brought in more immigrants to strengthen the white position but at the same time was determined to preserve Afrikaner control within the context of white-dominated South Africa.

This objective is central to understanding not only immigration policy but the whole range of the South African Government's policies during the 1960s. The appeal to a white nationalism became part of the overall social structuring to which Verwoerd and his disciples were committed. In this the early 1960s did not see a change of direction, but rather a clearer delineation of ideas

[1] H of A, 5 Feb. 1965, col. 636.

White immigration into South Africa

about 'race' and 'nation'. As early as the Sauer report of 1948, which had given currency to the word 'apartheid', a relationship had been recognized between 'race' and 'nation'.[1] The report had spoken of racial groups as 'separate national communities', an idea that Verwoerd developed in his years as Minister of Native Affairs. In the early 1960s he made his views more explicit, at least in the case of whites and Africans. The 'white race' was to be synonymous with the 'white nation', but this was not to be the case with Africans (the Bantu). According to the government's view, there were a number of 'nations' among the Bantu—the Xhosa, Zulu, Tswana, and so on. The case of the Asians and Coloureds was much less clear-cut, and it is easier to repeat the questions put to the government ministers than to find any certainty in their replies. Could the Asians who had come originally from India be said to form a separate nation? Were the Coloureds who had all their roots in South Africa a separate nation, and, if so, where was their 'homeland'? The answers were never clear. Dr. A. L. Geyer said: 'When I think of the Coloureds my thoughts arrive at a dead end and I prefer not to go any further. While I was High Commissioner in England I always preferred to give talks on the Africans rather than on the Coloureds because in the case of the Africans I knew the answers.'[2] Neither the Coloureds nor the Asians had articulated strong nationalist sentiments, but, however imprecisely conceived, the government claimed that each was a separate racial group aspiring to become a 'nation'.[3]

The government had set its face against national integration based upon a common South African identity. Instead it saw South Africa as a 'multi-national state'.[4] It was impossible, argued the government, to develop a sense of common identity among such a diversity of people. To attempt to do so would only lead to friction, bitterness, and a struggle for power among the different

---

[1] René de Villiers, 'Afrikaner Nationalism' in *The Oxford History of South Africa*, vol. II, p. 406.

[2] Quoted by H. W. van der Merwe, 'What Middle Road for the Coloureds?', *New Nation* (Pretoria), June 1971, p. 10.

[3] Munger calls the Indians, the Coloureds, and the English-speakers 'subgroups below the threshold of nationalism' (*Afrikaner and African Nationalism*, p. 18).

[4] Thompson calls South Africa a 'caste society' (*Politics in the Republic of South Africa*, p. 96), and this appears to me a more satisfactory basis of analysis for internal political development. In the text I am developing the government's own view.

groups. Much better, so the argument went, to accept the distinctions and let each group develop separately. Within the context of this thinking, African nationalism, as distinct from the nationalism of particular Bantu peoples, was not recognized. This assertion made a dramatic difference to the dispute about majority and minority rights. The African nationalists had called for universal adult suffrage, which would have given black men a clear majority of votes, but within the government's categorization there was no single majority group. Each national group was a minority of the whole and so no one nation could claim a preponderance in terms of numbers alone. Claims for majority rule therefore became irrelevant.

The contrasting views can be seen in the following tables—one divided into racial groups, the other into the government's 'national' groups.

POPULATION IN 1960 BASED ON MAIN RACES[1]

Africans	10,807,809
Whites	3,067,638
Coloureds	1,488,267
Asians	477,414
Total	15,841,128

MAIN 'NATIONAL' GROUPS—1960 FIGURES

Xhosa	3,423,000
Whites	3,067,638
Zulu	2,959,000
Coloureds	1,488,267
Northern Sotho	1,122,000
Southern Sotho	1,089,000
Tswana	863,000
Asians	477,414
Tsonga	366,000
Swazi	301,000

Although pressing the multi-national state argument, the government made clear that control of the South African 'state' would remain in the hands of the whites. The white government would continue to have responsibility for all the national groups until these groups became capable of managing their own affairs.

Just how far or how quickly this development would take place would depend upon the nations themselves. In the case of the

[1] Tables derived from IRR 1961, pp. 82 and 84.

Bantu nations they would have separate geographical areas ('homelands' based largely on the old native reserves), but the great bulk of what is now South Africa, roughly 87 per cent of the total geographical area, would be reserved for the white nation. The Bantu would come from their homelands to work or to visit in the white areas, but they could never gain full citizenship rights. The government was challenged on the artificiality of these claims. How, it was asked, could Africans who had lived all their lives in the white areas ever feel an identity with a remote and unknown homeland? And there were always the questions about the Coloureds and Asians. They had no homelands. Where would these 'nations' find their Zions? The challenges were never met. Verwoerd mused about the possibility of 'a state within a state', and political separation but mutual economic interdependence, but he was musing, he was not giving a clear answer.[1]

The distinction between 'country' (or 'state') and 'nation' came out clearly when Verwoerd spoke about the position of the Coloureds. He said:

One must distinguish between ... citizenship of a country and ... what the components of a homogeneous nation are. There is no doubt that the coloureds are citizens of this country. There is just as little doubt that they are not part of this homogeneous entity that can be described here as 'the nation'.... In South Africa various groups of the population who in the nature of things are different nations possess citizenship. ... For a long time we regarded ourselves as English and Afrikaners, etc. With the establishment of the Republic the unification of these two components into one nation became a possibility, and it is for that possibility that I plead. But, after all, the unification of both White population groups into one nation need not necessarily be accompanied by a further unification into one nation together with the Bantu.[2]

Verwoerd argued that the government was conscious of its obligations to all the national groups within South Africa and would endeavour to lead the separate nations to their own fulfilment. His insistence upon 'separate freedoms' was, according to de Villiers, his 'most important contribution to Afrikaner Nationalism'. He gave apartheid a coherence and respectability, which meant that the Nationalists, oppressed 'with an uneasy sense of guilt before the accusing eyes of the world', were able to hold up their heads again.[3]

[1] IRR 1961, pp. 135 and 141.
[2] IRR 1962, p. 119.   [3] de Villiers, op. cit., p. 414.

10

THE THREAT OF INTERNATIONAL
ACTION

One of the clearest dangers perceived by the South African Government in the early 1960s was the threat of international action. The threat grew with the changes in the world community following the emergence of new 'black' states in Africa, which substantially reinforced the ranks of South Africa's militant opponents both in terms of numbers and commitment. In attacking South Africa and her apartheid policies the Africans brought with them a burning conviction of right. They saw themselves, as Professor Ali Mazrui wrote, introducing a new morality and justice into international relations. 'The African feels that by fighting for himself he has been fighting for nothing less than the human personality itself.'[1] The sense of mission was never more clearly felt than in opposition to white minority rule in southern Africa. The great majority of the African states which gained independence at that time were in the 'middle belt' of Africa—physically separated from the Republic and independent of her for their economic welfare.[2] Their moral fervour was not, therefore, blunted by fears for their material well-being.

The new African states believed that the overthrow of white minority rule in southern Africa should be one of the principal tasks of international organizations. When they raised the issue at the United Nations or when they took a case to the International Court they were not aiming at a dialogue with the South Africans, or a compromise solution for conflicting interests, or a legal clarification of complex issues: they were out to attest their belief and to organize action against the racialist society. The African

[1] Ali Mazrui, *The Anglo-African Commonwealth* (Oxford, Pergamon Press, 1967), p. 86.
[2] The case of the black southern African states will be considered later—see ch. 16.

states brought new life and strength to the diplomatic attacks on South Africa and swung world opinion even further against the Republic. In itself this was an achievement, but the Africans wanted more than that. They wanted the international organizations to move away from 'advising', 'calling upon', or 'urging' the South Africans to a commitment to action. In their public statements the Africans were confident of their cause; confident that a society built upon apartheid could not stand; and confident that the international organizations would play a major part in bringing it down. Such confidence made assumptions not only about the compelling force of a moral cause, but also about the effectiveness of the international organizations.

Potentially one of the chief sources of danger for the Republic was the new African body, the Organization of African Unity (OAU). From its inception in 1963 the OAU examined the possibilities of organizing action against South Africa. Writing about its first meeting, Zdenek Červenka said that after condemning South Africa, 'The conference resolved to buy arms for the freedom fighters, give them all necessary military training in camps to be established in various independent African countries, and to offer them both shelter and transit on their way to and from the battlegrounds in the dependent territories and thus to launch full-scale guerrilla war against the colonial regimes and the white minority government.'[1]

This was a threat that the South African Government could not ignore, but by the time the OAU came into existence the South African Government had overcome the crisis of internal security. Reinforced by this success and by the realization of the country's increasing economic and military strength,[2] the South Africans were able to face outside dangers with much greater confidence. Also the OAU encountered considerable difficulties in translating its plans for military action into practice. From the beginning there were divisions within the organization which made co-operation difficult even on such a unifying issue as opposition to white minority regimes. Sometimes it appeared that opposition to white rule was the only question on which the members could agree.[3]

[1] Z. Červenka, *The Organization of African Unity* (London, C. Hurst and Co., 1968), p. 17.
[2] See ch. 13.   [3] Červenka, op. cit., pp. 12–13.

In 1964 a recommendation was put to a summit meeting of the OAU in Cairo for the establishment of an African High Command, and the hope was expressed that the South African Government would modify its racial policies when 'confronted with the prospect of a showdown with a well co-ordinated and determined African force representing the collective moral and material force of all the African States'.[1] This resolution was never approved because the immense problems involved in mounting a combined military assault on the Republic were clear to the new states. The OAU's contribution to military co-ordination became centred upon a Liberation Committee, established in 1963, which was concerned with providing aid for guerrilla fighters and resistance movements.

A further constraint on OAU activity was that while many of the states were prepared to give generous verbal support to the guerrilla fighters, they were reluctant to provide material and financial aid.[2] Because of this, and because of disputes about strategy and which of the African Nationalist groups should be supported, the Committee of Liberation was often ineffective.[3] Yet despite these difficulties, guerrilla warfare did develop in southern Africa, and, as will be discussed in a later chapter, the OAU was able to offer some support.[4]

Another form of direct action which the Africans planned to use against the Republic was economic boycott and sanctions. The pattern was set early. In November 1959 the African Trade Union Federation appealed to all Africans, to the International Free Labour Movement, and to democratic governments to use their influence and powers to refuse markets to South African goods. In January 1960 the All-Africa Peoples' Conference supported the boycott call and in the following June the Pan-African Federation Conference agreed to use commercial, diplomatic, and political sanctions against South Africa, and to exert particular pressure on South Africa's oil supplies.[5] After the establishment of the OAU, similar resolutions and calls for sanctions were always given overwhelming support.

---

[1] Červenka, op. cit., p. 74.

[2] There was a similar reluctance to give financial backing for the South West Africa case at the International Court. In 1965 the OAU Secretary General, Mr. Diallo Telli, complained that many members had failed to pay their contributions for the case. Cockram, *Vorster's Foreign Policy*, p. 21.

[3] Červenka, op. cit., p. 18.   [4] See ch. 16.   [5] IRR 1960, p. 274.

Almost all the middle-belt states declared boycotts of trade with the Republic, and refused to handle South African shipping or aircraft. The greatest inconvenience for the South Africans was caused by the refusal of overfly rights, which forced South African Airways to route its aircraft around 'the Bulge' of West Africa, adding about 900 miles to the flight to Europe. But the boycotts and sanctions were certainly not universally successful. They were not applied by all the African states (even by some who said they were imposing them). As the detailed trade figures are not published it is impossible to be precise, but Leo Katzen has estimated that if the twenty-five countries (mainly Afro-Asian) which had declared boycotts of South African goods had made them effective South Africa would have lost 4·5 per cent of the value of her exports. The first point to note about this figure is that however effective these boycotts had been they could not seriously have hurt the South Africans. To make a real impact the African states realized that they had to persuade South Africa's main trading partners to join them. The second point is that even these mini-boycotts were only partly successful. The loss in South Africa's exports in the period between 1959 and 1962 was about 1·7 per cent, excluding gold, and only 1 per cent if gold is included.[1] The South Africans absorbed this with ease.

As with other international organizations, the pressure on South Africa at the United Nations intensified during the early 1960s. The old issues of apartheid, South Africa's Asians, and South West Africa were discussed in an atmosphere which, according to a South African Government white paper, was 'charged with unbridled emotion as the result of the militant campaign carried on against the so-called evils of colonialism by the African grouped states, the communist powers and certain Asian powers'.[2] Louw declared that 'never except in a state of war had there been such concentrated opposition against a state'.[3]

It would be pointless and tedious to detail the streams of United Nations resolutions and votes which went against South Africa.

[1] IRR 1964, p. 124.
[2] The white paper is in the Printed Annexures to the Minutes of Proceedings of the House of Assembly, W. P. 1963, vol. III, *Report on the Proceedings of the 16th Session of the General Assembly of the United Nations on questions affecting South Africa, September to December 1961.*
[3] H of A, 26 Feb. 1960, col. 2334.

It was the pattern of the past, only more so. With the 'militants' reinforced and the Western states now openly critical, the best that the South Africans could hope was that the resolutions, although more sharply worded, would remain words and not be translated into direct action.

The bitterness of the attacks can be seen in the reactions which followed Sharpeville. The Security Council, with only France and Britain abstaining, resolved that South Africa's racial policies had 'led to international friction and if continued might endanger international peace and security'. United States support for this resolution marked a clear change of attitude, and the British abstention on this issue was quickly followed by a vote against South Africa in the General Assembly on a condemnatory resolution, requesting all states 'to consider taking such separate and collective action as is open to them, in conformity with the Charter of the United Nations, to bring about the abandonment of [apartheid] policies'.[1]

This change in Western diplomatic attitudes was particularly striking. The British, who previously had seen South Africa's race policies as an exclusively internal affair, now openly attacked apartheid, because, they argued, it had implications for the whole international community. The British delegate feared that apartheid 'would have disastrous consequences that would not only affect the peoples of South Africa but reach across its borders'. Not only was apartheid morally indefensible, but it would not succeed. Mr. Plimpton, the American delegate, joined the attack, declaring that all men were born equal, and that it was not only desirable but essential for a change of South Africa's apartheid policy. Louw characteristically replied that the Republic was a threat to nobody. He turned to ask the American delegate why, if all men were created equal, the Americans were still having integration troubles generations after the Declaration of Independence.[2]

Signs of increasing Western hostility were also found in bilateral relations. One that particularly disturbed the Nationalist government was the increasing estrangement from the Netherlands, the Afrikaner homeland. The Dutch Government had strongly criticized apartheid even before Macmillan's speech, and in

---

[1] Quoted by Spence, *Republic Under Pressure*, p. 106.
[2] The debates are outlined in the 1963 South African White Paper, loc. cit.

January 1960 the South African Ambassador at The Hague expressed his government's 'displeasure and serious concern' at the public criticism of apartheid by the Dutch Foreign Minister, which would harm relations between the Afrikaner people and the land of their forefathers.[1] Further friction was to follow. In 1964 a visit to South Africa by a delegation of the Netherlands Parliament was called off by Pretoria, because, according to Muller, the Dutch wanted to talk to Chief Luthuli which the South African Government would not permit as he was in restriction. One of the Dutch delegates drew a wider implication, stating that 'at the moment an attempt at dialogue between the Netherlands and South Africa on the basis of the old kinship and the old bonds is no longer possible and thus the old ties no longer have any functions in the present political tension'. Shortly after the visit was cancelled the Dutch Government further offended the South Africans by giving 100,000 guilders to the Defence and Aid Fund, which gives legal aid to Africans who have been arrested for political offences and help to their families.[2]

While there was this increasing criticism and hostility towards apartheid the picture of Western relations with South Africa continued to be a mixed one. There remained the attractions of economic links and the reluctance of the Western powers to break traditional contacts and become involved in the internal affairs of another state. The mixed picture remained, but during the 1960s South Africa became diplomatically more and more unpopular. In 1960 Macmillan could pay an official and 'friendly' visit. A few years later this would have been unthinkable for a British Prime Minister because of opposition in Britain as well as abroad. 'The Western nations are prepared to abandon the whites in Africa',[3] declared Verwoerd, while an editorial in *Die Burger* spoke of the Republic becoming 'a kind of Israel in a dominantly hostile Africa' and this 'may become our national way of life for as long as we can see ahead'.[4]

South Africa was internationally isolated by a gulf of attitudes. The moderates hesitated to take action, but they showed no sympathy for the racial ideas prevalent in the Republic. The clash of ideas and values explains much of the frustration and resentment

---

[1] IRR 1959–60, p. 277.
[2] Vandenbosch, *S. Africa and the World*, p. 259.
[3] H of A, 9 Mar. 1960, col. 3015.   [4] IRR 1962, p. 57.

felt both by the South Africans and their critics, moderates and militants alike. The Republic's policies were built on premises which were rejected by other states and so no genuine discussion or debate was possible. It was a slanging match from fixed and often mutually incomprehensible positions.

One of the many examples that can be used to demonstrate this came in 1964. In that year U Thant, the United Nations Secretary General, following a resolution of the Security Council, appointed a group to investigate methods of resolving the deadlock that had been reached on South Africa's racial policies. Mrs. K. Gunnar Myrdal of Sweden was appointed to lead the group and there were members from Britain, Yugoslavia, Ghana, and Morocco. As seen by the majority at the United Nations this was a well-balanced group, and the presence of two Western representatives gave it a 'moderate' flavour.[1] The South African view was very different. They did not think any group had the right to interfere in South Africa's internal affairs, and refused permission for the committee to enter the Republic.

In white South African eyes, the government's suspicions were fully confirmed by the committee's report, which assumed that majority rule must eventually come to South Africa. It stated: 'What is now at issue is not the final outcome, but the question whether on the way the people of South Africa are to go through a long ordeal of blood and hate.' To avoid this 'ordeal of blood and hate' the group suggested that a national convention should be summoned, fully representative of all the people of South Africa, charged with the task of setting the country on a new course based on racial co-operation and equality. Among the topics which it thought should be discussed were a Bill of Rights, a federal system of government, the removal of the 'mass of restrictive and discriminatory legislation', and the introduction of a fully representative system of government. The group also recommended the establishment of an education and training programme designed to 'enable as many South Africans as possible to play a full part as quickly as possible in the political, economic and social advance in their country'. It examined the logistics of economic sanctions.[2]

---

[1] In the case of Sir Hugh Foot, the British member, the group had one of the more 'militant' of the 'moderates'.

[2] IRR 1964, pp. 108–9, and Spence, *Republic Under Pressure*, p. 108.

It is difficult to imagine proposals which could have been more incomprehensible and reprehensible to the South African Government. The Nationalist government had no intention whatsoever of calling a national convention, and even less a convention to establish fully representative government. 'The report', said Verwoerd, 'consists to a large extent of a number of inaccuracies, distortions and erroneous conclusions based on false premises.'[1] Yet, however strong their feelings, the South Africans could not entirely ignore such a report, for the group had recommended that if the South Africans refused to call a convention the Security Council should apply economic sanctions.

The South African Government was not prepared to let its case at the United Nations go by default. It recognized that as it could now expect no support from the Western states it would face universal criticism. Therefore it concentrated upon emphasizing the difficulties, dangers, and costs of taking action against the Republic. In its diplomatic activities the South African Government continued to advance legalistic arguments, with occasional verbal counterblasts, which became less strident after Louw's departure, but there were also attempts to open up conciliatory dialogues. The most important of these was the visit of Mr. Hammarskjöld, the Secretary General of the United Nations, to South Africa in January 1961. Verwoerd explained that misunderstandings of South Africa's policies might be avoided if Hammarskjöld were able to gain personal knowledge of the country, and after the visit the South Africans said they were pleased with its results. A second visit by Hammarskjöld was being arranged when he was tragically killed in an air crash. No invitation was made to the new Secretary General, U Thant.

Economic sanctions were widely canvassed in the search for effective international action against the Republic. As already noted, the African states realized that to be effective they would require the support of the major Western trading countries. Within the West the debate about sanctions developed on two distinct planes. On one plane the concern was with moral issues, with questions of 'right' and 'wrong'. For those who believed strongly enough in these terms the issues were clear cut, the judgements absolute. Estimates of the effectiveness of sanctions

[1] IRR 1964, p. 110.

were dictated by the commitment of the person making the judgement. Ronald Segal, himself a strong advocate of sanctions, made this point. He wrote: 'Those who wanted sanctions dismissed all arguments against them as trivial or irrelevant, while those who opposed such action denounced it as illegal, impractical and economically calamitous. It was a dialogue of pulpits, with the phrases of revelation.'[1]

The other plane of the debate was hard-headed and pragmatic, concerned with calculating 'interests' and 'advantages'. It involved assessments of the impact of sanctions on world and bilateral trading relations, and the strategic implications of friendship or hostility with South Africa. On this plane the question was not 'What is right?' but 'How will our interests be affected?'

While there were people in the Western states who debated almost exclusively on one or other of the planes, most Western governments mixed the two, to ask both 'What is right?' and 'How will our interests be affected?' When the two questions were posed simultaneously a confused, complex picture emerged—a maze built from hedges of trading interests, moral judgements, legal considerations, strategic assessments, past ties and future predictions, emotions of blood, affection, and hatred. The difficulties of negotiating such a maze have been clearly outlined by Professor Dennis Austin.[2] Austin wrote about relations between Britain and South Africa, but the questions he posed are relevant for all the Western states with South African contacts. He asked such questions as: What are the likely consequences in southern Africa if sanctions are imposed? What will be the cost? How stable is white rule and will it be undermined by imposing sanctions? Is the moral issue so strong that some action must be taken whatever the cost? Is there agreement about an acceptable form of South African society? Will force have to be used to bring change, and if it is used what would be the likely results?

Persuading the Western states to take action was no easy task. Some of them, notably Britain, had much to lose, and none of them was fired by the moral fervour of 'the wretched of the earth'. In contrast to the characteristics which Professor Mazrui has suggested for the new African states, Professor Northedge

[1] Ronald Segal (ed.), *Sanctions against South Africa* (Penguin, 1964), p. 7.
[2] Dennis Austin, *Britain and South Africa* (London, Oxford University Press for the Royal Institute of International Affairs, 1966).

has seen the British 'style' in foreign affairs as venerating the *status quo*, and respecting law and the sanctity of treaties. 'As a rule', Northedge wrote, 'British Ministers do not concern themselves with the domestic arrangements of other countries; the question is rather whether foreign regimes are likely to last, whether their policies are, broadly speaking, in accord with British interests and whether they will honour their cheques.'[1]

In making their calculations about sanctions the Western states were brought face to face with the question of 'inevitability' in South Africa's political development. Militant critics of South Africa's racial policies stated that not only were these policies unjust and morally indefensible, but they were bound to fail. The argument was that the repression of the majority by the minority would inevitably lead to revolution unless radical reforms were introduced quickly. 'Sitting on a volcano' or 'standing on the edge of a precipice' were common images used about South Africa in the early 1960s, and events like Sharpeville were interpreted in this light. If the overthrow of white control was imminent then obviously this must be a major factor in Western calculations. Northedge had said the British were usually prepared to support the *status quo*, provided it was *likely to last* and honour its cheques. But what if white South Africa was not likely to last?

Another aspect of the 'inevitability' question was how the inevitable would happen. As the government gained the advantage over the African nationalists, the nature of that particular question changed. Successful internal revolution looked less and less likely, and as it did so the 'inevitable' rested more heavily on external action. This realization bred doubts all round. The memory of the Congo was still fresh and neither the Western nor the communist states savoured further intervention of that kind in Africa. For the Western powers, they might oppose apartheid, they might wish to see it abandoned, but in their scale of values was apartheid worse than the confusion, conflict, and even war that might follow intervention in southern Africa? If there were no imminent internal revolution might it not be better to wait for time to bring change, to hope that economic development would undermine racial barriers, to play a passive role and see what developed? Furthermore, there was the real danger that the result of any

[1] F. S. Northedge, *The Foreign Policy of the Powers* (London, Faber and Faber, 1968), pp. 163–4.

conflict in southern Africa would leave the Western powers in a weaker position than at the start. The South African economy might be wrecked, the country left with an unstable government; nor was there any guarantee that the government which emerged would be friendly towards the West. It was such doubts and fears that the South African Government sought to encourage.

The advocates of sanctions could claim a few successes in the early 1960s. Some pressure groups tried to prompt their governments into action, and even imposed their own limited sanctions. For example, the Trade Union leaders in Scandinavia called on their members to boycott South African goods between April and August 1960. In April 1964 the advocates of sanctions called an international conference in London, which drew delegates from more than forty states, including thirty official government delegations. The tone was set by Mr. Mongi Slim, the Foreign Minister of Tunisia and chairman of the conference, who said that 'economic sanctions are the last possible way of defeating apartheid peacefully'.[1] The sanctions advocates also had success in terms of advisory resolutions at the United Nations. For example in 1962 the General Assembly passed a sweeping resolution, by 67 votes to 16 with 23 abstentions, asking member states to break off diplomatic relations with the Republic, to boycott South African goods, to stop all exports to South Africa, and to close all ports and airports to her ships and aircraft.

Although these omnibus resolutions were largely ignored by South Africa's major trading partners, there was hope of an important development in the sanctions campaign in December 1963 when the Security Council called on all member states to ban the sale of arms and ammunition to South Africa. But again the resolution was not universally accepted or implemented. Britain and France, asserting that a clear distinction could be drawn between weapons for internal and external use, said that while they would not sell weapons which could be used to impose apartheid they would continue to sell arms for external defence. The British Conservative Government of the day also confirmed that it would continue to sell arms which were required for the defence of the Cape sea route, in the spirit of the Simonstown Agreement.[2]

[1] Ronald Segal, op. cit. Quoted on back cover of book.

[2] Less conspicuously, other countries also continued to sell arms. The Italians, for example, did not withdraw their licence for the manufacture of the Impala jet aircraft in South Africa.

In 1964 there was a change in British attitudes when a Labour government came into power. The Labour Party had always been more critical of South Africa and more inclined to consider the imposition of sanctions than their Conservative opponents. Although, after initial hesitation, the new government agreed to fulfil an order for sixteen Buccaneer strike aircraft, Mr. Harold Wilson, the British Prime Minister, announced that no further arms would be sold to the Republic. Despite Britain's change of heart, France continued to supply arms and substantially increased its sales to fill the gap left by Britain.

The international action sketched above was inconvenient for South Africa, and in the case of the arms ban it could have created a dangerous situation, but a major sanctions confrontation did not develop. The United Nations, the organization in which the African states had placed so much faith, had revealed its chronic inability to move further than its individual sovereign members were prepared to move. Ironically, it had been an African problem, the involvement in the Congo, which demonstrated these limitations very clearly. While the precise issues in the dispute were not directly relevant to South Africa's situation, its impact on the organization was. There was a series of open rifts among the UN members, which resulted in one third of the members refusing to pay any of their dues. Other states, including South Africa, refused to contribute to the Congo operations. It was an early lesson for the new African states that organizing international action was more difficult and confused than issuing strongly worded, moralistic statements.

The fear of extended conflict and disorder influenced both the major Western and Eastern states. The Congo experience had alerted them to the complexities and dangers of African 'adventures', and they were eager to contain their already extended commitments rather than seek involvement in new problem areas. In a very real sense the white South Africans were fortunate in being remote from existing centres of East/West confrontation, but they reinforced their luck by their intransigence. The South Africans left no doubt that any external action would be resisted, and resisted fiercely, so that a challenge even by a major power would be a substantial undertaking. In relation to economic sanctions, it was concluded that they would involve a long-drawn-out campaign with the threat of violence and the danger of serious escalation.

As another possible line of attack, the Republic's militant opponents saw South Africa's legalistic approach to international disputes as a double-edged weapon. These opponents aimed to fortify their moral cause with the authority of law by gaining favourable judgements at the International Court and mandatory decisions at the Security Council. Thus there was a situation in which both the South Africans and their militant critics concentrated much of their energies on legal arguments, although neither of them believed that these arguments were compelling in themselves. They were both convinced of the justice of their own causes, but they used legal arguments because for one side it seemed to offer the hope of effective international action, while for the other it was a way to counter that action.

The dispute over South West Africa continued as the clearest example of the use of legal pressures. It entered a new and potentially very dangerous phase for the Republic in November 1960 when Ethiopia and Liberia, as ex-members of the League of Nations, asked the International Court of Justice to declare:

(*a*) that South West Africa is still a Mandated Territory;

(*b*) that the 1920 Mandate is still a treaty in force under the ICJ;

(*c*) that South Africa is still under the obligations imposed under Article 22 of the Covenant;

(*d*) that South Africa has practised apartheid in the territory and that this is contrary to Article 2 of the Mandate and Article 22 of the League of Nations Covenant;

(*e*) that South Africa has failed to promote the well-being of the peoples of South West Africa and has impeded opportunities for self-determination;

(*f*) that South Africa must cease these violations and meet its obligations.[1]

Although these were the precise terms on which the case was fought, both sides knew that the aim of the two African states was to use the legal dispute as a direct attack on white South Africa. The danger of this new case for the South African Government was that, unlike earlier ones which had asked for advisory judgements, Liberia and Ethiopia were now seeking a binding judgement. If this went against South Africa, the government

[1] Austin, op. cit., pp. 108–9.

would be left in a serious situation. If it took the improbable step of implementing the judgement by repealing apartheid legislation in South West Africa it could undermine the policy in the remainder of the Republic and end all hopes for the integration of South West Africa. Alternatively, if the government failed to take action, it was probable that the case would be reported to the Security Council with a request for enforcement. It is impossible to predict what the Council's response would have been, but had this position been reached the South Africans would have been unable to fall back on their usual legalistic defence of denying United Nations rights to interfere.

A judgement against South Africa could have told strongly with the Western powers, as they tried to balance the advantages and disadvantages of interfering in the Republic's affairs. Spence has written that the Western states would have had 'the choice of supporting a resolution designed to give effect to the judgement, or appearing to flout the decision of the International Court for reasons of marked self-interest. This would have been a difficult decision to justify in the face of a self-evident breach of international law, and more particularly if the prestige of the United Nations as a law-enforcing agency could be shown to be in jeopardy.'[1]

The significance the Western states attached to the court's findings is shown by the pressure that Britain and America put on South Africa to delay the full implementation of the Odendaal Report (a development plan for South West Africa)[2] until the judgement was handed down, and by the action of the United States Government shortly before the judgement was known. The Americans sent a note saying that they hoped that the South African Government would recognize the court's findings as the Americans would themselves feel bound by it.[3]

The South African Government, recognizing the importance of the case, had sent a powerful team of lawyers to represent the Republic, but in 1962 an interim judgement was given which went against them.[4] In this interim judgement the South African application that the Court had no jurisdiction in the case was

[1] Spence, *Republic Under Pressure*, p. 112.   [2] See p. 156.
[3] Personal communication.
[4] For an outline of the South African case see the Hon. Mr. Justice J. T. Van Wyk, *The United Nations, South West Africa and the Law* (University of Cape Town, 1968).

turned down by 8 votes to 7. This decision, allied with the previous 'advisory' decisions which had also gone against South Africa, created a firm assumption in international circles that the final judgement would also be against the Republic.

While the court case was being argued, the pattern of accusation and counter-accusation about South West Africa continued at the United Nations. As in the past, the legal complexity of the issue prompted the South Africans to adopt a more conciliatory attitude than on the broader issue of apartheid. In 1961, although the government refused permission for the United Nations Committee on South West Africa to visit the territory, it suggested personal visits by three past presidents of the General Assembly. The government said that it was prepared to publish the ex-presidents' opinions and impressions of the territory in full. The suggestion was rejected by the Trusteeship Council, which instead set up a new seven-nation committee to investigate South West Africa. The South Africans refused entry for the whole committee, but they did grant permission to Mr. Victorio Carpio of the Philippines, who was the committee's chairman, and Dr. Salvador Martínez de Alva of Mexico, the vice-chairman. Their visit provided a near comic interlude in an otherwise gloomy relationship. At the end of their visit Carpio and de Alva apparently agreed to a communiqué which was favourable to South Africa, but even on this there was some confusion as Carpio was in bed, said to be sick, when the communiqué was drafted. However, as soon as they left South Africa they recanted and issued another report which called for sanctions, and if necessary force, if the Republic did not change her policies.[1]

While the United Nations' challenges and criticism continued, the South African Government pursued its policy of treating the territory virtually as an integral part of the Republic. In 1964 the Odendaal Commission,[2] which had been charged with preparing a five-year development plan for the territory, made its report. It recommended that the territory be divided up, in a similar way to the Republic, between a 'white' area constituting about 44 per cent of the territory, and ten 'homelands' or Bantustans occupying about 40 per cent. In the homelands local authorities would be established, but these authorities would be responsible to the South

---

[1] IRR 1962, pp. 233–7.
[2] The Commission took its name from the Chairman, Mr. F. H. Odendaal.

African Government. If the proposed territorial pattern of settlement were to be achieved it would involve some purchase of land from whites, and the movement of substantial numbers of non-whites (about 28 per cent of them). In addition a major development programme was outlined which, if it were implemented, would cost R114,450,000 in the first five years. The British and United States Governments sent notes pointing out that any attempt to carry out the Commission's proposals for the establishment of Bantustans while the Court case was still unresolved would probably result in Liberia and Ethiopia applying for a Court injunction restraining South Africa. The notes stated that if the injunction were not granted quickly the Security Council might decide to take action by establishing a United Nations presence in South West Africa.[1]

Referring to these notes, Verwoerd said that while he did not dispute the right of friendly governments to say what their reaction would be if certain developments were to take place, they were based on two false assumptions. The first of these was that the South African Government was not taking account of the International Court case in assessing the Odendaal Report; the second, that if an interdict were applied for and granted, the South African Government would behave in such a way as to lead to Security Council action. At no time had the government given any indication that it would challenge the Security Council on such an issue. The cautious tone, with an emphasis on legal niceties, which can be detected in Verwoerd's speech can also be found in the government's white paper on the Odendaal Report. In this paper the government announced its decision to go ahead with some aspects of the report, and notably the proposals for economic development, but to delay decisions on proposals affecting the *status quo* of South West Africa and the implementation of Bantustans. But while there was delay, there was no doubt that the government looked favourably on the Bantustan proposal. South Africa, said Verwoerd, was 'not forcing the policy of separate development on South West Africa'. It was merely preserving the separate homelands which were based on the historical differences of peoples within the territory.[2]

The Odendaal Report, in its conception and in the government's

---

[1] IRR 1964, pp. 366-7.
[2] H of A, 5 May 1964, col. 5446, and IRR 1964, pp. 366-8.

handling of it, reflected the established South African attitude towards South West Africa. The government, while going ahead with practical steps to bring the territory into line with the remainder of the Republic, and while generally treating the territory as a component part of South Africa, avoided formalizing the position because this would have jeopardized the claim that South Africa had respected international law and had fulfilled the terms of the mandate.

In 1966 the immediate danger over South West Africa was removed. By the casting vote of the President, the International Court rejected the claims of Ethiopia and Liberia because, it argued, they had no legal rights or interests in the matters before the Court. It was an extraordinary decision and appeared to go against the previous advisory decision. After years of legal argument, debate, and dispute, it was a 'non-finding'. The Court said nothing about the substantive issues that had been raised, nothing about apartheid and racial discrimination. So in this sense the South African policies in South West Africa were as open to challenge and criticism as ever, but, rightly from their point of view, the white South Africans celebrated the 'non-finding' as a triumph.[1] Verwoerd said it was a 'major victory'. 'The purpose of Ethiopia and Liberia', he said, 'had been to obtain a decisive decision against South Africa, and if the judgement had not been complied with, to exert pressure on members of the Security Council to apply coercive measures.'[2]

The hopes of the militants that the judgement would give them a tool to attack the Republic had been frustrated. They still had no doubt that their cause was just and right—they had no need of an International Court to tell them that. What they had wanted from the Court was a means of gaining United Nations action. Naturally they were infuriated by the result. It convinced them more strongly than ever that 'It is better to be carried away by emotions than bogged down by legal sophistication.'[3] Pushing aside the Court's finding, a resolution was rushed through the General Assembly stating that the mandate for South West Africa was terminated and South Africa's right to administer the territory was cancelled.

[1] For a South African view of the case see Van Wyk, *The United Nations, South West Africa and the Law.*

[2] Quoted by Cockram, *Vorster's Foreign Policy*, p. 22.

[3] Observation by Pakistan delegate to General Assembly in 1952. Quoted by Spence, *Republic Under Pressure*, p. 103.

A committee was appointed to recommend ways in which South West Africa could be administered so that the people could exercise self-determination.

The anger of the African states at the Court's findings was part of a wider anger at the frustrations they had met in their attempts to organize international action against the Republic. Despite their success in excluding South Africa from many international organizations and in maintaining continuous verbal attacks, their failure to mount an effective military or economic challenge against the Republic, either directly themselves or by persuading others to undertake it, had highlighted the limitations of their moral crusade. They had successfully used the United Nations and other international forums as a means of institutionalizing diplomatic hostility against South Africa and maintaining verbal and moral pressure on the Western states. As a result the Republic had been forced into ideological isolation, her diplomatic contacts had been restricted and those which remained had often been strained, but all this fell far short of the militant action the African states felt was justified. For them there was the disappointment of discovering how little many states, including African states, were prepared to do if they did not perceive their immediate and direct interests to be involved, and how little the verbal attacks at international gatherings achieved in terms of action.

For all the sound and fury at the General Assembly over South West Africa, the South Africans realized that the immediate danger had passed. The Western powers would not feel bound by the Assembly's resolution as they would by a Court finding. The long-term danger of international action still remained, but the South African Government had weathered another storm.

11

A BLACK CONTINENT

During the early 1960s the South Africans were forced to recognize that the process of decolonization in Africa would be quicker and more comprehensive than they, or indeed the colonial powers, had previously anticipated. Even small territories, like the British Protectorates in southern Africa, which had previously been considered too small and impoverished to become sovereign states, were now being groomed for independence. Of the colonial powers with large possessions in Africa, only the Portuguese stood out against the revolutionary tide, and who, other than the Portuguese themselves, was bold enough to say that their empire would survive when more powerful colonial powers had given way? In April 1960 Louw gloomily and accurately predicted that white rule in Africa would soon be confined to the Portuguese territories, Southern Rhodesia, and South Africa itself. Even Northern Rhodesia was, he said 'practically over the wall'.[1]

The South African ministers never spoke of decolonization without criticism and hostility. They accused the colonial powers of pursuing a policy of appeasement, of betraying the white man and his values, of handing over power to immature states and so leaving Africa open to communist penetration. Verwoerd declared that the colonial powers had given way far too easily to the dual pressures of African nationalism and international opinion. South Africa, he said, was exposed to the same pressures, but she would never bend before them for to do so was to invite self-destruction. If necessary, South Africa would stand alone.[2]

The South Africans, powerless to intervene in the decolonization, could only criticize. Naturally it was the British, whose colonial past was a part of South Africa's own history and who still had colonial possessions on South Africa's borders, who came in

[1] H of A, 20 Apr. 1960, col. 5626.   [2] H of A, 24 Apr. 1964, col. 5018.

for the most extensive criticism. In April 1964 Verwoerd said that while the British claimed their policy was to counter communism in Africa, already the communists had footholds in Ghana and Zanzibar.[1] In a later speech he said that British colonial policy had gone through three stages—first 'baaskap', second 'partnership and integration', and finally 'running away'.[2] He accused the British of deserting the white man in Africa, and said that 'non-racialism' was a euphemism for promoting black interests at the expense of the whites. The British said they found apartheid abhorrent, but, said Verwoerd, he found the British treatment of white men in Kenya and Tanganyika abhorrent.[3] He doubted if black men were capable of running a modern state and yet the Western powers were prepared to sacrifice the white man in 'the auction sale of appeasement'.[4]

While the South Africans continued their protests they reluctantly adapted to the changing situation. In 1959 Louw, in one of his more sanguine moments, claimed that friendly relations were being established with black states and that South Africa was demonstrating how it was possible to co-operate with states like Ghana and Nigeria.[5] These hopes for co-operation continued to rest on the assumption of Louw's 1957 'Pretoria' speech.[6] Verwoerd specifically mentioned this speech in 1962 when he outlined the broad principles of the Republic's African policy—to remove mutual suspicion, to accept the new black states, but in turn to demand acceptance of the Republic as a fellow African state, and to build co-operation on common economic and technical interests.[7] The South Africans were not at this time very specific about how co-operation could be achieved. The few tentative moves made in the late 1950s had failed to develop,[8] and while the South Africans always emphasized that they wanted to co-operate in technical and economic ventures, and were prepared to send experts to less developed countries, these offers had always to be matched against white South African suspicions of the new states.

The benefits of limited co-operation which seemed so obvious to the South Africans were much less obvious to most African states. The exceptions were to be the black states of southern

[1] ibid.   [2] H of A, 5 Feb. 1965, col. 628.
[3] H of A, 29 Mar. 1962, col. 3455.   [4] H of A, 11 Apr. 1962, col. 3761.
[5] H of A, 20 Mar. 1959, col. 2944o. See also ch. 8, p. 107.
[6] See ch. 8, p. 106.   [7] H of A, 11 Apr. 1962, cols. 3756–8.
[8] See ch. 8, p. 107.

Africa,[1] but the major political changes of the early 1960s came in the 'middle belt' of Africa.[2] There the new states had not inherited strong links with the Republic, and for the future South Africa seemed unlikely to be able to offer advantages that were not being offered elsewhere, and certainly no advantages that could counteract the smear of co-operation with a racialist state. To have accepted the vague South African offers of co-operation would have required an act of political will, an initiative in establishing new links. The new states were not prepared to exercise that will. In the broadest terms they came to see South Africa not as a potential ally in economic development, but as *the* symbol of racialism.

The South Africans had hoped that a clear divorce could be achieved between economic and political issues. The reactions of the black states during the early 1960s suggested that this could not be done, but even then there were a few signs that South African persistence might succeed. The first came when Katanga under Moise Tshombe tried to break away from the remainder of the Congo. Two Katangese ministers visited South Africa in August 1961 for discussions with the government. In Katanga's case there were some existing links with South Africa through the major mining companies and these provided a useful channel of communication, but the main Katangese aim was to gain political allies and material support in their attempt at secession. The Katangese had the political will because in their exposed position they were pleased to find support anywhere. The secession attempt failed, but in 1964 came an even more exciting proposition for South Africa when Tshombe became Prime Minister of all the Congo. Again he made contact with the Republic to ask for medical aid and food supplies but again he failed to hold on to power, and with his failure the contact disappeared.[3]

---

[1] In this study southern Africa is taken to be the Portuguese territories of Angola and Mozambique; the territories of the Central African Federation which in 1963/4 split up into Zambia, Malawi, and Rhodesia; the three High Commission Territories which were later to gain independence as Botswana, Lesotho, and Swaziland; South West Africa; and South Africa itself. In identifying 'southern Africa' in this way I am already anticipating the emergence of a southern African bloc and the 'Outward Policy', although Zambia did not become a member of the bloc (see ch. 14 and 15).

[2] I have taken the 'middle belt' to be the section of the continent that lies south of the Sahara and north of southern Africa.

[3] Spence, *Republic Under Pressure*, p. 76.

The Congo incidents were important in this context because they diverted attention away from the south, and because they revealed a rift in the black African ranks, thereby encouraging the South Africans in their belief that limited co-operation could be achieved. But more important for the future were the attitudes of Malawi and Zambia. These two countries, which had important economic links with the Republic, gained independence after the break-up of the Central African Federation. In contrast to the 'middle belt' states, it required an act of political will by them if they were to break off contact with the Republic. There were early signs that Dr. Hastings Banda of Malawi was not prepared to do this. In July 1964, at the OAU's conference in Cairo, he refused to support the call for a complete economic and diplomatic break with South Africa and the Portuguese colonies. A year later Arthur Wina, the Zambian Minister of Finance, although much more critical of South Africa than the Malawians, said that his country could not afford to break its trade links with the Republic.

The chief obstacle to good relations with African states was again South Africa's internal racial policies. These were not only offensive to the new states but created practical difficulties. For example, if South Africa wanted co-operation it seemed obvious that diplomatic relations would have to be established. But how would the black diplomats be treated? Would they share white facilities? Would they live in white areas? Would their children go to white schools? These questions taxed and vexed white South Africans because many of them feared that this could be the thin end of the wedge undermining the existing social structure.

The representation of black states in South Africa was an issue debated at Commonwealth conferences. Verwoerd denied that it was important in forcing South Africa out in 1961, and that was probably true, but it certainly caused resentment and bitterness and made the other Commonwealth members less inclined to seek an accommodation with the Republic. There is evidence of this in correspondence between Sir Robert Menzies, the Australian Prime Minister, and Verwoerd which followed the 1960 Conference. At the Conference, attended by Louw, there were informal discussions about South Africa's policies. Menzies, who had never met Verwoerd, wrote to give his impression, and raised the specific issue of diplomatic representation:

Nkrumah was obviously hurt by the current failure to receive a High Commissioner from Ghana at Pretoria. As I understand the position, you don't receive Diplomatic Missions from what I will call the 'coloured' countries. This, I think, is regarded as disagreeable and unco-operative by our colleagues. I spoke very earnestly to Eric Louw in private about it. He said that if such Missions were received and in consequence a considerable number of Asian and African diplomats and their staffs were established in Pretoria and Cape Town, it would run counter to the policy of separateness. I said to him, as I now say to you, that since we all meet in London on terms of equality and conduct close and inti-mate and friendly discussions with each other, it must be impossible for those other governments to understand why similar discussions on the ordinary diplomatic level cannot occur in your own country.[1]

Menzies, perhaps naively and certainly optimistically, suggested that a great deal of the heat would go out of the conflict if South Africa was prepared to receive Afro-Asian diplomats, but Verwoerd in his reply disagreed. First, he argued that it was untrue that South Africa was not prepared to receive 'coloured' diplomats. South Africa already received diplomats from Egypt[2] and China (Taiwan), she was prepared to consider exchanging representatives with Pakistan and India again if these states so wished, and she was now discussing the possibility of representation with Japan. But when Verwoerd turned to the black African states, his letter revealed doubts and fears both about what they were trying to achieve and the impact of having their diplomats inside South Africa. Verwoerd wrote:

You mentioned the case of Nkrumah. It must not be forgotten, how-ever, that before there was any talk of representation, he had made known that Ghana would do everything in its power to aid black men everywhere in Africa, including South Africa, to take over the reins of government. Apart from other considerations, it could not be expected that we would receive a mission which could easily become the centre of agitation where those would foregather, white and non-white, who wish to create a multiracial or Bantu government here. South Africa has had such an experience with Soviet Consular-Generals and had to request the closing down of that Consulate rather than invite further trouble. It was, therefore, felt that representation by Ghana and others should be postponed until conditions of separate development in this country, less active interference by others in our domestic affairs,

[1] Sir Robert Menzies, *Afternoon Light* (London, Cassell, 1967), pp. 200-1.
[2] The Egyptian (United Arab Republic) mission was withdrawn in 1961 (IRR 1961, p. 285).

clear indications of goodwill by African states and worthwhile relations with them, had created the right atmosphere. If Ghana and the others were at all politically mature, they should have accepted as a first step the many proofs of goodwill shown and co-operation in technical matters given by the South African Government. . . . Naturally, we also have our own particular problem to consider if members of these missions from black states moved in Government social circles. What justification would there be for the same not happening to educated Bantu here, or to the leaders of the big Bantu national groups, whose followers are almost as numerous as the population of Ghana? Yet until separate development has progressed far enough for this to be possible, without endangering the whole position of the white man as described above, we have to tread warily.[1]

Verwoerd continued to 'tread warily' at the 1961 Commonwealth Conference. When he was pressed on the exchange of diplomatic representation with Afro-Asian states he said that such relations could not be established with unfriendly countries.[2]

Diplomatic representation of African states was certainly not an issue on which the South Africans were prepared to move as a concession to Commonwealth opinion, but it would be a mistake to think that they ignored the problem entirely, or failed, according to their lights, to search for ways to overcome it. From time to time the old idea of a diplomatic suburb, set apart from the rest of society, was unsuccessfully canvassed. In 1964 Verwoerd said he favoured Malan's earlier scheme of a roving ambassador. His suggestion was that South Africa would appoint an ambassador to keep up contact with the black states, while ambassadors or ministers from the black states could fly to South Africa for day visits, as the Katanga ministers had done during their brief hour of glory.[3] Verwoerd argued his case in terms of saving the expense of formal diplomatic representation, but this was the thinnest of thin veils to hide the difficulties that he had outlined in his letter to Menzies.

Verwoerd's suggestion for a roving ambassador followed an initiative from Dr. Kenneth Kaunda, shortly before Zambia's Independence. In a press statement Kaunda said that Zambia would be prepared to exchange representatives with South

[1] Menzies, op. cit., pp. 206–7.
[2] Menzies commented that this had a bad psychological effect. 'It seemed to be carrying it pretty far' (IRR 1961, p. 6).
[3] H of A, 24 Apr. 1964, col. 4901.

Africa provided Zambian diplomats enjoyed the same rights and treatment in the Republic as South African diplomats would expect in Zambia.[1] As this was only a press statement it appears that Verwoerd did not reply directly, but rather made his parliamentary statement about the roving ambassador. However, Kaunda's initiative had again revealed the narrow limits set by the South Africans for co-operation with black states. 'It must', said Verwoerd, 'be very clear to representatives of other countries that while we shall act in their countries in accordance with their customs, we . . . expect them to act in South Africa in accordance with South Africa's customs.'[2] It seemed to many African leaders that they were being asked to accept *the custom* of white racial superiority. (Verwoerd's response to Kaunda in 1964 may have lost the opportunity of a diplomatic breakthrough, which only a few years later the South Africans were anxiously seeking to make.)

In the early 1960s the South Africans, far from extending their diplomatic contacts with the new states of Africa, quickly lost the few ties that had been established in the colonial days. The Egyptian representative withdrew in 1961 and when the South African Consul General was recalled from Kenya in 1963, shortly before Independence, the last direct link with black Africa was severed. The diplomatic links which remained in the continent were with Southern Rhodesia and the Portuguese territories.

Whenever the United Party criticized the government for failing to establish contacts in black Africa, the ministers retorted that it was impossible because the black states refused to co-operate. In 1961 Louw said that all the government's attempts to establish good relations had been frustrated. South Africa had not been invited to the Independence celebrations in Nigeria or the Congo, and in the case of the Congo, she had been asked to withdraw her Consul General.[3] In Ghana, South African goods were being boycotted and South African visitors refused entry unless they signed a declaration condemning apartheid. Liberia and Ethiopia had instigated the South West Africa case, and Dr. Julius Nyerere was establishing himself as a major opponent of South Africa, even before Tanganyika gained independence.[4]

[1] IRR 1964, p. 125.
[2] H of A, 24 Apr. 1964, col. 4831.
[3] The Katanga attempt at secession came after independence, and Tshombe's brief period as Congolese Prime Minister did not start until 1964.
[4] For example, see Louw's speech, H of A, 24 Feb. 1961, col. 1940.

Yet a question hangs over the genuineness of the South African offers of friendship and co-operation at this time. They often behaved as though the offers were ritual exercises and little else. They found it impossible to throw off lightly the conviction built up over generations that white men ruled and black men were ruled. Yet it would be wrong to dismiss entirely the South African hopes of co-operation. Given their restricted terms, they were probably genuine in their belief that over the years values would change, and that the strong commitment against white supremacy would disappear, to be replaced by an emphasis on economic development and technical co-operation. In 1964 Verwoerd said that once the maelstrom and chaos of the early years of independence were over good relations would be established with other African states, and, as originally predicted, the foundations would be built on South Africa's economic and technological strength.[1] In the following years he said that South Africa's very efficiency would in time create the right conditions. 'The fruits of this', he said, 'will still be reaped one day. . . . Nevertheless the time is not yet ripe when they will come to us to seek sound co-operation; the climate is still against it, but the undercurrents are noticeable.'[2]

Partly from lack of choice, partly because of the long-established ties and mutual interests, South Africa's main attempts at co-operation became concentrated on her neighbours in southern Africa. In the early 1960s, when the world's attention was captured by the emergence of independent black states, there was a common international assumption that the pattern of the 'middle belt' would be duplicated in southern Africa. In retrospect, it is clear that this was a misperception. Conditions in southern Africa were very different from those elsewhere in the continent. In the south was a group of territories with large white populations, ruled by local white governments with very different views of African developments from those of the European colonial governments. With the important exception of the Central African Federation (which at its dissolution gave birth to the independent black states of Zambia and Malawi),[3] the tide of independence challenged but did not radically change the existing power structure. In addition

---

[1] H of A, 21 Jan. 1964, cols. 55–7.   [2] H of A, 5 Feb. 1965, col. 624.
[3] In Southern Rhodesia the 1962 election brought to power the Rhodesian Front Party which was determined to hold on to exclusive white control. See the author's *Rhodesia: the Road to Rebellion* (London, Oxford University Press for the Institute of Race Relations, 1967), ch. VII.

to these political circumstances, southern Africa was tied together by strong economic and communication links to form a more cohesive economic unit than any other part of Africa.

Although (with the exception of the old Federation) there was less political change in southern Africa than in the remainder of the continent, in a very real sense there was greater uncertainty. Elsewhere Independence brought some confusion and birth pains, but the general course of the developments seemed relatively clear. A series of new black states had emerged which could anticipate major economic problems and difficulty in establishing satisfactory patterns of government but they were there to stay. In southern Africa there was less certainty. The whole structure of governments, territories, and states seemed open to question. Could the South African Government suppress the internal resistance movements? Could the white minority hold on to power in Southern Rhodesia? Would international action be taken against the white governments? What would happen in the Portuguese territories? Would Malan's old fears about the High Commission Territories be justified?

With regard to the High Commission Territories, there remained doubts in South African minds about their future constitutional development until late in 1963. This was partly due to the uncertainty of British policy, with its hesitation about the ability of the Territories to stand on their own feet and the fears of hostile South African reactions.[1] The South African Government ministers continued to stress that in their opinion the Territories would be much better off within the Republic, developing along similar lines to the Bantustans. In 1963 Verwoerd made a final plea for Britain and South Africa to co-operate in planning the orderly development of southern Africa, including the three Protectorates, with a view to the consolidation of white and black areas. He said:

We would aim at making them democratic states in which the masses would not be dominated by a small group of authoritarians ... the whole population [would be led to] democratic rule over its own country ... we would steer away from the principle of multi-racialism. ...

---

[1] See Stevens, *Lesotho, Botswana and Swaziland.* In relation to Basutoland Stevens says that even in mid-1963 the British were not prepared to mention full independence (p. 75).

Where Whites would be needed and must remain for some time in those areas and occupations, they would become voters in the Republic of South Africa, just as the Bechuanas, the Basutos or the Swazis will, when they work in the Republic, be voters in their respective homelands.[1]

This plea met no response and later in the year, when the British made clear that they had decided to grant independence, Verwoerd finally announced that South Africa had given up hope of incorporating the Territories.[2] The government, he said, would accept the position as it was and work for friendship with the small emerging states.

In accepting the situation, the old South African fears did not miraculously disappear, and in the early 1960s the fears seemed well founded. The Territories temporarily became havens for political refugees, and potential centres for organizing resistance against the white government.[3] The borders between South Africa and the Territories were the scene of dramatic escapes by African nationalists, and dramatic arrests by the South African police, who on occasions crossed into the Territories to seize their prisoners.[4] The British were criticized by both sides. The African nationalists criticized them for vacillation and ineffectiveness in helping the refugees, while the South African Government was incensed at the British preparedness to accept political refugees at all.

As the flow of refugees and political opponents into the Territories increased, the South African Government threatened to close the borders completely. Although they never carried out this threat, they substantially increased their control and vigilance over movements. In 1962 the government had decided that in future passports would be required to cross into Basutoland. In 1963 legislation was introduced which gave greater powers over people who committed offences against the Republic from outside its borders, more controls over Africans entering and leaving the

---

[1] Quoted by Spence in the *Oxford History of South Africa*, vol. II, p. 501.
[2] IRR 1963, p. 126.
[3] For example in 1963 A. K. Leballa set up a Headquarters in Maseru, Basutoland, to control the PAC underground movement in South Africa (Gibson, *African Liberation Movements*, p. 93).
[4] See Jack Halpern, *South Africa's Hostages* (Penguin, 1965), ch. 1, and Gwendolen Carter, *Five African States, Responses to Diversity* (Cornell University Press, 1963).

Republic, and tighter control of aircraft movements. The government insisted that aircraft flying to and from the Territories had to land at certain designated airports in the Republic. East African Airways, which had transported refugees out of the Territories, was refused a licence to fly to South Africa. A new extradition treaty was agreed with Rhodesia. In the face of these restrictions the British Government was not prepared to react forcefully. 'They were unwilling', wrote Stevens, 'to elevate the difficulty to full international level.'[1] Instead they tightened up their own regulations in the Territories with the Prevention of Violence Abroad Proclamation of 1965 which made it a crime to plan, aid, instigate, or incite acts of violence outside the Territories and restricted the political activities of refugees.[2]

In the changing circumstances the South Africans sought to establish a satisfactory relationship with the Territories by holding out the stick with one hand and the carrot with the other. The South African position was very strong. Stevens wrote that: 'Each of the three states is particularly vulnerable to economic pressure from South Africa. These pressures need not take the form of directly hostile actions. Rather the potential danger is that they might be strangled through slow, undramatic administrative and economic measures, all of which might be entirely legitimate.'[3] The South African Government's message was that friendly co-operation would not only avoid this but give the Territories all the advantages of association with a powerful, rich neighbour. The major parties in the Territories recognized this and Mr. Q. M. Malapo of the Basutoland Congress Party expressed a very common view when he said: 'We are going to have to live with South Africa, whether we like it or not. Our geographical position makes sure of that. It is, therefore, vitally important that we get busy as soon as possible laying the foundations of satisfactory relations with the Republic.'[4] For some of the African leaders in the Territories it was a bitter pill to swallow, a realization that they really were 'South Africa's Hostages'.[5]

Shortly after his announcement in 1963 that South Africa had abandoned hopes for the transfer of the Territories, Verwoerd

[1] Stevens, op. cit., p. 75.
[2] Spence in *Oxford History of South Africa*, vol. II, p. 502.
[3] Stevens, op. cit., p. 11.　　　　[4] IRR 1964, p. 126.
[5] Title of Jack Halpern's book.

changed the emphasis of all previous policy statements by claiming that South Africa would probably benefit by their independence. He argued that Britain with her wide-ranging world responsibilities had subordinated the interests of all the inhabitants of southern Africa to these wider aims. This would not happen with the rulers of the new states whose interests would be firmly fixed in southern Africa.[1] Verwoerd's statement probably reflects the South African awareness that moderate, and even 'conservative', African political parties were developing in the Territories, but another way to argue his point would be to say that these small new states would have no choice but to accept a close and a subordinate relationship with their powerful neighbour. Verwoerd never said it quite that bluntly, but he came near to it when he spoke to the Senate in June 1964. Independence, he said, could bring some difficulties, but:

As long as Britain was the overlord they [the people of the Territories] could even be hostile towards us and reckon that anything they lose here in the form of employment or revenue will be made up by Britain. The Father must look after the children: But as this fatherly hand disappears more and more and they become more and more responsible for their own future existence and collect their own funds and see to it themselves that their own people have work, they must consider their neighbour. If this is their place of employment, if this is the source of their revenue, if our co-operation in connection with customs revenue is in their interest, then any individual government that is established there must maintain friendship with its neighbours in the interest of its own people.[2]

The major point to make is that with the confidence which came from its success in suppressing the internal resistance movements, the South African Government had begun to see that decolonization opened up new opportunities as well as new dangers. It saw that in the new relationships which were being created in Africa the Republic would have the opportunity to behave as a powerful state, especially in southern Africa. As the realization grew the South Africans identified the Bantustan policy more clearly with decolonization in the Protectorates, although they still recognized distinctions. The South Africans accused the British of pushing the pace too quickly, of mistakenly encouraging inter-racialism and white investment, but the broad similarities

[1] H of A, 23 Apr. 1963, cols. 4599–600.
[2] Quoted by Halpern, op. cit., p. 437.

of preparing small black states for independence were given increasing prominence.

The changed emphasis was also part of Verwoerd's response
to the 1960 crisis. His insistence that the crisis had given the
government the opportunity to go ahead more quickly and more
thoroughly with apartheid ended with a commitment that the
Bantustans would move to independence. There has, however,
always been some doubt about what the South African Government means by 'independence' for the Bantustans. For example,
in 1961 after Verwoerd had announced that independence was the
objective, the Minister of Bantu Affairs drew a distinction between
self-government and full independence. He claimed that the mass
of Bantu did not want complete separation from the rest of South
Africa, but if eventually a stage were reached when they wanted
full independence it would have to be considered.[1]

The terms in which Verwoerd saw the development of the
Bantustans re-emphasized the interrelationship of domestic and
foreign policies. The core objective of both policies was the
preservation of the white state. If this meant accepting that small
sections of the Republic would have to be cut away and given to
the Bantu nations then that was unfortunate, but it was a price well
worth paying. In explaining his policy Verwoerd accepted that
dangers were involved. The Bantustans, he admitted, could
become Zanzibars or Cubas on the Republic's borders:

A Cuba or a Zanzibar beyond the borders of the white State may be
dangerous (not only inconvenient, but dangerous) but if three million
whites have to live together in one State with four times as many of
those same people who are liable to create a Cuba surely it is much more
dangerous. Then you are living together with them in that Cuba
together with the further difference that you will constitute the oppressed
minority inside that Cuba or Zanzibar.[2]

Verwoerd was prepared to accept the dangers involved not only
because of the Republic's internal situation, but because of external pressures. In one speech he admitted that granting independence to the Bantustans 'is not what we would have liked to
see. In the light of pressures being exerted on South Africa there
is, however, no doubt that eventually this will have to be done,
thereby buying for the white man his freedom and the right to

[1] IRR 1961, p. 99.   [2] H of A, 23 Apr. 1964, col. 4817.

retain domination in what is his country.'[1] Although this statement indicates that one aim of the Bantustan policy was to blunt
or buy off international pressures, it would be quite wrong to suggest that this was the only aim. In its contribution to the grand
design of preserving white South Africa and ensuring exclusive
political control for the white man in his own 'homeland', the
Bantustan policy was designed to solve many internal problems.
It was to help separate the races, provide an outlet for African
ambitions, and give a framework for future economic development.

The way in which the Bantustan policy came to be seen as part
of the pattern of relations with neighbouring black states was
revealed when Fouché, the Defence Minister, was asked whether
defence arrangements had been made to counter the potential
danger of independent Bantustans. Fouché replied that it would
be very wrong to plan on the assumption that friction and conflict
with the new states was inevitable. The aim should be to build up
friendship. Far from seeing dangers, he said that good relations
with the Bantustans could be a springboard for better relations
throughout Africa. He admitted that so far the Republic had not
had much success with other African states, but it must continue
to work for a breakthrough. There was no better opportunity than
that provided by the Bantustans, for, whatever their political
status, they would have no choice but to co-operate with and be
dependent on South Africa.[2]

Fouché's was a public statement and it would be naive to suggest
that the South African Government did not calculate the defence
implications of the Bantustan development. But the most interesting aspect of the statement was the revelation that the South
Africans were feeling their way to a situation where, with the
British presence removed, the Republic would be the dominant
power in southern Africa. While in 1960 Louw had been gloomy
about the chance of regional co-operation, three years later when
Verwoerd replied to a question about future relations with Southern Rhodesia he took the opportunity to outline a possible wider
pattern of co-operation across southern Africa. He spoke of the
possibility of a 'common market', or even a 'commonwealth'. He
was careful to avoid a commitment of support for any particular
government in Rhodesia. He said: 'If in the future Southern
Rhodesia should become an independent state, whether governed

[1] IRR 1962, p. 97.   [2] H of A, 24 June 1963, cols. 8622–3.

by a multiracial government as now or for that matter by a white or a black government, co-operation between sovereign independent states would be welcomed whether in some form of organized economic interdependence according to the example of the European Economic Community or whether for common political interests taking the Commonwealth as an example. Whatever the consultative set-up might be for economic or political purposes it could not consist of any arrangement having a central government.'[1]

In the development of ideas about southern African co-operation the reference to a 'commonwealth' is an interesting one. Because of existing economic inter-relationships a 'common market' seemed an obvious development, and in part already existed, but a 'commonwealth' suggested more. Although Verwoerd had specifically rejected any idea of a central government, a commonwealth implies a form, even if a very loose form, of political co-operation. The word 'commonwealth' may itself offer a clue to the South African Government's thinking. For the South Africans it almost certainly conjured up images of the British Commonwealth, with its acceptance of sovereign independence for each member but a centralizing, pre-eminent role for the most powerful state. The National Party had always resented British pre-eminence, but in a Southern African Commonwealth the Republic would be the natural leader. It was a thought to be savoured.

As South African confidence increased so the government's thinking about co-operation developed further. In June 1965 Muller, the Foreign Minister, welcomed the moves in the High Commission Territories towards independence. He repeated that South Africa had no ambition to dominate any neighbouring states. She was keen to co-operate in relationships in which mutual sovereignty would be respected. From this reference to the High Commission Territories, Muller expanded the picture to take in the whole of southern Africa. He said: 'I believe that the time has come when all the territories in Southern Africa will co-operate in all matters of common interest with a view to tackling their common problems and solving them in the interests of all the inhabitants of each particular territory.' When he was asked what he meant by 'Southern Africa', he said he was not prepared to draw precise boundaries, but, perhaps with the memory of

[1] H of A, 23 Apr. 1963, col. 4599.

Tshombe in mind, he drew his speculative frontier far to the north. 'I draw the line very vaguely,' he said, 'I even include the Congo (Léopoldville). I am explaining my view as to the future and I do not think the honourable member can expect me in these circumstances to draw a very clear line of demarcation.'[1]

While Muller would not draw precise lines, the future policy of the South African Government had become reasonably clear by 1965. Confident of her increasing strength, the Republic was starting to canvass more energetically for friendship and co-operation in the continent. At best the South Africans hoped that this would lead to effective technical co-operation. At worst they hoped for a 'live and let live' attitude from others. The first steps would be taken in southern Africa by gaining the acceptance of neighbouring states and developing the Bantustans. Once this base was firm, attempts could be made to extend co-operation further north. The task of gaining acceptance and even more the co-operation of the black states would be difficult, but in a mood of increasing confidence the South African Government was coming to believe that given relative stability, and quiet diplomacy, it could be achieved. Shortly after Muller's optimistic speech the hopes of stability and quiet diplomacy were dealt a sharp blow by the Rhodesian Government's Unilateral Declaration of Independence (UDI) in November 1965.[2]

There were aspects of the old Central African Federation which the South African Government had never liked, and especially the acceptance of multi-racial government, but the Federation had had its attractions. It was ruled by a predominantly white government which had put its emphases on stability, order, and economic growth rather than rapid political change. Verwoerd said that the disintegration of the Federation in 1963 had caused deep distress in South Africa.[3] He accepted the judgement of the Federation's Prime Minister, Sir Roy Welensky, that the responsibility lay with the British Government and its policy of appeasement.[4]

[1] H of A, 4 June 1965, cols. 7276–80.
[2] See the author's *Rhodesia: the Road to Rebellion*.
[3] H of A, 23 Apr. 1963, col. 4597.
[4] For contrasting views of the Federal break-up see Sir Roy Welensky, *400 Days* (London, Collins, 1964) and Lord Alport, *Sudden Assignment* (London, Hodder and Stoughton, 1965).

Although in the period of the Federation there was a white-controlled territorial government in Rhodesia, relations with South Africa during the 1950s and the first years of the 1960s were ambivalent. The two countries appeared to be moving in different directions, with South Africa imposing its racial separation while Rhodesia, as a member of the Federation, slowly implemented a policy of racial 'partnership', which included a limited African voice in government. Even in 1962, when the Federation was showing clear signs of disintegration, Lord Malvern, the doyen of the United Federal Party, rejected thoughts of a close association with South Africa. 'The day is coming', he said, 'when things are going to change for South Africa so that type of escape from reality does not really exist for Rhodesia.'[1]

Malvern's view did not prevail. As doubts increased about the future of the Federation the white Rhodesians reassessed their situation, halted their faltering steps towards a multi-racial partnership, and late in 1962 voted into office the Rhodesian Front (RF)—a party dedicated to gaining independence with white minority rule. In 1963 the British Government formally broke up the Federation, leaving Rhodesia in a constitutional limbo. It no longer had any formal connections with the two northern territories of Zambia and Malawi, and in these territories black governments came to power, rejecting 'partnership' and throwing their support behind the Rhodesian African nationalists' demands for 'one man, one vote'. On the question of Rhodesia's independence, an impasse was quickly reached in negotiations between the Rhodesian and British Governments. Rejecting the Rhodesian Government's view, the British Government, which was the constitutional sovereign power but had no forces in Rhodesia to impose its will, insisted that legal independence could only be granted if there was guaranteed progress to majority rule.

In 1964 Mr. Ian Smith became Rhodesia's Prime Minister. In the realignment of forces in southern Africa he realized that a white Rhodesia had to move closer to South Africa, and so shortly after becoming Premier he visited the Republic with the express purpose of improving relations. One of Smith's major concerns was how the South African Government would react if the Rhodesian Government illegally seized independence. He may have hoped for a promise of active support but more probably he

[1] *Cape Argus*, 5 Dec. 1962.

was sounding the ground in anticipation of a benevolent neutrality. Smith appears to have gained little encouragement from Verwoerd. According to the South African Press he received 'tea and sympathy' and little else. But the Smith visit is only part of the story. Later in that year a five-year trade agreement was signed by the two governments, lowering trade tariffs and giving South Africa equal preferences with Britain in selling machinery, textiles, foodstuffs, and a wide range of manufactured goods to Rhodesia. Naturally, with her lower transport costs, South Africa now had an edge over Britain. Early in the following year, Dr. Dönges, the South African Minister of Finance, announced that Rhodesia had been given a R5 million loan which he said would help South Africa's exports as well as helping a friendly neighbour. The impact of the trade agreement was immediate and 1965 saw a rapid increase in trade between the two countries. The South Africans saw it as an opportunity to expand their markets and increase their contacts to the north. The Rhodesians saw it as an indication that South Africa had a stake and confidence in their future. In this sense it may have encouraged the Smith government to seize independence, but this had certainly not been the intention of the South Africans. They wanted more trade, not an international crisis on their borders.

Smith's government declared independence in November 1965. This unilateral and illegal action had many disadvantages for South Africa. It was a setback to her attempts to create a more acceptable international image. The South African Government did not want to be seen merely as the champion of the white-controlled states, and therefore by inference the main barrier to African nationalist movements outside as well as inside the Republic's borders. In his April 1963 speech, Verwoerd had carefully avoided a specific commitment to support a white government in Rhodesia. After UDI this posture of non-involvement and non-commitment could not be sustained. There was no choice but to react to the situation, and, as the white South Africans saw it, no choice but to react in favour of their fellow whites in Rhodesia.

At a time when the South African Government had been hoping for greater flexibility in its relations with other African states, UDI polarized attitudes and held out direct dangers for the Republic. It had created in southern Africa the very atmosphere of tension, uncertainty, and instability that the government had been striving to avoid. At the United Nations there were loud appeals for Britain to use force to overthrow the Smith government. The British rejected this. Instead, with United Nations support, they chose economic sanctions as their weapon for forcing the erring colony to abandon its illegal act. For years the South African Government had struggled against the threat of sanctions. Now they were being applied on her very borders. The United Nations' resolutions called on South Africa to break existing trade and commercial ties with Rhodesia, and when she refused there was an outcry for sanctions to be extended against her. Despite the assurance of George Brown, the British Foreign Secretary, that 'Britain cannot and will not contemplate an economic war with South Africa',[1] the South Africans realized that the danger did exist.

They also appreciated that the British decision not to use force was no certain guarantee that fighting and violence would not break out. The British might change their minds, or there might be internal revolution in Rhodesia, or other states might intervene. The situation was full of threats and dangers, and the dangers seemed all the greater because the South African Government was unable to fall back on its usual legalistic defence. Whatever else might be said about UDI, it certainly was not legal. By ignoring United Nations resolutions and by supporting the Rhodesians the South African Government was furthering the illegal act.

Verwoerd had foreseen these problems and although he publicly denied having advised against UDI, he certainly regretted the step. But once it was taken the South African Government never hesitated. It immediately gave its support to the Rhodesians. It clothed this in a claim that UDI was a domestic issue between Britain and Rhodesia, which should be settled exclusively by them without involving the international community. The South Africans argued that they had always stood on the principle of non-interference in internal affairs and they would not now interfere in the internal affairs of others, except to offer help to reach a settlement. There was no doubt about this eagerness for a settlement, but equally, there was no doubt where white South Africa's sympathies and support lay. Simply by its decision to retain existing services, to keep open trading, banking, commercial,

[1] *The Times*, 27 Sept. 1967.

and communications channels, the South African Government had provided one of the major weapons by which the Rhodesians were able to counter sanctions. Verwoerd said: 'I need not go into details, but anyone will realize that maintaining regular relations, especially economic relations, with a neighbouring state means everything to a state which is isolated, as Rhodesia is today.'[1]

The South Africans were prepared to help the Rhodesians partly because they saw it in terms of direct self-interest. It seemed obvious to them that if economic sanctions succeeded in overthrowing white rule in Rhodesia, the Republic would be next on the list. Refusal to participate in any form of international sanctions had been one of South Africa's guiding principles in the post-war world. Verwoerd insisted upon keeping to the principle, even in Zambia's case, when ironically that country in imposing sanctions on Rhodesia was forced to seek more trade with South Africa. 'I have been attacked', said Verwoerd, 'for saying that we would be prepared to send coal to Zambia if coal were ordered. But this is a symbol, a clear-cut symbol, of our preparedness to uphold this principle towards all sides.'[2]

In his public statements, Verwoerd often tried to give the impression that the South African Government's response to the Rhodesian crisis was simply based on a hardheaded calculation of South Africa's self-interest. 'It was clearly in South Africa's interests', he said, 'not to be dragged into the conflict if avoidable or as long as avoidable. It was clearly in our interests to try to have the conflict restricted to those directly implicated, the United Kingdom and Rhodesia. . . . It was clearly in South Africa's interests not to make enemies unnecessarily', and to stand by her principles of non-interference and refusal to participate in sanctions.[3]

The hardheaded calculation of self-interest was certainly there, but white South African reaction to UDI was not just careful calculation. There was an immediate and overwhelming emotional response in favour of the Rhodesians. The South Africans saw an image of themselves in the struggle of the white minority community to the north. In his New Year message for 1966, Verwoerd said that South Africa did not want to be involved in the dispute

[1] H of A, 25 Jan. 1966, col. 53.
[2] Quoted by Cockram, *Vorster's Foreign Policy*, p. 177.
[3] Quoted by Cockram, op. cit., pp. 176–7.

but 'it would be idle to hide that most South Africans are convinced that it would neither be just, advantageous nor wise to white or black in Rhodesia to seek to hasten black government, whether at the pace Russia professes to support it or at the somewhat slower rate [to which] the United Kingdom Government seems to be committed.'[1] He also recognized the ties of blood and race, of 'kith and kin'. 'The declaration of independence in Rhodesia with whom bonds of friendship and economic ties have grown through the years, has created a situation from which the Republic cannot escape. We have blood relations over the border. However others may feel or act towards their kith and kin when their international interests are at stake, South Africans on the whole cannot cold-shoulder theirs.'[2]

For the South African Government UDI had created serious problems. In its response of studied self-interest combined with instinctive, emotional sympathy, it had the widespread support of the white population. If anything the United Party, now thoroughly disillusioned with the British, was even more sympathetic to the predominantly English-speaking Rhodesians than the government. Sir de Villiers Graaff stated that pressure from the party may have made the government marginally more sympathetic in its attitude towards the Rhodesians.[3] If this is so it can only have been marginal. The South African Government refused to involve itself in a major legal tangle by giving Smith's government formal recognition, but short of that it treated Rhodesia as a friendly and as an *independent* state.

For all the threats created by UDI, no South African Government would ever have thought of supporting sanctions against a neighbouring white government or even standing idly by while they were applied. It was unthinkable in terms of self-interest, it was unthinkable in terms of white reaction inside South Africa, and it was unthinkable in terms of the values and premises on which the white societies in Rhodesia and South Africa are built.

[1] *Cape Argus*, 2 Jan. 1966.
[2] South African Minister to UN. Fact sheet, 'South Africa and the Question of Rhodesia', p. 4.
[3] Private communication.

12

THE ACCEPTANCE OF ISOLATION

By the late 1960s the white South Africans had emerged from the
dangers and challenges of the earlier years apparently stronger
and more confident than before. Many threats remained, but the
fires of the early 1960s had forged a confidence in their ability
to survive and even prosper. Some explanations for this have
already been discussed—the drawing together in the face of common dangers, the ineffectiveness of the international pressures,
the increasing opportunities as well as disadvantages perceived in
emergent Africa—while the importance of economic and military
strength will be discussed in the next chapter. Enduring the period
of crisis also involved substantial changes in white attitudes, with
an acceptance of isolation and living with danger. One of the
government's tasks was to breed a conviction inside and outside
the Republic that radical change was not 'inevitable', that South
Africa's critics were wrong in asserting that revolution must come.

In an attempt to counter hostile international publicity the
South African Government substantially increased its information
and propaganda service. In 1962 a separate Department of
Information, with its own Minister, was created to take over the
work of the old State Information Office. The objectives of the
department were to promote a favourable impression of the
government both in South Africa and abroad, where the department's work was reinforced and supplemented by the South
Africa Foundation. The Foundation, which was formed in December 1959 and which claims to be a non-political body, has strong
support from business organizations. Its aims are, first, to promote
'international understanding of South Africa, her people, their way
of life, achievements and aspirations'; second, to organize 'positive
campaigns which shall present to the world at large a true picture

of South Africa'; and, finally, to demonstrate opportunities for investment and to help South African exports.[1]

The Department and Foundation concentrated their efforts on the Western states which have strong links with the Republic. Within these states they concentrated on the influential and potentially sympathetic and on young people. In 1969 Dr. C. P. Mulder, the Minister of Information, said that the Department had tried to achieve its objectives by concentrating on the 'rulers of tomorrow'. The aim was to reach young people and to do this implied making contacts with those who controlled the communications media, such as journalists and broadcasters. In addition the Department had paid attention to those who mould opinion and who are the authors of policy, including 'academic people, industrialists, businessmen and politicians'. The success of the Department was, he said, shown by the United Nations concern about its activities.[2]

The main messages which the Department and the Foundation project are that South Africa is strong and successful and that it would be both difficult and painful to wage war, including economic war, against her; that she is stable and provides a secure ally and base for the Western states; and that the picture of the internal situation painted by militant opponents is a gross distortion, that conditions for non-whites as well as whites are better in the Republic than anywhere else in the continent.

Inside the Republic the government aimed at reassuring the white society that isolation from international organizations was of no great importance. It was argued that many of them were dominated by communists and new, immature states. In 1960 Louw predicted that in ten years' time the Western states would have broken away from the United Nations to avoid being swamped.[3] Meanwhile the Republic was forced out of many international organizations, as the Afro-Asian states used this as a further form of pressure on South Africa. In this they were often opposed by the Western powers and those states, like Japan, that had strong contacts with the Republic. These states were quick to emphasize that they did not support apartheid, and used arguments that were

[1] IRR 1960, p. 177, and Spence, *Republic Under Pressure*, p. 20.
[2] H of A, 6 June 1969, cols. 7482–4.
[3] H of A, 20 Apr. 1960, col. 5625.

either legalistic (e.g. that the particular organization did not have the power to exclude members) or based on claims that it was by retaining contact that influence for change could be exerted on the Republic. The Afro-Asian states put much less stress on the legalistic approach, and they countered the 'change through contact' argument by stating that despite all the previous international contact and the appeals for change, South Africa had not abandoned apartheid.

In general the South Africans attempted to retain membership of international bodies, provided their 'dignity' and 'national pride' were not offended. Some organizations they favoured more strongly than others, for example the World Health Organization, which Verwoerd argued was beneficial to mankind as a whole, and in which the Republic had received co-operation and support from some members.[1] In the case of the United Nations the arguments which had persuaded the South Africans to retain membership in the 1950s were still accepted. There were no signs of a voluntary withdrawal. In many other international organizations, however, the South Africans were forced to resign or withdraw their membership. These included the Commission for Technical Co-operation in Africa (CCTA) and the Economic Commission for Africa (ECA). Exclusion from these two bodies emphasized that more than inconvenience or a blow to pride could result from this form of pressure. The South Africans had always seen such organizations as important channels for building up co-operation and friendship in Africa by the provision of technical and economic aid.[2]

The severing of the Commonwealth link, by far the longest standing of South Africa's formal external contacts, was the clearest indication of increasing isolation. On becoming a Republic South Africa had to reapply for Commonwealth membership. The application came to the 1961 Conference, which Verwoerd himself attended. Like all Nationalists he had reservations about the

[1] IRR 1964, pp. 130–2.

[2] South Africa has been expelled or has withdrawn from the following international organizations: the Commonwealth, UNESCO, the Committee for Technical Co-operation in Africa, the Scientific Council for Africa, the Economic Commission for Africa, the International Civil Aviation Organization, the International Telecommunications Union, the International Labor Organization, the Food and Agriculture Organization, and from the Congress of the Universal Postal Union, but not the Union itself. (Vandenbosch, *South Africa and the World*, p. 257.)

Commonwealth, but when he set off for the conference he almost certainly believed that the advantages of retaining membership outweighed the disadvantages. As well as the advantages which the Nationalist government had recognized in the 1950s, Verwoerd was determined to unite the whites after the divisive referendum campaign, and one of the ways to do it was to remain in the Commonwealth. In the letter he had sent to the voters urging them to vote for the Republic, he had written that 'it would be a democratic Republic within the Commonwealth'.[1]

During the referendum campaign the United Party, traditionally committed to strong support for the Commonwealth, emphasized the disadvantages of being excluded. They argued that there would be serious economic consequences from losing trading preferences,[2] that defence ties would be loosened, and that generally the country would become even more isolated. In pushing ahead with the Republic Verwoerd accepted that Commonwealth membership was jeopardized, but naturally he hoped that South Africa could have it both ways, that she could achieve Republican status and remain inside. He believed that he could persuade the other Commonwealth leaders by a personal explanation. Before leaving for the conference he said he would endeavour to the best of his ability to retain membership. But then he added a critical proviso. 'It must remain understood', he said, 'that South Africa will not be prepared to pay the price for this of allowing interference in her domestic policies, of sacrificing principles on which her Government has been repeatedly elected since 1948 or of submitting to any reflection on her sovereignty or her national honour.'[3]

At the conference, Verwoerd agreed to a discussion of South Africa's race policies, but while some Prime Ministers were prepared to separate that discussion from the question of continued membership, others were not.[4] Verwoerd had expected opposition from the Afro-Asian members, but, according to Sir Robert Menzies, it was Mr. Diefenbaker of Canada who made the first attack. He came, said Menzies, 'armed with a resolution of his

---

[1] The full letter is quoted by Hepple, *Verwoerd*, pp. 177–8.

[2] In fact trading preferences with Britain were retained despite the departure from the Commonwealth.

[3] IRR 1961, p. 4.

[4] See J. D. B. Miller, 'South Africa's Departure', *Journal of Commonwealth Political Studies*, vol. 1 (1961–3), pp. 56–74.

Parliament and presented his views with immense emotion'.[1] Before this outburst Menzies thought that there was a chance that the Afro-Asian states would accept South Africa's continued membership, but once the Canadian position had been put, major critics like Nehru of India and Nkrumah of Ghana joined the attack.[2] While, with the exception of Canada, the old Commonwealth members—Britain, Australia, and New Zealand—hoped to keep South Africa in the Commonwealth, there was no suggestion that they would band together in unqualified support of the new Republic and her policies. After long and fruitless attempts to reach a form of compromise, Verwoerd withdrew South Africa's application. He had failed in his objective to persuade the members that a state which practised apartheid could be a member of a multi-racial community. South Africa had been forced out of the Commonwealth.

Yet even if Verwoerd had succeeded in 1961 it is difficult to see how South Africa could have retained membership for more than the briefest period. By the early 1960s all the Commonwealth members had come to accept that it 'must be an ideological as well as an historical community',[3] and the ideological base was a rejection of racial discrimination. Short of abandoning their policies the South Africans had no place in the new Commonwealth. As Menzies wrote: 'Technically Dr. Verwoerd withdrew. But in substance he had to withdraw unless he was prepared to depart from the policies which, however criticized, are the settled policies of his own government.'[4]

When Verwoerd gave his explanation to the House of Assembly, he said that his concept of the Commonwealth was of an international group which built its strength on common interests and points of view and tried to avoid differences and disputes. It was a multi-racial group in the sense that the member states came from different racial stocks, but not in the sense of insisting that each member followed multi-racial policies in its internal affairs. He rightly claimed that the constitutional issue, the question of

[1] Menzies, *Afternoon Light*, p. 213.
[2] There were also reports that Julius Nyerere, the Tanganyika leader, had said that his country, which was shortly to become independent, would not join the Commonwealth if South Africa was still a member.
[3] P. Calvocoressi, *South Africa and World Opinion* (London, Oxford University Press for the Institute of Race Relations, 1961), p. 13.
[4] Quoted by Miller, 'South Africa's Departure', p. 63.

whether South Africa was a republic, had been unimportant in the conference debate. The central issue had been South Africa's internal racial policies, and he had seen a challenge to these as a challenge to the Republic's sovereign dignity. He thought that four possibilities faced him. First, he could have given way to the pressures by agreeing to radical policy changes inside South Africa. Second, he could have stood his ground against any change but have accepted that the conference would issue a communiqué critical of South Africa. Third, he could just have sat back to let the others fight it out over South Africa's membership. Finally, he had the choice of withdrawing the application. The first two possibilities he dismissed because they infringed South Africa's sovereign rights. The third he rejected because he said it would place South Africa's friends, like Britain and Australia, in the impossible position of having to take sides in a divided Commonwealth. This, he asserted, would have destroyed the whole organization. He concluded, therefore, that the only step left, which would retain both South Africa's dignity and her strong bilateral ties with individual Commonwealth members, was a voluntary withdrawal.[1]

Verwoerd returned to South Africa having failed in his objective, and yet he was greeted by his supporters as a hero. At the airport he told an enthusiastic crowd:

We do not come back as people who have had a defeat. It's a happy day for South Africa. What happened was no less than a miracle. So many nations have had to get their complete freedom by armed struggle. . . . But here we have reached something which we never expected. We struggled for the establishment of our republican ideal and we were prepared to pay a price to the extent of remaining a part of the Commonwealth.[2]

This airport statement only makes sense if it is set in its context: first by remembering the strain and emotionalism of white South Africa in 1960, and second by realizing that it was the faithful of the National Party who were at the airport. Taken outside this context, the statement appears ludicrous. Verwoerd spoke of South Africa gaining 'complete freedom'. Did this imply that she did not have 'complete freedom' before the conference? And what did he mean by referring to 'a miracle' and to 'reaching something we never expected'? Verwoerd's aim had been to remain in the

[1] H of A, 23 Mar. 1961, cols. 3501–2.   [2] Quoted by Hepple, op. cit., p. 9.

Commonwealth and that 'miracle' he had failed to achieve. What he was doing was to build victory from defeat, and if there was any miracle involved it was how quickly he persuaded his followers that it was a victory.

At meetings like that at the airport, Verwoerd could play on the traditional Afrikaner fears of outside domination. When he spoke of freedom it was interpreted as freedom from the old imperial masters. But Verwoerd in his eagerness to build a wider white nationalism wanted more than that. He wanted to convince the great majority of white South Africans, including the English-speakers, that withdrawal from the Commonwealth was in their interests. One way was to play down the Commonwealth's advantages. Verwoerd said it was an illusion to suggest that it offered South Africa any military protection, and even in diplomatic terms there was no real loss because Macmillan had already warned him that Britain would not continue to support South Africa at the United Nations.[1] Later he even claimed that relations with Britain had improved since leaving the Commonwealth, they had become clearer and more relaxed because Britain no longer felt obliged to steer South Africa into line with the other members.[2] Finally, Verwoerd emphasized that the gloomy predictions of economic recession had been unfounded, that South Africa's trading and economic relations with Commonwealth members and notably Britain had continued to flourish, and that trading concessions had been retained.

Verwoerd had naturally overstated his case. There were disadvantages for South Africa in leaving the Commonwealth. Within the government these were felt most acutely by the Department of Foreign Affairs.[3] When the break was made the flow of information which Britain provided for all Commonwealth members stopped. There was no way to replace this comprehensive information and intelligence service, nor was there any way of replacing the informal contacts which a group of this range and diversity provided. South Africa no longer enjoyed the benefits and contacts which came as a member of a major international group, including

[1] H of A, 10 Apr. 1961, col. 4187.   [2] H of A, 29 Mar. 1962, col. 3466.
[3] The title of the Department and its Minister changed from 'External' to 'Foreign' when South Africa left the Commonwealth. John Barratt has written: 'This emphasized the break, as the term "External Affairs" is particularly associated with the Commonwealth.' (Worrall (ed.), *South African Government and Politics*, pp. 334–5.)

some defence benefits. For all Verwoerd's claims, Britain was more likely to give military support, to supply arms, and to offer training facilities to Commonwealth members than to a Republic outside the Commonwealth.

Although it is possible to draw up a balance sheet of the advantages and disadvantages of Commonwealth membership, once the decision to withdraw was made the debate inside South Africa died. It died because, whatever other considerations might be taken into account, most white South Africans accepted Verwoerd's view that the Republic could not retain membership without either abandoning her policy of white supremacy or having it under constant attack. Verwoerd's appeal to Nationalist Afrikaner tradition had impressed his own party, but it was the broader appeal to white supremacy that really killed the Commonwealth issue. The most striking change came in the attitude of the United Party. After an initial protest the party rapidly accepted the decision. It came to realize that its image of the Commonwealth—the crown, flag, being 'British', and the clubby intimate atmosphere of like-minded men—had become irrelevant. As with other international contacts, the great issue for South Africa had become race relations. The United Party, despite its old loyalties, its more flexible policies, and its emphasis on retaining external links, was as determined as the Nationalists on this score. Speaking at Pietermaritzburg in June 1961, only a few months after the Commonwealth decision, Sir de Villiers Graaff said that there were certain prices the United Party would not be prepared to pay for readmission. One of these was the traditional pattern of white leadership.[1] In August 1961 the annual party conference agreed that if it came to power it would reapply for membership, but only if this was 'in South Africa's interests'. The proviso was introduced by Mr. D. E. Mitchell, who previously had been one of the strongest advocates of the Commonwealth and who, after the Republic had been declared, had said that Verwoerd 'is placing us in jeopardy, where we could have remained completely secure in the Commonwealth'.[2] After the 1961 party conference little was heard from the United Party about South Africa re-entering the Commonwealth.

[1] Colin De B. Webb, 'Foreign Policy of the Union of South Africa' in J. E. Black and K. W. Thompson (eds.), *Foreign Policies in a World of Change* (New York, Harper and Row, 1963), p. 499.

[2] IRR 1961, p. 9.

Once it was seen as a simple choice between retaining white supremacy or membership of the international organization, Verwoerd could speak for almost all white South Africans when he said: 'Without any hesitation my choice is to have fewer friends and ensure the survival of my Nation.'[1] The great Commonwealth debate which had threaded its way through decades of South African history died with scarcely a whimper.

Verwoerd's success in reconciling white South Africa to leaving the Commonwealth can be set in the broader context of a new white South African self-image—a small, civilized people abused and misunderstood even by old friends and standing alone in a continent of potentially hostile states in which power had been handed over to immature black men. The government preached a new gospel of strength in isolation. In March 1962 Verwoerd made an important speech in which he retracted sharply from previous perceived aims. He said that Portugal's experience in Goa, where her NATO allies had failed to assist her, had demonstrated the small value that could be placed on formal military alliances. He asked rhetorically whether South Africa could have expected any Commonwealth assistance if she had been attacked by India, and concluded that states would only work together if it served their interests. Formal alliances, he asserted, were pointless, and particularly so in South Africa's case for the only way to gain admission to an alliance would be to drop the central objective of government policy—the commitment to white supremacy. Unless, therefore, the Western states abandoned their policy of continually placating the non-white states, South Africa could expect no alliances, and given the circumstances, she was better off this way. Verwoerd quoted Kuyper, a Dutch statesman, who had said that 'in isolation is your strength', and he argued that 'as far as South Africa is concerned I want to repeat it in respect of our colour policy—in isolation in the sphere of colour policy lies our strength. If we were to agree to the demands of other Nations because in that sphere we were afraid of the world isolation then we would go under. But isolation in this one sphere does not mean complete isolation. There is a lot of co-operation gained from states in other spheres.'[2] Verwoerd was on particularly strong ground if in the 'other spheres' he was referring to continuing economic contacts.

[1] H of A, 29 Mar. 1962, col. 3457.   [2] H of A, 29 Mar. 1962, col. 3452.

13

THE MILITARY AND ECONOMIC
RESPONSE

White confidence and an acceptance of isolation were built on the very tangible assets of military and economic strength. Strength in these two areas continued throughout the 1960s, and so in this chapter the whole of the decade will be considered, overlapping both the 'Years of Crisis and Doubt' and the 'Years of Confidence'.

At a time when white South Africa 'lived with fear and anxiety',[1] she faced military as well as diplomatic isolation. The government, therefore, undertook a major redirection of resources and effort to build up military strength. In June 1961, J. J. Fouché, the new Minister of Defence, gave three reasons for the expansion of the forces. First he said it was to preserve internal security. 'The trained soldier will be available for the maintenance of internal security in the same way as our untrained men are also available for it.' His second reason was the old idea of involvement in a Western military alliance. The South African Forces would be built up 'so that they can fight on the side of the West against Communism', and 'so that we have something decent to offer the West' in terms of contribution to an alliance. Finally, he said that the forces must be able to meet any external invasion; to ensure, among other things, that no 'insignificant little state' would think it could bully South Africa.[2]

The possibilities of external attacks were elaborated in 1962 by Sydney Waterson, a United Party M.P. and an ex-minister of Smuts's Cabinet. The main threats he identified were: an attack by the 'black' states aided by the communists; a major East versus West conflict in which South Africa would be involved on the Western side; and, what he thought the most likely threat, combined international action on 'the pretext' of enforcing international

---

[1] H of A, 6 Feb. 1964. [2] H of A, 6 June 1961, cols. 7398–9.

laws. In facing any of these dangers, he said, the United Party would stand firm with the government.[1]

Verwoerd accepted Waterson's three broad areas of danger. He said that although the threat of a major East versus West clash had diminished, South Africa saw international communism as a continuing and in some ways increasing threat.[2] Fouché reinforced this in 1964 when he said that the communists had already infiltrated East Africa (he was probably referring to Zanzibar), and this had been anticipated by the government. 'We know', he said, 'what the breakthrough means to us. We know that now for the first time in our history the communists have a base in the Indian Ocean along the East Coast.'[3]

As to direct military action by the black states, it was never made clear what form an attack might take (the guerrilla fighters were to come later). But the picture of black armies marching on Pretoria was not inconceivable at that time. So much had changed and was changing in Africa that virtually anything seemed possible.

Finally, the South African Government recognized the danger of international action. Again, there was no precise picture of the shape this might take—would it, for example, be economic sanctions, or could it be some form of military action, or could it be both? In planning to counter such threats the South Africans, having abandoned hope of Western support, now aimed at persuading the Western states to remain inactive. In 1962 Verwoerd referred to speculation that the United States might consider supporting international action against the Union. He could not believe this for it would be against American economic and strategic interests.[4] But perhaps the most significant point was that he had to deal publicly with such speculation.

In retrospect many of the military dangers can be seen as paper tigers, but at the time they seemed real enough. The government faced the delicate task of retaining white confidence and morale while at the same time preparing to meet the dangers. In February 1964 Fouché said that the government fully realized the size and complexity of the threats that were faced: 'the problems we have to face are manifold and as far as I can see we can only face these dangers if we as South Africans stand together in the sphere of

---

[1] H of A, 26 Mar. 1962.   [2] H of A, 29 Mar. 1962.
[3] H of A, 6 Feb. 1964, col. 871.
[4] H of A, 29 Mar. 1962, cols. 3450–1.

defence.'[1] Verwoerd tried to soothe away worries by comparing the military build-up with a man taking out an insurance policy against injury—the man does not expect to be injured, but covers himself for the unexpected. If the analogy can be stretched a little further, Verwoerd was saying that South Africa was prepared to pay heavy premiums in terms of capital and manpower to provide some form of military insurance.

The high premium was very clear in the rapid increase in defence expenditure. Throughout the 1960s there was a substantial and sustained increase in the budget allocation for defence (see page 193), and defence absorbed a much higher proportion of the government's overall expenditure. For example in 1959/60 the expenditure on the armed forces was 7 per cent of the total (R39·2 million out of R602·8 million), while by 1966/67 it had risen to 17 per cent (R216·3 million out of R1,252·2 million).[2]

In 1963 Fouché explained that 'the present time may almost be regarded as a period of cold war calling for a large expenditure over a relatively short period on expensive defensive equipment'. The increased vote 'is the formidable price we are called upon to pay for our protection against aggression' and he feared that the price would 'have to be paid for some years to come'.[3]

The rising expenditure was soon reflected in enlarged stocks of military 'hardware'. The government aimed not only to increase the amount of military equipment available but to diversify and safeguard the sources of supply. Another answer was to expand South Africa's own arms industry, and this became much more compelling after the Security Council's 1964 arms ban Resolution. Even before the Security Council's Resolution the South Africans had acted quickly and positively. In 1961 alone they had negotiated 127 licences for the manufacture of military equipment from a wide range of countries.[4] The Defence White Paper of 1964 revealed that while in 1960/61 R315,000 had been spent on the manufacture of munitions, by 1964/65 the estimate for expenditure had risen to R33,000,000—a hundredfold increase in four years! In September 1964 the first automatic rifles to be made entirely in South Africa were produced.[5] Then in the following year the government claimed that South Africa was now

[1] H of A, 6 Feb. 1964, col. 871.   [2] South African Year Book 1969.
[3] IRR 1963, p. 33.   [4] IRR 1965, p. 24.
[5] *African Institute Bulletin* (Pretoria), Nov. 1964.

South African budget estimates for defence

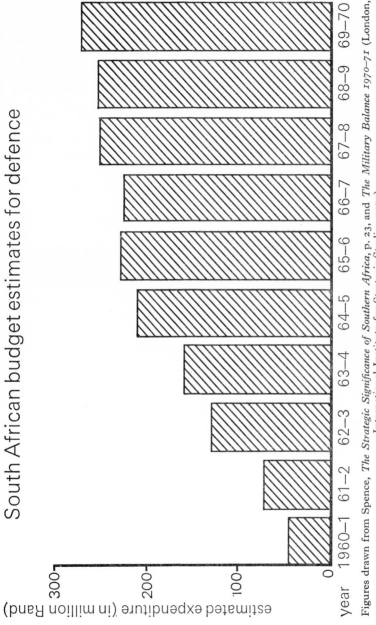

Figures drawn from Spence, *The Strategic Significance of Southern Africa*, p. 23, and *The Military Balance 1970–71* (London, International Institute for Strategic Studies, 1971).

virtually independent in the manufacture of small arms and ammunition, and that stock-piling had started to meet the requirements of full-scale mobilization. The establishment of an aircraft industry was also announced. The aircraft industry, which is government-supported, has concentrated on producing the Impala, an aircraft made on licence from the Italian Macchi Company and based on a jet trainer. By the end of 1966 the first of these aircraft were leaving the factory. A further extension in South Africa's arms repertoire was the establishment of a National Institute for the Development of Missiles which was announced in 1965.[1]

In June 1964 Fouché said, 'We need nothing—and when I say nothing, I mean nothing—at all to maintain internal order.' The reason he gave for buying additional equipment overseas was 'to make us a reliable force in the Western defence group',[2] but there also remained fears that South Africa might have to face external attacks alone. For these the government wanted large and sophisticated weapons which could only be purchased abroad. In 1965 Fouché said that ground-to-air missiles, submarines, surface ships, and certain types of aircraft were wanted. Had the UN arms ban been fully effective South Africa could have obtained none of these, but in the event the ban proved to be no more than an inconvenience. The South Africans were able to counter it, first because not all the suppliers accepted the Security Council's Resolution, second because even those states which stopped selling new arms continued to supply spares and replacements, and third because South Africa benefited from an illicit international trade in arms. In spite of the arms ban the Auditor General's Report for the 1969/70 Financial Year revealed that R53,161,578 had been spent on the purchase of armaments overseas.[3]

The extent of the illicit trade is impossible to quantify but certainly arms were routed to South Africa under cover of false destinations, and by using 'middle men'. One example came to light at the trial of six men from Switzerland's largest armaments firm (Oerlikon-Buehrle) in 1970. It was alleged that between 1963 and 1968 the firm had illegally exported arms worth about £8½

[1] IRR 1965, p. 25.
[2] Quoted by L. M. Thompson, *Politics in the Republic of South Africa* (Boston, Little, Brown and Co., 1966), p. 215.
[3] IDAAF, Jan.–June 1971, p. 448.

million, of which more than half had been sent to South Africa. The accused admitted that arms were being sent to South Africa via France. In addition it was noted that the firm had *legally* sent ninety heavy guns to South Africa from a factory it had opened in Italy.[1]

While the illicit trade was of some importance, the main break came from the French decision to defy the ban. For the French arms industry it was something of a bonanza, with South African orders for submarines, aircraft, and helicopters.[2]

The expansion of the armed forces also involved a large increase in the number of South Africans under arms. It was the white nation mobilizing to defend itself. With the exception of the Cape Coloured Corps, which the Nationalist government re-formed after previously disbanding it, the armed forces were exclusively white. When it was suggested that Africans might be recruited, Fouché replied that it 'would clash with our way of life'.[3] By 1964 there were more than 120,000 in the regular or reserve armed forces. They consisted of regular and conscripted armed forces, a part-time rural militia ('Commandos'), and an armed police force. The legislation for compulsory military training was introduced in 1961 when Fouché called on white mothers to 'give up their sons in defence of their land'.[4] At first there was a selective intake of 7,000 men, for nine months' service, into the Citizen Defence Force, but this was gradually extended so that by 1964 there was an annual intake of 16,500. In addition to the conscripted forces, a vigorous effort was made to expand the regular forces. In 1960 these stood at about 9,000 men, and by 1964 they had increased to approximately 15,000. The mobilization included not only the expansion of the existing regular forces, and compulsory military service for young men, but an increase in school training corps and women's rifle and pistol clubs. In 1964 27,250 women were members of such clubs, and there were plans to double the numbers of schoolboys who received military training from 60,000 to 120,000.[5]

Initially there was a danger for the government that the very speed and urgency with which the armed forces were built up would increase the already strong tension and fears. This phase soon passed. The new military strength became an important

---

[1] *The Times*, 24 Nov. 1970.   [2] See p. 198.
[3] H of A, 18 May 1961, col. 7005–7.   [4] ibid.
[5] Thompson, *Politics in the Republic of South Africa*, p. 214.

factor in reinforcing white morale. At first the government was not prepared to give details of military developments. Verwoerd explained this in 1964 by saying that it was wrong to draw a comparison between the secrecy maintained by South Africa and the public displays of strength made by a country like the United States. America, he said, was outstandingly powerful and 'such information as it does make public is disclosed for the very specific reason that the world and possible opponents may know with what they have to reckon should the occasion arise'. In the case of a small country like South Africa which was facing so many dangers, it would be folly to disclose information about defence forces and equipment.[1]

Even though the government would not reveal details, there was a gradual but clear increase in confidence. For example, in June 1963 Fouché was still prepared to admit that he was worried by the threat of attack by African states, but then he went on to say: 'We must not become unnecessarily anxious or worried about these African threats. In the first place if these people want to attack us soon, they will have to build up tremendously long lines to reach us. . . . In the second place it is still going to take a long time before they can attack or before they would dare to make such an attack', by which time South Africa would be 'considerably stronger'.[2] In the following year he dismissed even the possibility of an attack by the black states. He read out and endorsed a newspaper headline which said: 'Black Africa has missed the bus to attack South Africa. They are too late.'[3] And so the confidence grew. By 1965 the days when Fouché had admitted that 'anything may happen' seemed far away.

Growing confidence was built upon a revision of perceived dangers as well as the increase in military strength. Although the three areas of danger identified by Sydney Waterson remained, they grew blurred and improbable as the years slipped by. The new threats which were recognized seemed on a smaller scale. In 1963 Fouché told the Senate that the chief threat to the Republic came from 'small wars'.[4] He did not define what he meant by small wars but the reorientation in military thinking is important, for if the threat of a major international challenge was removed

---

[1] H of A, 27 Apr. 1964, col. 5008.
[2] H of A, 24 June 1963, cols. 8625–6.   [3] H of A, 6 Feb. 1964, col. 871.
[4] Senate Debates, 15 Mar. 1963, col. 1759.

South Africa could probably deal with the new dangers by herself, whether they came in the form of guerrilla warfare or the revival of internal resistance movements, or both.

In the expansion and retraining of the armed forces Fouché succeeded in instilling a new confidence and pride which had been absent in the 1950s. By the time P. W. Botha succeeded to the Ministry in 1965 it was possible to think of even more ambitious schemes. Botha saw the opportunity provided by conscription to reinforce the values of the white society. There was much more, he said, to training than teaching to kill. 'We must convince the youth of our country that through a spirit of *esprit de corps* and ruthless efficiency they must live for their country.' He denied that there was any party indoctrination in the forces. The young men were trained 'so that they may rise and deal with the methods which will be used against them', and were taught 'civics and knowledge in regard to world trends and knowledge of dangers threatening them and knowledge of the cunning methods used by those people who want to subvert the free world'.[1]

The rapid expansion of the Republic's armed forces continued during the later years of the 1960s. Again the statistics speak for themselves. In the financial year 1959/60 R40,000,000 had been allocated to defence. Ten years later it was R271,000,000. The 1969 Defence White Paper revealed that R660,325,000 had been spent on armaments since 1960, far outstripping similar expenditure in any comparable period, and it was noted that the estimate of expenditure for the next five years was R1,647,000,000.[2] This would include the building of a submarine base and a major communications centre for defence of the Cape route.

There was a similar story for the number of men under arms. The Defence Amendment Act of 1967 (no. 85 of 1967) abolished the ballot system, made military service compulsory for all medically fit young men, and extended the period of full-time service to twelve months. Introducing the new legislation, Botha repeated the arguments that South Africa needed strong armed forces to deter potential aggressors and to contribute to the defence of the Western world. 'Europe', he said, 'can be overthrown in Africa.' By 1969 the Republic could call on 200,000 armed and trained

[1] H of A, 29 Sept. 1966, cols. 3241 and 3245.
[2] IRR 1969, pp. 31–2.

men.[1] The expansion in size was matched by a continued supply of sophisticated and powerful weapons. Part of this was achieved with outside help. The French continued as the main collaborators with direct supplies of arms and co-operation in joint projects.[2] For example in 1969 it was announced that France and South Africa had developed a unique ground-to-air missile for defence against low-flying aircraft. Co-operation in such ventures was one of the fruits of the heavy South African investment in weapon research and development. Among other fruits was a missile base for experimental tests and launching established on the Zululand coast; South Africa's own napalm bomb; a night sight for rifles; anti-tank and shrapnel shells; and a computer-controlled early warning system.[3]

The message from all this was plain. In a decade South Africa had revolutionized her military capacity and in the context of Africa become a major military power. One measure of this is to match the Republic's expenditure on armed forces against those of other African states.[4]

The combined OAU states had a substantial advantage over South Africa in terms of manpower, but it had become clear by the late 1960s that there was little if any chance of the black states overcoming the geographical and logistic problems involved in combining their forces to attack South Africa. Also, far from planning external enterprises, many African aims were frustrated by internal political disputes. The confidence of men like Fouché and Botha that the threat of invasion by a black African expeditionary force had disappeared was echoed outside South Africa. In 1966 David Wood wrote that the developments in Rhodesia, where the OAU had decided that direct military intervention was not possible, 'have served to illustrate the essential military weakness of the independent African states in the starkest possible way'. He wrote

[1] These were made up of (a) regular forces 13,200; (b) citizen force undergoing full-time training 26,500; (c) commandos 58,000; (d) police force 32,700 full-time, 15,000 reserves; (e) citizen reserve 45,000 (previously trained in national service scheme).
[2] Weapons supplied by France after the UN 1963 arms ban included 3 submarines (the first South African submarines); 2 squadrons of Mirage II-E fighter-bombers; 50 Alouette helicopters; 16 Super Frelan helicopters; and 9 Nord Transall troop carriers. Previously the French had supplied 2 squadrons of Mirage II-C interceptors and 50 Alouette helicopters. (Spence, *The Strategic Significance of Southern Africa*, p. 23.)
[3] IRR 1969, p. 32.   [4] See table, p. 199.

THE MILITARY BALANCE IN SUB-SAHARAN AFRICA 1970[1]
(MEASURED IN UNITED STATES DOLLARS)

	Expenditure	Men under Arms	
Congo (Zaïre)	60,000,000	38,250	
Ethiopia	35,948,000	45,400	
Ghana	48,140,000	15,900	
Guinea	9,470,000	5,400	
Ivory Coast	15,570,000	4,500	
Kenya	17,900,000	5,400	
Malagasy Republic	13,450,000	4,500	
Nigeria	99,430,000	185,000	
Rhodesia	23,630,000	4,600	
Senegal	18,060,000	5,850	
Somali Democratic Republic	9,008,000	12,000	
South Africa	359,940,000	43,800	(Full-time armed forces excluding commandos)
Tanzania	10,900,000	10,350	
Uganda	20,030,000	6,700	
Zambia	20,050,000	4,400	

of the problems of logistics, of combining mixed forces and equipment, and of heavy expenditure, and concluded that set against the strength of the Rhodesian and South African forces, 'these are the stuff of the balance of military power in Africa today'. William Gutteridge was equally clear when he wrote: 'Direct military intervention from outside in the affairs of Africa south of the Zambesi would be a major military operation probably impracticable without the generous backing of a super power.'[2]

Ministers would still refer to the Republic as a 'small power', but this had a hollow ring as it became increasingly obvious that in the context of post-colonial Africa the Republic was a 'great power'. Even in relation to the East/West confrontation there was a new tone of assurance and assertiveness as government ministers chided the Western states for refusing to co-operate with the Republic. In May 1968 Botha said that the Republic still wanted co-operation with others, and repeated that the Cape route would

---

[1] This table is drawn from *The Military Balance 1970–71*. The figures are the most recent available but are not all for 1970 expenditure. See also Claude E. Welch (ed.), *Soldiers and State in Africa* (Evanston, Northwestern University Press, 1970), pp. 268–9. He gives statistics for 1966.

[2] David Wood (introduction by W. F. Gutteridge), *The Armed Forces of African States* (London, Institute for Strategic Studies, Adelphi Papers 27, 1966), pp. 4 and 2.

be a prime target in any East versus West conflict. But if the other Western states were not prepared to see this, South Africa would have to make her own preparations. He continued:

The prime responsibility of the Government is to take into consideration the security and the protection of the Republic, and if certain interested Western nations do not want to lend a hand in the protection of the Cape sea route, then the Republic will have to go it alone, firstly for the sake of its own national interests and secondly for the sake of what we believe to be the interests of the free world, because we have interests in common with the free world.[1]

The government also became notably less diffident in its statements about the strength of the armed forces. By the late 1960s there was an eagerness 'to lift the veil', as Botha put it. For example, the whole of the June 1969 edition of *Report*, a monthly review published by the Director of Information of the South African Embassy in London, was given over to the Republic's strategic importance and accounts of the strength of its armed forces.[2]

With the three original threats largely removed, what dangers did the South African Government perceive by the late 1960s? Vorster said there were two things that South Africa would not tolerate: communist domination in southern Africa and 'terrorism'. In the eyes of the government the two dangers were linked, for, in addition to direct communist military expansion, the communists provided some of the training and backing for the terrorists (guerrillas), and used them as a means of spreading their beliefs and their influence. The training offered to guerrilla fighters in Russia and China, the supply of communist-made arms, and the communist literature carried by guerrillas was proof enough for the South Africans. 'Attempts are being made under communist leadership', said P. W. Botha, 'to infiltrate into Southern Africa to an increasing extent by means of terrorists and to paralyse the country by involving it in a continual fight against terrorists which must eventually lead to guerrilla war.'[3]

The military response to guerrilla warfare and the Russian naval expansion of the late 1960s will be examined in later chapters.[4] But the general point to be made is that while the South

---

[1] H of A, 27 May 1968, col. 6028.
[2] *Report—South Africa and World Strategy* (London, June 1969).
[3] H of A, 3 Apr. 1968, col. 3328.   [4] See chapters 15 and 16.

African Government continued to tread a narrow path, its military strength meant that it could tread with a new certainty, believing that 'the world respects a country which is militarily powerful'.[1]

Increasing military strength was one of the pillars on which white South Africa's confidence was built during the 1960s. Another, and perhaps the most important, was the continued success of the economy. Without this the South Africans would not have had the capacity to develop their expensive policies to counter external threats—policies like the expansion and rearmament of the forces and the promise of development of the Bantustans. Furthermore, South Africa's economic relations provided an intricate network of trading and business contacts. Whatever their views of apartheid, the states which traded with South Africa, whether economic giants like the United States or poor, undeveloped countries like Malawi, had a stake in retaining a prosperous South Africa. Here the South Africans were able to make a telling point. They argued that a *prosperous* South Africa could only be achieved by a *politically stable* South Africa and this in turn implied accepting the *status quo* which provided both the prosperity and the stability.

In assessing political stability, the economy was itself a barometer of confidence in white South Africa. There was a direct but complex causal relationship. The health of the economy rested partly on confidence in political stability. Equally, confidence in the economy helped to build up confidence in the political structure. The South Africans never entirely eliminated the fears of outside investors that a special element of risk was involved in the Republic and therefore high profits were demanded, but the government clearly recognized the importance of the economic performance. As Dr. T. E. Dönges, the Minister of Finance, explained in March 1964: 'I think it is clear to all of us that but for the soundness and strength of our economy, we should have been hard put to maintain ourselves, to protect the integrity of our land and the independence of our people against the openly expressed aggressive designs of certain states.'[2]

The South African economic barometer was set for storms

---

[1] Editorial comment in *Die Volksblad*, 6 May 1969. Quoted by Spence, *The Strategic Significance of Southern Africa*, p. 27.

[2] Quoted by Spence, *Republic Under Pressure*, p. 45.

in 1960 and 1961. During the 1950s the economy had steadily
expanded. Although there had been a slowing down of activity
in 1957 and 1958, 1959 had seen the start of another upsurge,
but this was abruptly halted by the crisis of 1960 which undermined economic confidence. A clear indication of this was the
large outflow of foreign capital. Between January 1960 and May
1961 gold and foreign exchange reserves fell by more than half—
from R312 million to R153 million. Over the whole of 1960 there
was a net outflow of R194 million. The Reserve Bank traced
R176 million of this outflow and discovered that R148 million
had been a repatriation of foreign indirect investment via sales
of listed securities, while R28 million was capital which had
previously been resident in South Africa being placed abroad. In
the first half of 1961 there was a further outflow of R45 million.
The government countered by increasing interest rates, restricting
credit, and refusing to grant loan facilities to foreign-controlled
subsidiaries which wanted to repatriate funds. Eventually, South
African citizens were totally prohibited from exporting funds for
the purchase of securities, while non-residents were prohibited
from repatriating money.[1] These steps were important in stopping
the immediate flow, but the long-term health of the economy rested
in restoring confidence.

The economic troubles of 1960 and 1961 appeared to demonstrate the vulnerability of South Africa's economy to external
pressure. Professor Houghton has written: 'Economic policy in
South Africa had never been isolationist. For the past hundred
years it has ranked high among those countries in which international trade represents a major portion of the total economic
activity.'[2] Accepting Houghton's judgement, directly contradictory arguments can be advanced about whether this heavy reliance on external trade is a source of strength or of weakness in
international relations. Those who argue its strength say that the
economic links give South Africa a wide range of contacts, and
give many countries a stake in preserving the Republic's stability
and economic health. But in the early 1960s it seemed equally
cogent to argue that these same links made South Africa vulnerable. Threaten to cut them, so the argument went, and the white

[1] Merton Dagut, 'The South African Economy Through the Sixties',
Southern Africa, 3 Jan. 1970, p. 13.
[2] Houghton, *The S. African Economy*, p. 181.

government would be in serious trouble, because South Africa was more reliant upon others than they were upon her.

The arguments about the vulnerability of the South African economy have never been satisfactorily resolved. Once the crises of 1960/61 were over the cumulative process started to work, whereby the revival of political confidence bolstered the economic system which in turn reinforced the growing political strength. The economic revival started late in 1961. Houghton writes: 'Few economists at that time would have predicted 1961 as the prelude to one of the greatest waves of economic expansion that this country has experienced.'[1] He called the years between 1961 and 1965 'The Great Boom', and the boom continued into the late 1960s. Dagut dates the rapid expansion slightly later than Houghton, but he is equally clear about its importance. Writing in 1969 he said that 'The performance of the economy since 1962 has been such as to suggest that in six years South Africa has hoisted itself on to a new plane of growth'; this was explained 'by a change of mood within the country, backed-up by internal demands, and by a marked acceleration in world trade. The measures taken by the government had restored the belief that the stability of the country would continue and the stock exchange began to recover its nerve.'[2]

There is ample statistical evidence to support these claims. Between June 1960 and June 1965 South Africa's gross national product rose from c. R5,200 million to c. R7,700 million, an increase of 48 per cent.[3] By 1967 it had risen to c. R9,600 million.[4] In 1969 Dr. Carel de Wet, the Minister of Planning, announced that between 1963 and 1967 the average economic growth rate had been 6·4 per cent per annum.[5] The index of the physical volume of manufacturing production, which had stood at 100 in 1956/57, had risen to 193 in 1966 and 211 by 1968,[6] and, as in the past, the Republic continued to exploit her enormous mineral wealth. In the latter half of the 1960s 'the average annual growth rate of mineral sales value (other than gold) had been a spectacular 13·5 per cent'.[7]

The economic expansion cannot be explained simply in terms

[1] Houghton, op. cit., p. 198.   [2] Dagut, op. cit., p. 13.
[3] Houghton, op. cit., p. 198.
[4] IDAAF, Jan.–June 1968 (Economic Section, p. 43).
[5] Southern Africa, 8 Mar. 1969.   [6] Bulletin of Statistics, Dec. 1969.
[7] Von Maltitz, op. cit., p. 221.

of a return of confidence within white South Africa. Dagut has suggested that it was also related to the increase in world trade from 1962, opening up substantial new markets, but without the confidence, South Africa would not have been able to benefit. When the expansion came, it in turn increased the confidence.

Horwitz has shown how the South African Government was able to use the existing strength of trading and investment links to stimulate manufacturing industries within the Republic and also to draw in more capital. This was done by import substitution legislation, by which foreign firms with existing heavy commitments were induced to make further investments to protect those commitments. Horwitz used the example of the motor industry. By the early 1960s several major foreign motor companies had established assembly plants in South Africa, but the great bulk of the vehicle parts were imported. In 1964 the government introduced legislation which lifted import restrictions on parts for cars which were classified as 'South African made'—that is, those assembled in the Republic and containing a minimum proportion of parts manufactured in South Africa. Late in 1961 the average imported content of cars assembled in the Republic was 87·5 per cent by weight. The 1964 legislation, with its 'import control formula', laid down that classification as 'manufactured in South Africa', and hence exemption from import control permits, implied that 45 per cent of the car's parts by weight had to be made in South Africa, and within three and a half years this proportion had to rise to 55 per cent.[1] The manufacturer, faced with the choice of severe import restrictions, pulling out altogether, or investing a great deal more in the motor and ancillary industries of South Africa, chose more investment. The Republic's car market was sufficiently attractive to ensure this, while the additional investment in turn marked a further commitment to supporting the existing economic structure, and by inference the existing socio-political structure.

Although the government was prepared to take such direct steps to strengthen the country's economy, questions are left concerning, first, the extent of the government's contribution to economic development, and second, the extent to which the government has used economic factors in pursuing foreign policy goals. On the first of these questions—the government's contribution to

[1] Horwitz, *The Political Economy of South Africa*, pp. 362–4.

economic development—the United Party frequently argued that it was despite the government's policies, and especially its rigid attitudes towards the employment and movement of non-white labour, that the economy developed. Certainly in a mixed economy like South Africa's the private sector of commercial and industrial enterprise, as distinct from the government sector, has a major role, and if there is credit to give for expansion much of it must lie there. Also the government can claim no credit for the combined circumstances of South Africa's rich resources plus favourable world markets. But, even accepting these points, and accepting that apartheid policies may have held back further economic expansion, the South African Government's role in economic development cannot be dismissed. The government helped to create the confidence and the political framework in which expansionist policies could be pursued. Also in the mixed economy the government is heavily involved in such sectors as communications and power. While these services have not always been renowned for their efficiency, economic development has required a combined, if not always harmonious, relationship between government and private enterprise. Concerning the second question—the use made of economic factors to achieve policy goals— the government consciously and obviously did this in southern Africa,[1] and hoped to extend it elsewhere in the continent. Outside Africa the economic contacts were used to retain and reinforce other contacts, and in particular to blunt attempts to organize action against the Republic. In this way the government was able to benefit substantially from economic circumstances which were only partly of its own making.

The resilience of South Africa's economic links provides a clear contrast with her diplomatic difficulties. If South Africa's foreign relations can be seen as webs of interaction, then the threads of the web which represent formal diplomatic ties, contacts with international organizations, and military co-operation, were under great strain during the early 1960s. There were few new strands, and many of the old ones showed clear signs of weakness and some had even broken. In contrast, the threads of the economic web, after showing strain in 1960 and 1961, were strengthened and extended, and this strengthening process continued throughout the late 1960s. Old threads like those going to Britain and the

---

[1] See ch. 16.

Common Market were thicker and stronger than ever, and there were important new ones like that going to Japan. The analogy of separate economic and diplomatic webs is not entirely satisfactory as the various threads interact upon each other, but the contrast which can be drawn is instructive.

The strength of economic contacts is shown in the following trade tables:[1]

SOUTH AFRICA'S IMPORTS 1960–1970 IN R MILLION—
SHOWING TOTAL IMPORTS AND MAIN SOURCES OF SUPPLY

Year	Total Imports	UK	EEC	USA	Africa	Asia
1960	1,111	315	210	214	77	156
1961	1,005	292	205	177	69	139
1962	1,002	309	198	169	70	154
1963	1,212	361	239	204	81	168
1964	1,525	423	309	292	90	219
1965	1,719	480	358	397	90	239
1966	1,590	448	328	362	110	222
1967	1,914	497	433	395	141	268
1968	1,878	449	461	391	121	287
1969	2,128	500	504	371	121	367
1970	2,540	561	659	424	131	410

SOUTH AFRICA'S EXPORTS (EXCLUDING GOLD) 1960–1970
IN R MILLION—SHOWING TOTAL EXPORTS AND MAIN MARKETS

Year	Total Exports (excluding Gold)	UK	EEC	USA	Africa	Asia
1960	884	223	138	66	141	71
1961	948	255	164	81	129	86
1962	869	241	181	93	119	107
1963	905	272	193	102	107	103
1964	953	301	194	82	114	118
1965	832	297	176	109	116	107
1966	1,125	403	227	163	196	106
1967	1,361	421	241	134	223	203
1968	1,503	476	265	137	249	235
1969	1,527	511	286	109	225	189
1970	1,634	447	279	129	264	219

[1] These figures have been extracted from the South African Year Books (Johannesburg, Da Gama Publishers).

Within the overall picture provided by the trade figures were some interesting individual developments. These included increasingly important trading links with Japan and West Germany. Again, the figures make this clear:[1]

SOUTH AFRICA–JAPAN TRADE
(IN R MILLION)

	1955	1960	1966	1968	1969
Exports to Japan	11	30	97	250	213
Imports from Japan	20	36	91	121	198

SOUTH AFRICA–WEST GERMANY TRADE
(IN R MILLION)

	1955	1960	1966	1969	1970
Exports to West Germany	32	35	150	103	243
Imports from West Germany	58	112	174	293	389

Trade is only one measure of economic links. Another, which has already been used as an indicator of confidence, is capital investment. South Africa was largely able to overcome the problems of being a risk area by the high profits that were to be gained. Britain continued to be the main source of capital. In 1969 the total value of foreign investment in South Africa was estimated at R4,990 million, of which 61 per cent came from the Sterling Area and 15 per cent from the Dollar Area.[2] Although American investment in the Republic was smaller than British, it was particularly profitable. In 1967 United States earnings from capital investment in the Republic were $128 million or 20 per cent of the book value of the investments and 30 per cent of all US earnings from Africa.[3] In 1970 the *Wall Street Journal* reported that 260 American companies had stated that their South African invest-

[1] Based on *Union Statistics for 50 years 1910–1960* and IDAAF, Jan.–June 1967, p. 7E; July–Dec. 1970, p. 103E; and Jan.–June 1971, p. 115E.
[2] IDAAF, Jan.–June 1971, Economics Section, p. 111E.
[3] F. Taylor Ostrander, 'US Private Investment in Africa', *Africa Report*, Jan. 1969, vol. 14, no. 1, p. 39.

ments were the most profitable overseas investment proportionate
to capital involved.[1]

The attractions for British capital were equally obvious. The
1970 Report of the United Nations Unit on Apartheid described
British earnings in South Africa as 'quite remarkable'. It pointed
out that although Britain had greater investments in areas like
Australia and the United States, earnings from South Africa were
higher. The average earnings on British capital between 1964 and
1966 were: South Africa £60 million, Australia £56 million,
United States £53 million, India £21 million, and the EEC
countries £19 million.

The prospects of high profits continued to draw in foreign
capital.

FOREIGN INVESTMENT IN SOUTH AFRICA[2]
(IN R MILLION)

	1959	1964	1969
Sterling Area	1,921	2,076	3,074
Western Europe	446	469	1,065
Dollar Area	458	405	741
International Organizations	162	138	59
Other	13	21	51
Total	3,000	3,109	4,990

The South Africans were quick to use the economic success
in political terms. The propaganda of the Information Department
and the South African Foundation has persistently highlighted the
strength of the economy and the opportunities it offers for foreign
trade and investment. They also argue that this economic strength
benefits all South Africans, non-whites as well as whites. Spence
quotes one Foundation publication which claimed that British
investment 'will in the long run provide more work and higher
wages and better standards of living . . . for the Africans'.[3] The
government also made clear that economic action against South
Africa would adversely affect the non-whites as well as the whites,

[1] IDAAF, Jan.–June 1970, Economic Section, p. 94.
[2] IDAAF, Jan.–June 1971, Economic Section, p. 111E—based on a table
published in the *Financial Mail* of Johannesburg.
[3] Spence, *Republic Under Pressure*, p. 56.

and would be extended to South Africa's black neighbours who rely so heavily on the Republic.

The direct corollary of South Africa's economic success was to keep alive the questions and doubts that had always plagued those states which would be most directly involved if sanctions were imposed. The argument that white South Africa was on the verge of collapse, which had seemed so realistic in 1960 and 1961, became less and less convincing. The price of taking a 'moral' stand steadily increased. To add to this, when, after November 1965, Rhodesia succeeded in weathering sanctions, their effectiveness as a political weapon was brought into serious doubt. By the late 1960s external economic interests seemed to point more strongly than ever to a policy of non-interference in South Africa's internal affairs.

PART FOUR

THE LATE 1960s —
THE YEARS OF CONFIDENCE
(1966–1970)

14

WHITE CONFIDENCE AND SIGNS
OF FLEXIBILITY

There is no precise division between the periods I have called 'The Years of Crisis and Doubt' and 'The Years of Confidence', but the South Africans clearly recognized the change. Speaking at the celebrations for the seventh anniversary of the Republic, Mr. John Vorster, who had succeeded Verwoerd as Prime Minister in 1966, said: 'It seems as if it was only yesterday that supporters, as well as opponents, of the Republic wondered what the future of the Republic would be. Now, after seven years, South Africans have the answers to most—if not all—of their questions. Doubts have gone and fears have vanished.'[1]

The South African Government did not become so euphoric that it failed to perceive continued hostility and difficulties, and ministers warned against confidence growing into complacency. P. W. Botha, speaking in 1968, said he hoped people were 'aware of the fact that a threat against South Africa does in fact exist; that we cannot simply lean back blissfully and say that all is well and that there is no danger threatening'.[2] Despite such warnings the white South Africans' confidence in their ability to survive and prosper despite external threats had become very strong.[3]

The confidence had built up gradually over the decade. It had been reinforced as perceived dangers like the military threat from the black states disappeared and more particularly as the internal resistance movements had been suppressed. It was a confidence

[1] *Southern Africa*, 10 June 1968, p. 371.

[2] H of A, 3 Apr. 1968, col. 3326.

[3] C. W. de Kiewiet, describing South African attitudes, said: 'The threats and vituperations against South Africa become part of a fictional script, but not any part of their own real world. . . . Quite clearly in the Afrikaans press, but also in the more critical and reflective English language press, one gets the impression of a scoreboard of both domestic and international success and failure on which the balance is in favour of South Africa.' (*Africa Report*, Feb. 1969, p. 4.)

founded on a sense of strength—of economic and military power, and of white unity in the face of external opposition. A senior civil servant commented: 'The outside world may not like us, but we have become so strong that, like Russia, we have to be accepted whether they like it or not.'[1] In a journal published by the Information Department, Martin Spring wrote that South Africans were amazed at how little outsiders appreciated the strength of the Republic. 'This is a young society, like America in the 20's, with a proud capitalist Protestant ethic and complete confidence in its future. Planners in and outside government see no reason why South Africa cannot continue to push up its real income at a rate of at least $5\frac{1}{2}$ per cent a year for an indefinite period—which will bring national income *per capita* up to the current British level in just 16 years time.' Then he turned to military power and claimed that 'South Africa is virtually impregnable to any conventional attack except one made on a massive scale by, or backed by either the U.S. or Russia—a possibility which can be ruled out.'[2]

Another, unsigned, article in the same journal gave a further indication of the South African Government's thinking. The author wrote: 'In 1968 *realpolitik* replaced ideology as the unifying factor among the world's contending powers.' During much of the post-war period 'ideology alienated men from their kith and tied them to the alien: hard reality gave way to diffuse aspirations in determining political affiliations'. This period was now over, and in a radical reshaping of international relations 'power and self preservation' had become the main criteria for behaviour.[3] It would suit the South African Government to be judged in terms of 'power and self preservation', for South Africa is well endowed with the tangibles of *realpolitik*. It is on the intangibles, of rights, freedoms, and equality, that the government founders.

In their re-evaluation of the external environment the white South Africans began to draw a close analogy between their position and that of the Israelis. When *Die Burger* had done this in 1960 it was as a warning of the isolation and dangers that lay ahead.[4] By the late 1960s, and especially after the Israelis' dramatic victory in the Six Day War of 1967, the comparison was drawn

---

[1] Personal communication.

[2] Martin Spring, 'How Strong is South Africa?' in *Report from South Africa*, June 1969, p. 7.

[3] ibid., pp. 3–4.   [4] See ch. 10, p. 147.

in terms of two small states which had demonstrated their ability to survive by guts and determination. The Israeli experience confirmed the South African view that apparently overwhelming odds can be overcome by a combination of economic and technical strength, a dedicated citizen army, and a concerted national effort.[1]

Although there is no one incident which represents a sharp breaking-point between the early period of anxiety and the later period of confidence, the International Court's findings on South West Africa is as good a signpost as any. It removed the threat of Security Council action, the last *immediate* threat the South Africans had feared they might not be able to contain. 'We must ask ourselves', said Muller, 'what would have happened to us if that Court had found against South Africa and in favour of the applicants.'[2] But having recorded the victory, Muller again warned against complacency. He said that it would be quite wrong to think that the judgement in the South West Africa case had seen an end to all South Africa's problems.[3] In another speech he even argued that South Africa's very success in resisting external hostility had stimulated her enemies to greater activity. 'This vehement reaction', he said, 'proves how cunning and dangerous and influential the agitators against South Africa are. One finds this agitation quite incomprehensible, inexplicable, illogical and totally in conflict with the splendid and lofty ideal of the United Nations Organization.'[4]

Another event which paradoxically demonstrated the new confidence of white South Africans was the death of Verwoerd. He was assassinated in September 1966 by one of the white attendants in the House of Assembly. For all the shock, sorrow, and sense of loss felt by white South Africans, there was no sign of panic, no fear that the white society as a whole was threatened.

Verwoerd was succeeded as Prime Minister by Mr. Balthazar Johannes (John) Vorster. Vorster's past record and image suggested that once again the National Party in choosing a leader had shifted further to 'the right'. Vorster was remembered for his

---

[1] See C. W. de Kiewiet, 'The World and Pretoria' in *South Africa International*, vol. 1, no. 1 (July 1970), p. 3 (published by the South Africa Foundation).
[2] H of A, 23 Sept. 1966, col. 2798.   [3] H of A, 22 Mar. 1968, col. 2724.
[4] H of A, 16 Feb. 1968, col. 718.

wartime record as a leading member of the anti-British *Ossewa-brandwag*, and in the government his reputation had been built up as a ruthless Minister of Justice who had suppressed the non-white resistance movements by tough, uncompromising measures. In office Vorster proved to be more flexible than his record had suggested. He has even been accused of weakness in handling his government and party, and certainly he failed to gain the immense authority that Verwoerd had exercised over his colleagues. One outside view of the two men was given by Chief Jonathan, the Prime Minister of Lesotho, who said that Vorster was 'a bit more realistic and practical' than Verwoerd. Verwoerd had been 'a bit difficult, indeed very difficult', for he was a philosopher 'and philosophers want you to accept their philosophy', while Vorster had been more reasonable 'perhaps because he is a lawyer and they are more amenable'.[1]

The 'granite' phase of South African politics was over. Changing circumstances, aided by the change in personalities, had created a more fluid situation in internal as well as external politics. Soon after Vorster became Premier a division appeared in the National Party. In its broadest terms it was a split between the 'verkramptes' (bigoted) and the 'verligtes' (enlightened). Although the dispute may have grown from recent sociological changes within the Afrikaner community, it revived memories of the splits of pre-1948 days.[2] It was bitter, it was highly personalized, and it was centred upon the purity and survival of the Afrikaner people. Explaining the distinction between the two groups, Leo Marquard said:

The verkramptes are those who maintain that Afrikaner nationalism grew strong through its isolation; it should not bow the knee to the foreign and false gods that appear in seductive guises as 'moderation', 'co-operation between the Christian Churches' and so on. These are really liberalism in disguise. The Afrikaner should glory in his isolation.

[1] Quoted by Cockram, *Vorster's Foreign Policy*, p. 124.
[2] Denis Worrall has written that although on the surface it was an ideological split it had important socio-economic dimensions. The move of Afrikaners into the cities, and the success of some as businessmen, had altered attitudes including those towards the authority structure. Business enterprise gained a glamour at the expense of the church and politics. (Denis J. Worrall, 'Afrikaner Nationalism: A Contemporary Analysis' in C. P. Potholm and R. Dale, *Southern Africa in Perspective*, New York, Free Press, 1972, p. 23.)

The verligtes (especially as seen by the verkramptes) are those who think that Afrikaner nationalism not only can afford to relax its exclusiveness but that it will be compelled to do so in order to preserve itself as a white group on a black continent.[1]

The 'verkrampte' case was championed by Dr. Albert Hertzog, who until 1968 was a cabinet minister.[2] On 14 April 1969, in a famous House of Assembly speech, Hertzog said: 'The focal point around which everything revolves in South Africa is that we as a white people, the civilized people, the knowledgeable people, dare to rule as a minority.' Within the white people there are two distinct groups, both of which have enormous strength and vitality and reinforce each other, but the two groups have distinctive characteristics. The Afrikaners, he said, 'are permeated by that great complex of principles called Calvinism, that code of moral, ethical and religious principles. They form part of our being, of our upbringing. We cannot be anything else.' From this Calvinist tradition had developed a particular set of values, which included a recognition of the diversity of creation, a love of freedom for their own people, and a preparedness to stand firm against any who challenged authority in an unlawful way. It was because of these ideals and principles 'that the Calvinistic Afrikaner, the Nationalist, makes such a good, such an ideal fighter and such a good soldier for white civilization'. Hertzog then turned to the English speakers. For all their great qualities, he said, they do not share the Calvinistic tradition and instead are basically 'liberal'. 'This liberalism is so deeply ingrained in our English-speaking compatriots that they, themselves, find it difficult to take action against those communistic and leftist movements when these movements make an attack upon them.' Without the Calvinists the English speakers would have collapsed before the wave of liberalism announced by Macmillan. It is the Calvinist, declared Hertzog, who is 'the champion', 'the soldier' of his own and the English speakers' white civilization, and for the future, as in the past, it is on the Calvinists that the major reliance for preserving that civilization must be placed.[3]

The government, which was eager to attract greater English-

---

[1] IRR 1968, p. 1.
[2] Vorster excluded Hertzog in a cabinet reshuffle because of his opposition to government policies.
[3] H of A, 14 Apr. 1969, cols. 3879–83.

speaking support and to reinforce white unity, attacked Hertzog and his followers. As the struggle within the National Party developed it became clear that it overlapped internal and external affairs. In an attempt to distinguish the 'verkrampte' goats from the party's faithful sheep the government asked for a vote of confidence on four specific issues at the Transvaal National Party Congress of 1969. The issues were, first, continued co-operation with English-speaking South Africans; second, support for the government's immigration policy; third, support for its attempts to improve relations with black states; and fourth, its acceptance, under certain conditions, of racially mixed sports teams visiting the Republic.[1]

The government in its 'outward policy'[2] was attempting to extend its external influences from a firm domestic base, but the 'verkramptes' saw the implications of the policy in reverse terms. They feared the impact that these external policies would have inside the Republic. They feared that the purity of the Afrikaner would be destroyed by extensive immigration and co-operation with the English-speakers. They feared that the foundations of apartheid would be undermined by black diplomats sharing white facilities and racially mixed sports teams touring the Republic. And they feared the ideas of leading 'verligtes' like Advocate D. P. de Villiers, who had represented South Africa at the International Court. He stated that behind the government's 'outward policy' was the presumption 'that it must also work "inward" to change white–black relations inside South Africa'.[3]

The divisions within the National Party led to a formal break in 1969, when the most committed 'verkramptes' left to form the Herstige Nasionale Party (HNP) under Hertzog's leadership. Following the formation of the HNP Vorster called an election in April 1970 to crush the new party. In this he succeeded. No HNP candidate was returned or even came near to being returned. But while Vorster and his governing party had countered the HNP threat, they had been reminded of the limits within which a predominantly Afrikaner party had to work. Decisions about who are 'verkramptes' and 'verligtes' depend on shading and degree.

---

[1] IRR 1969, p. 4.   [2] See ch. 15.
[3] Quoted by Patrick O'Meara, 'Tensions in the Nationalist Party', *Africa Report*, Feb. 1969, p. 44.

The firmest 'verkramptes' may have broken away, but many of those who remained in the National Party shared some of Hertzog's views. The government had been reminded that it could not ignore the roots from which it sprang.

Despite the fears and objections of the HNP, the government continued to pursue a vigorous immigration policy although again there were clear constraints imposed by National Party objectives. The broad aims of immigration policy were outlined by Senator Trollip in 1968—'to ensure an adequate work corps of skilled and trained persons in order to maintain our economic progress', to help all the races to 'enjoy a decent standard of living', and 'to strengthen our white population'.[1]

The importance of strengthening the white population in relation to the growing number of non-whites was emphasized by the preliminary figures for the 1970 census.

POPULATION BY MAIN RACIAL GROUPS 1960–1970

	White	African	Coloured	Asian
September 1960	3,088,000	10,928,000	1,509,000	477,000
May 1970	3,799,000	14,893,000	1,996,000	614,000
Percentage increase	22·4	36·3	32·3	28·7

While the figures reveal the relatively slow growth of the white population they do not reveal that, but for immigration, the white performance would have been very much worse. During the 1960s immigration had become a more important factor than birthrate in increasing white numbers. Between 1960 and 1970 there were 180,000 white immigrants to South Africa, compared with 145,000 births.[2] Yet despite the gains made by immigration and despite the absence of permanent immigrants from any other racial group, the white proportion of the South African population fell from 19·3 per cent in 1960 to 17·8 per cent in 1970.

The attractions for the government of a vigorous white immigration policy were therefore obvious, but the government also recognized the dangers. When the United Party called for a more open policy, with immigration on the Australian scale, the government replied that it was impossible in South African circumstances.

[1] Cockram, *Vorster's Foreign Policy*, p. 97.　　　[2] ibid., p. 92.

It argued that immigration had to be restrictive and confined to skilled whites, for if a large pool of unskilled and semi-skilled white workers were imported there would be serious social problems, with increased racial antagonism and the old spectre of 'the poor white' looming ahead. Moreover the old Afrikaner fears, which had been protested so loudly by the HNP but which were not exclusive to them, still held good. The government was aware of this. The Minister of Immigration, Dr. C. P. Mulder, said in September 1970 that, while most immigrants used English as their home language, the government was taking steps to ensure bilingualism, and 'that the ratio between Afrikaans-speaking and English-speaking South Africans is not disrupted by immigration'.[1]

The inherent conflict remained for the government of trying to expand the white population while retaining exclusive Afrikaner values, and ensuring that the Afrikaners remained the core element of white society. In point of fact the Afrikaner way of life had clearly changed. They were no longer predominantly rural dwellers, and with their move to urban areas they had entered the old English-speaking preserves of business and industrial enterprises. Such development had brought the Afrikaners and English speakers closer to a common life style, and changed some traditional values and behaviour patterns. But much of the past remained. The Afrikaner exclusiveness, bred from a distinctive culture and history and now reinforced by long years of power, was little if at all easier to break. However sympathetic an immigrant or an English-speaking South African might feel towards the Afrikaners and the Nationalist government, they could never 'belong'.[2]

The 1970 election not only crushed the HNP but saw the first signs of a revival by the United Party since its electoral defeat of 1948. At each of the subsequent elections the United Party had lost ground, but in 1970 this decline was halted and some ground was even reclaimed.[3] The United Party hailed this as the start of a new era in South African politics. It was hardly that. There was

---

[1] *Southern Africa*, 26 Sept. 1970, p. 175.

[2] For example Edwin Munger found this among Dutch immigrants. See his 'In Dutch with the Dutch' in *African Field Reports 1952–1961* (Cape Town, C. Struik, 1961), pp. 471–8.

[3] 1970 election results, with 1966 results in brackets: National Party 117 (126); United Party 47 (39); Progressive Party 1 (1).

a very long way to go before the United Party could think of winning an election. The 1970 results may have shown no more than a temporary disenchantment with the government, especially among the English speakers, because of the recent internal disputes in the National Party. And even if a shift to the United Party had significance inside South Africa, it was not a signal for any change in foreign policy.[1]

The United Party and the government both acknowledged the common ground that existed in foreign policy. 'Fortunately,' said Dr. Muller, 'as far as the political parties of South Africa are concerned, there exists a very large measure of unanimity concerning the objectives of our foreign policy.'[2] Dr. Gail Cockram has written of a 'drawing together', or 'toenadering'. She quotes Vorster as saying that 'toenadering' did not imply that he consulted the Leader of the Opposition before the Cabinet agreed policy, but it did imply that they discussed 'the dangers that threaten all of us' because it was in the interests of all to do so.[3]

The government claimed that the common stand on external affairs was built upon its continued success in ensuring stability and order within South Africa. The resistance movements had not been entirely eliminated and during the late 1960s there were fears that the guerrilla fighters might infiltrate into the Republic to link up with internal pockets of resistance. The government never relaxed its grip. It never allowed the African nationalist parties to raise their heads again. Backed by severe legislation, the police moved ruthlessly to suppress any suspected opposition.

The severity of the South African Government's security measures continued to incense its most bitter international opponents and to cause a revulsion even among the more moderate. An enormous burden of individual suffering was imposed by the government in ensuring order and in thrusting on with the policy of apartheid.[4] This was deplored by almost every other govern-

---

[1] This view would almost certainly not be shared by the United Party, and Sydney Uys, writing in *Africa Report* (Nov. 1970, vol. 15, no. 8) under the head 'South Africa Shifts', thought the 1970 election was of much greater significance than I have suggested. He thought the National Party was losing its emotional hold over its followers and 'an even more deep-seated change is taking place in South African politics: the ideology of apartheid has come into conflict, finally, with the economic facts of life'.

[2] Quoted by Cockram, op. cit., p. 215.   [3] ibid.

[4] See IRR 1967, pp. 37–9 dealing with 'The Control of Persons', 'Political Trials', 'Terrorism', and 'Other Matters Relating to Justice'.

ment but, however unpopular, the South Africans never flinched. For all their unpopularity, the harsh laws and police action had worked in preserving white supremacy. The government had, and was seen to have, a tight grip on the country. No longer was it widely believed inside or outside South Africa that revolution was imminent or inevitable.

The imposition of order in South Africa had created an international sense of acceptance, even if the acceptance was a reluctant one. South Africa was seen as one of those chronic international problems for which there is no immediate solution. The South African Government realized, however, that this would evaporate immediately if there were serious internal troubles. In 1966 Verwoerd had said that the government had shown how to deal with internal threats and it would continue on its path whatever the criticisms. 'The Government is prepared to take necessary steps, even unorthodox steps . . . no matter how it is vilified.'[1] It was a commitment which his successors faithfully followed.

The assurance of stability and faith in the *status quo* continued to provide an excellent climate for economic activity. Vorster said that 'There is confidence in South Africa, not only because South Africa has the potential, but because these people know that there is a Government in power here which will keep matters in order. . . . We know only too well that . . . the first question an industrialist asks himself before investing in a country, particularly before he invests in Africa, is this: Is there a stable government in that country?'[2]

While the government had succeeded in countering previous external threats, it became increasingly aware of a very different but potentially serious one. This would arise if external influences were to create a substantial shift in the attitude of young white South Africans towards racial discrimination. Vorster voiced the fears of his generation when he said: 'The permissive spirit of our time is undermining our moral fibre and we shall have to take measures against it—drastic measures.'[3] If young South Africans were to follow the path of young people in Western states the existing racial structure of the society could be undermined by their rejection of the assumptions on which it is built. But are there any real grounds for this fear? Although young white South

[1] H of A, 25 Jan. 1966, col. 67.   [2] H of A, 6 Feb. 1968, cols. 67–8.
[3] *Southern Africa*, 14 Nov. 1970, p. 272.

Africans are certainly influenced by external cultural changes, the influence may be very selective, and they may still retain the firmly established attitude towards the racial structure of their own society. There is little evidence on which to base an assessment. Opinion polls were hardly used in South Africa until the late 1960s and even then they were uncommon. One of these rare polls of white opinion, taken in 1968, indicated little difference in terms of 'liberal' opinion between those over and under 35 years.[1]

If substantial changes in attitude are to come in the white society the student body would seem the most obvious group to take a lead. At the predominantly English-speaking universities there have been clear signs of challenge to the government's policies. For some years there has been a running feud between the government and the National Union of South African Students (NUSAS), mainly on racial questions.[2] These clashes made regular newspaper headlines, but it could be argued that NUSAS activities represented little more than the frustrations of young English-speaking South Africans who realized that political power was firmly in the hands of the Afrikaners. Seen in this light the NUSAS protests would not so much reflect dissatisfaction with the racial structure of South Africa as dissatisfaction with the distribution of political power within white society. This narrow interpretation is certainly unfair to the NUSAS leaders but it serves to highlight the point that if effective change is to come in white attitudes it probably has to come through the Afrikaners.

In 1970 Professor Ben Vosloo and Mr. Jeffrey Lever conducted an opinion survey of student attitudes at the University of Stellenbosch, the most famous of the Afrikaans-language universities. The great majority of students came from Afrikaans-speaking homes (81 per cent in 1970), but there are minorities from English-speaking (9 per cent) and from bilingual homes (8 per cent).

---

[1] For example, in answer to the question 'Do you or don't you think South Africa should withdraw her membership from the United Nations?', 42 per cent of the under-35s thought she should *not* withdraw as against 45 per cent of those over 35. In answer to the question 'Do you or don't you think South Africa should give financial help to her neighbouring black states?', 58 per cent under 35 thought she should help as against 60 per cent over 35. (Public Opinion Survey Nov.–Dec. 1968. Prepared for The South African Morning Group of Newspapers by Market Research Africa (Pty) Limited, Johannesburg.) I am grateful to the Editor of the *Cape Times* for permission to use this survey.

[2] NUSAS is largely confined to the English-speaking universities.

Student activities at Stellenbosch during 1969 and 1970 set off
speculation that a readjustment of attitudes might be taking place,
especially when the Stellenbosch students rejected the lead of the
Afrikaanse Studentebond by resolving to retain some contacts
with Coloured students. Vosloo and Lever tried to find out if
there was any substance in the speculation. One of their findings
confirmed the generally held belief that the English-speaking
students tended to be more 'liberal' than the Afrikaans-speakers.
For example, in reply to the question 'Do you think that the
government's ban on mixed sport in South Africa should remain or
should it be changed?', the answers were:[1]

	Afrikaans-speaking students	English-speaking students	Students from bilingual homes
	%	%	%
Ban should remain	61	19	23
Ban should be changed	38	81	77

Nor was there much sign of a 'liberal' awakening among the
Afrikaans-speaking students when they were asked to respond to
the statement: 'Even if he has equal opportunities for develop-

[1] In the 1968 public opinion poll (see p. 223 above) a similar question had
brought a similar distinction between the language groups. To the question
'Do you or don't you agree that overseas-born non-white sportsmen should be
allowed to compete against white sportsmen in South Africa?', the answers were
as follows (in this case English and other languages were grouped together):

	English/ other languages	Afrikaans/ bilingual
	%	%
Agree—should be allowed to compete	49	19
Disagree—should not be allowed to compete	45	74
Don't know	6	7

(Public Opinion Survey Nov.–Dec. 1968 prepared for
The South African Morning Group of Newspapers by
Market Research Africa, Johannesburg.)

ment, the non-white will not be able to attain the same achievement as the white.' The responses were:

	Afrikaans-speaking students	English-speaking students	Students from bilingual homes
	%	%	%
Strongly agree	21	3	17
Agree	38	16	23
Uncertain	10	13	3
Disagree	22	34	27
Strongly disagree	9	34	30

After noting that the great bulk of Stellenbosch students remain supporters of separate development, Vosloo and Lever concluded that 'If the much abused word "verligte" is taken to mean someone of decidedly liberal views on race, and who harbours strong doubts as to the feasibility and fairness of the policy of separate development, then Stellenbosch students must be considered not markedly "verlig".'[1] However, they did note that there was a considerable discrepancy between what the students thought *should* happen in the future and what they thought *would* happen. They found that more than half the students thought there would be less separation and that about 70 per cent agreed with the statement that: 'The whites in South Africa will have to make many concessions to the non-whites in the near future.' The student view on this issue can be contrasted with a survey of attitudes among the existing power-élite undertaken by Heribert Adam in 1966–7. He questioned members of parliament, businessmen, and senior civil servants. Asked for their predictions about future developments, only 37 per cent thought that 'substantial political and economic concessions' would have to be made to non-whites, while 48 per cent thought that 'on the whole everything continues as it is at the moment'. There was a very clear distinction between Afrikaans and English speakers, with 55 per cent of English speakers but only 17 per cent of Afrikaans speakers believing that concessions would have to be made.[2]

---

[1] Vosloo and Lever, 'Student outlook at Stellenbosch', *New Nation*, Feb. 1971, p. 21.

[2] Heribert Adam, 'The South African Power-Elite: A Survey of Ideological Commitment', p. 96. This study is contained in *South Africa: Sociological Perspectives* (London, Oxford University Press, 1971) which Adam edited.

These attitude-surveys give little encouragement to those who believe that change in the white society will create its own momentum, but they may encourage those who argue for continuing pressure on South Africa to gain the concessions that the majority of Stellenbosch students and the English-speaking power-élite believe they will have to make.

15

THE OUTWARD POLICY AND
THE BANTUSTANS

The foundation for the outward policy lay inside South Africa—
in the country's economic and military strength and the confidence of the white society in its ability to overcome dangers
and retain control of the state. From this domestic base the government projected outwards to influence and improve the external
environment in which the Republic's foreign policy was shaped.[1]
The broad policy objectives were similar to those which South
African governments had pursued over generations—a leading role
in Africa, military security, especially in southern Africa and the
surrounding oceans, an extensive network of economic contacts,
identification and co-operation with the West, and the exclusion
of external interference in internal affairs. What distinguished the
outward policy was, first, the increased capacity of the government
to influence the external environment (this came both from the
increased resources available to it[2] and the changing pattern of
international relations, especially in southern Africa, which opened
up new opportunities for the South Africans), and, second, the
confidence and urgency with which the policy was pursued.

South Africa's external environment can be viewed as a series
of concentric circles—first southern Africa, second the African
continent in general, and finally the international community as a
whole with special regard to the Western states. Each circle will be
examined separately,[3] but the South Africans realized that a
success in one circle could lead to successes in the others, and that
in the late 1960s opportunities were opening up for them in each
of the circles. The government sought to seize the initiative in

[1] In James Rosenau's terms it is a 'conscious policy input' into the external
environment—see *Linkage Politics* (New York, Free Press, 1969), p. 45.
[2] An increased 'power output', to use Modelski's phrase. George Modelski,
A Theory of Foreign Policy (London, Pall Mall Press, 1962), part 2.
[3] See ch. 16, 17, 18, 19.

exploiting these opportunities and, although not always successful, this marked a new, more confident and militant stage in the Republic's foreign policy. Her opponents were quick to take the point. 'Apartheid is on the offensive,' said President Kaunda,' . . . the Boer Trek is still on.'[1]

The new outgoing mood was captured by Muller in 1968 when speaking about the Republic's place in the United Nations: 'Particularly of late, we have deliberately tried to act in a more positive way and to move away from the negative and formalistic attitude which very sound reasons compelled us to adopt in the past . . . we are going to make a special effort to bring the true facts about South Africa to the notice of the world.'[2] And when he spoke at a conference to celebrate twenty years of Nationalist rule he asserted that the 'outward policy' was not something new, but rather 'a determined effort to return South Africa's international position to normal—to what it should be. The principles and the aims of our foreign policy remain unchanged, but the methods and the strategy depend on changing circumstances.'[3] Muller's idea of what 'should be' would give South Africa an active, positive international role with particular emphasis on Africa, where she would take her 'rightful place' as a continental leader.

When asked to give greater precision to the 'outward policy' South African Government officials usually give two answers. First they say it is an African policy, and second a policy which grows from the expanding economy with its search for trade and commerce.[4] Ironically, a similar connection is suggested by some of South Africa's sternest critics, including some who base their analysis on Marxist principles. While the South African officials would argue that the other African states will benefit from greater contacts, the critics interpret the outward expansion as a form of exploitation. The critics' case is that the South Africans are being driven to project outwards because of their internal economic problems. It is argued that the South Africans face increasing balance of payment problems, and also have an inadequate home market to absorb their increase in capital funds and the output of their manufacturing industries. One of the chief constraints within

[1] Cockram, *Vorster's Foreign Policy*, p. 126.
[2] H of A, 16 Feb. 1968, col. 714.   [3] *Southern Africa*, 27 May 1968.
[4] Personal communication.

the home economy is the uneven distribution of wealth which leaves the non-white majority with very limited spending power. Rather than attempting to increase this spending power by re-distributing wealth at home, the South Africans have tried to solve the problem by extending the size of their market through contacts with other African states. Sean Gervasi wrote: 'Since the stability of the economy is dependent upon an ability to in-crease sales of output, economic stagnation is a real danger. The classic solution to this problem, at least for a time, is to expand exports of goods and of capital. South Africa is now attempting to create the political conditions which will make that possible.'[1]

While there is substance in these arguments, they certainly do not offer a complete explanation for the outward policy. First, although the South Africans have consciously attempted to ex-ploit the opportunities offered by a larger African market, most African states are too underdeveloped to offer large trading or investment opportunities. The Republic must continue to look to the rich states for its principal opportunities for economic expansion. Another important proviso is that it is a misperception simply to see the South African Government being driven to pursue policies by economic forces it cannot control. Rather it is attempting to use its economic (and military) resources to gain political objectives. In this sense it is the Republic's economic strength and not its economic problems which provides the founda-tion for the outward policy.

Aid to African states is one of the ways the South African Govern-ment has consciously attempted to use its resources in foreign policy. It has always stated that it cannot compete with the major Western powers in quantity of aid, but it sees itself ideally equipped to offer 'qualitative' technological and economic aid based on experience of similar conditions to those faced by the black states. Pursuing this policy in the late 1960s, the government reduced its contribution to pooled international aid schemes and channelled its main effort into bilateral arrangements in which the aid would be clearly identified as South African. The decision was formalized in March 1968 when Dr. Diederichs, the Minister of Finance, announced the establishment of a loan fund which initially would stand at R5 million. The fund would be used to promote economic

[1] Sean Gervasi, 'South Africa's Economic Expansionism', *Sechaba*, vol. 5, no. 6, June 1971.

co-operation and give direct assistance by low-interest loans to developing countries in Africa which were well disposed to South Africa. The Minister said that previously South Africa had contributed to international funds on a multilateral basis but had often received no recognition and even been slandered by the countries which benefited from the aid. In future the government had decided to reduce its support for multilateral schemes and offer more assistance on a bilateral basis.[1]

One unique aspect of South Africa's external relations during the period of the outward policy has been the conscious attempt to develop a new pattern of international friendship in the Southern Hemisphere, on an East–West axis stretching from Australia and New Zealand across the southern oceans to South America. The traditional view of South Africa's interests lying along a South–North axis, through Africa to Western Europe, was not abandoned, but the new initiative added a further dimension to foreign policy. When Muller reported to the House of Assembly in September 1966 he picked out for special mention his visit to four South American countries. 'We must', he said, 'regard these people as our neighbours.'[2] In 1969 Dr. Diederichs said that he not only wanted to expand trade links immediately, but he looked to a future when there would be a Southern Oceans trading bloc. He speculated on the possibility of a common market emerging before the end of the century comprising southern Africa, Australia, New Zealand, and a South American state.[3]

Progress in developing the Southern Hemisphere contacts was not as rapid as the South Africans would have wished, but some links were established and Muller made a virtue of moving forward cautiously. At a dinner in 1969 attended by six South American states he said: 'I believe there is no need for any unnatural or hasty attempts to force the pace in our relations with each other. What I envisage is a joint search for common ground or areas in which co-operation between South Africa and her neighbours across the Atlantic will seem logical and mutually beneficial.'[4]

The significant point to emphasize is that the 'outward policy'

[1] IRR 1968, pp. 77–8. The legislation giving effect to this was the Economic Co-operative Promotion Loan Fund Act.
[2] H of A, 23 Sept. 1966, col. 2801.
[3] *Southern Africa*, 12 July 1969, p. 15.
[4] H of A, 7 May 1969, col. 5451. Muller was reporting to the House.

5. 'The Wind of Change' —Macmillan addressing a joint meeting of the House of Assembly and the Senate in February 1960. On Macmillan's immediate right and left are the Speakers of the Senate and the House of Assembly. On Macmillan's far left are Dr. Verwoerd and Sir de Villiers Graaff, leader of the opposition United Party. The painting above is of the Union Conference of 1910.

6. Verwoerd speaking at Cape Town shortly after his return from the 1961 Commonwealth Conference. Behind him are Louw (partly obscured) and Dr. Eben Dönges, leader of the Cape Nationals and Minister of Finance. The banner reads 'Believe in God—Believe in your People—Believe in Yourself'.   *Cape Times*

is not a specific policy. It is not just 'an economic policy' or 'an African policy', or even both of these married together. It is a broad-based attempt by the South African Government to improve its international status and position. In their most optimistic moments the South Africans would hope that a whole series of interconnecting improvements would result from their initiatives. For example, in making friendly gestures to an African state the South Africans would not only hope to establish good relations with that particular state but would hope to influence other black states to follow suit. If this were to happen the critics outside the continent would be confounded and the government's prestige at home would receive a boost. This could not all be achieved at once, but the ambition was there, and with patience the government believed it could be realized. 'It is not my intention', said Vorster, 'to try to build Rome in one day, but slowly and systematically to establish relations to our benefit and the benefit of neighbouring states in Southern Africa and further north where saner attitudes prevail.'[1]

The South African Government continued to see the Bantustan policy as one of the most important bridges between internal and external affairs. Vorster's government continued to follow the road plotted by Verwoerd of relating the development of the Bantustans to policy towards neighbouring black states. They were to be the first link in a chain which started in the Republic, led through the small neighbouring black states, and then outwards to the rest of the continent and the wider international community.

Inside the Republic there was no shrinking back from the commitment to apartheid. In practice the government's aims of racial separation had often to be seriously modified because of economic and physical circumstances, but the commitment remained. 'If one wants peace,' said Vorster in 1969, 'then the development must not be towards each other, but must be away from each other.'[2] The government continued to tighten up apartheid legislation. Whether it concerned job reservation, or rights of residence and movement, or shared facilities, the government

[1] Quoted by John Barratt, 'Dialogue in Africa: A New Approach', *South Africa International* (published by South Africa Foundation, Johannesburg), vol. 2, no. 2, Oct. 1971, p. 101.
[2] IRR 1969, p. 1.

worked for greater separation. In 1968 the last small breach in the wall of exclusive white participation in parliamentary government was removed when the remaining Coloureds were taken off the voters' roll and political parties of mixed race were prohibited.

Apartheid is implemented on two planes. One is the 'grand design', with its broad, bold sweep and its commitment to the development of separate national units. The other plane is 'petty apartheid'—the separation of people in their day-to-day activities— with separate buses, living areas, social amenities, and the thousand and one other regulations designed to keep apart non-white and white. Both aspects have their implications for foreign policy. 'Petty apartheid' has always produced strong international hostility and has created serious practical problems in such matters as accepting black diplomats in South Africa. But it is the 'grand design' on which the government has built its hopes for inter-national acceptance. It has argued that the Republic's relations with the emerging Bantu nation-states will be a model for relations with other black states.

One of the questions that this immediately poses is how firmly the 'grand design' is supported by white South Africans. The government asserts that apartheid is all one piece, that separation must be enforced at all levels, whether it is using separate entrances at a post office or building separate nation-states, but there are white South Africans who question this view. William Greenberg wrote: 'Petty apartheid as it happens is really all the separation that the mass of white South Africans want. . . . Grand apartheid by comparison with petty apartheid has always been a non-starter in popular appeal and every realistic politician knows it.'[1] Men like Greenberg would argue that for most whites the grand design is a remote and uncertain venture. There are doubts about its practicability, its costs, its dangers, and the capacity of black men to govern themselves. While the grand design attracts the support of the National Party's intellectual élite, it is petty apart-heid, so the argument goes, which is seen by most whites as the defence of their privileged position, their high standards of living, and their security. If this view has substance, if it is petty apart-heid and not the grand design which is deeply rooted in white support, then on this score alone doubts must persist about the

[1] William Greenberg, 'The UP and the Labour Issue', *New Nation* (Pretoria), vol. 4, no. 5, Dec. 1970, p. 5.

Bantustan policy. Greenberg's subjective judgement appears to be supported by Adam's attitude-survey of the white power-élite. Adam points out that the people he questioned are likely to be less dogmatic and more flexible in their attitudes on race than most whites because they are less threatened, but generally they viewed the African 'as an immature child, who needs the help and supervision of the ruling father'. When they were asked whether within ten to twenty years the situation in the Transkei would be mature enough to offer complete independence, 79 per cent said 'No', 17 per cent 'Yes', and 4 per cent were undecided.[1]

Developments in neighbouring states could have a critical influence on the independence decision. Verwoerd had said that it was better to have hostile elements outside the Republic— Cubas on the borders rather than enemies within—but if there was a clearly perceived danger of instability in the new states, or a danger of close links being established with the Republic's enemies, then there could be no certainty that white South African opinion would accept such a view.

The government continued to proclaim its commitment to the grand design. Vorster told the House of Assembly in September 1970 that 'Any Bantu state is free to come to this Parliament and say that its time has arrived and that it wants to follow its own course. This Government or whatever other Government may be in power will deliberate and negotiate with the state.' He said he would prefer to see these discussions deferred until the black states were more developed, but it was not a condition that they had to be viable before they could approach the government. 'This is an inalienable right which they have to exercise tomorrow if they want to do so.'[2] Dr. Koornhof, the Deputy Minister for Bantu Affairs, said that the government meant 'real independence', and that the Bantu states could become members of the United Nations after the Republic had granted them independence.[3]

These statements clearly accept that independence is possible for the Bantustans, but in Vorster's case the only undertaking to which he committed the government was to have discussions. The way in which these discussions could develop had been outlined two years earlier when the Prime Minister was questioned

---

[1] Adam, 'The South African Power-Elite', op. cit., pp. 81 and 91.
[2] H of A, 15 Sept. 1970, col. 4211.
[3] *Today's News* (South African Embassy, London), 10 June 1971.

by Mr. Warwick Webber of the United Party. After Vorster had said that the government would allow the Bantu people to follow their own course, Webber asked 'What if they prefer independence?' 'If they prefer independence,' replied Vorster, 'and if they are ripe for it, this Parliament will decide and this Parliament will grant them independence.' Webber asked for clarification about precisely who was to decide whether they were ripe, and was told: 'This Parliament in consultation with the people concerned.' 'What if they do not agree with Parliament?' 'Then', said Vorster, 'it is a question of negotiations. Then it depends on whether this Parliament allows itself to be intimidated and shunted about, as the Leader of the Opposition would be shunted about under these circumstances.'[1]

The government was treading a narrow path. The National Party had staked an enormous amount on the success of the Bantustans, but in implementing its policies the government was always conscious of the constraint within which it operated. For every statement from the government which declares that independence will be granted, another can be found urging caution or laying down a series of exacting provisos. In 1969 M. C. Botha, the Minister of Bantu Administration, set out five determining factors for independence. First was 'the human capabilities of the Bantu'; second, the urge of the Bantu towards self-determination; third, the means in terms of money and manpower; fourth, 'public consent and support, i.e., on the part of the white population of South Africa'; and fifth, the limitations of time.[2] Yet another constraint was added by Dr. Koornhof in October 1970 when he spoke about defence considerations with particular reference to the coastline of the Transkei. The tone of this statement was very different from the one in which he spoke of United Nations membership for the Bantu states. He explained that if independence were granted to the Transkei it would be by treaty, and, as he claimed that the coastal waters belonged to South Africa, he left open the possibility that control of the coastline itself would also have to be determined by the treaty. 'This National Party Government will not be so irresponsible . . . as to let the coastline cause any problems or dangers for this country.'[3]

When in 1968 the United Party again pressed the Minister of

[1] H of A, 23 Apr. 1968, cols. 3947–8.
[2] IDAAF Jan.–June 1969, p. 258.   [3] IDAAF, July–Dec. 1970, p. 401.

Defence both about the coastline and the danger of the Bantustans harbouring guerrilla fighters, Botha was at first evasive. He said that the defence of the homelands was still the responsibility of the South African Parliament. He resented having such a question dragged into open debate. 'Why burden our defence policies with questions in regard to which we have up to now been agreed that all sections of the white population must present a united front?' Then he came closer to the ground. He said that it was now widely realized that to counter guerrilla activities the goodwill of the local people was essential and this the South African Government intended to retain, as it had secured the goodwill of other African people such as those in Lesotho.[1] In a speech later in the same day Botha was even more specific. He accused the United Party of working on the assumption that black people will be enemies whether inside or outside South Africa. This need not be. Some African states would have no choice but to accept South Africa's friendship. 'I take the view that for economic, military and other reasons it will be necessary for the emergent states to retain South Africa's friendship and to reciprocate such friendship.' Finally, he used the Verwoerd argument that if South Africa was to have black opponents it was better to have them outside than inside the gate. He said that the United Party's policies 'would create in South Africa a black proletariat of millions, which would be the breeding ground for communist agitation and chaos around our cities and which we would only be able to suppress with the aid of security forces'.[2]

For all its public confidence, the government obviously had its worries about the potential military risks of the Bantustan policy. The government's main hope was, as P. W. Botha had said, that the small black states could not afford to be unfriendly to South Africa, but this still left a delicate balance which M. C. Botha, the Minister of Bantu Administration, recognized when he spoke at the opening of the Ovamboland Legislative Council in October 1968. 'You are now the rulers of your own homeland. In making your decisions you will be offered two types of advice. One will be well-meant advice, aimed at the furtherance of your national and territorial interests. The other type ... will be aimed at furthering the ideals of foreign powers.' He warned them to be on their guard. 'You will yourself realize that these people who are

---

[1] H of A, 27 May 1968, col. 6031.   [2] ibid., cols. 6072–3.

thousands of miles away from you and have no contact with the people of Ovamboland do not know what is of benefit to the Ovambo Nation. Undoubtedly, your best friend is your neighbour whom you know and who knows you best, the Government of the Republic of South Africa.'[1]

Another worry which the government attempted to play down was the growing number of Africans in the urban areas. P. W. Botha's assertion that the United Party's policies would produce a large and potentially dangerous black proletariat in South African cities presupposes that the Nationalist government's policy has avoided this. It has not. If the grand design had really taken its planned course of developing the African homelands, drawing the blacks back to them out of the white areas, Botha's assertion would have had firm foundations. But this has not happened. There has been great difficulty in attracting capital investment and industrial development, and generally in breaking the pattern of rural poverty. Development in the Bantustans has gone so slowly that most Africans living there have remained near subsistence level, while the 'white' urban areas have expanded and developed rapidly, drawing in more African labour. The implications of these problems in terms of black population movements was revealed by the preliminary figures for the 1970 census. These figures are open to different interpretations and naturally the government chose an interpretation most favourable to its policy. The government emphasized that while in 1960 only 37·5 per cent of the African population lived in the homelands, by 1970 it had risen to 46·5 per cent. These figures appeared to indicate a substantial achievement in moving Africans out of white areas into their homelands. But there are important provisos to be made. First, the African population had grown so rapidly that although the proportion living in the white areas had fallen there were substantially more Africans in the white areas in 1970 than had been there in 1960—7,975,000 against 6,827,000.

Other important provisos must be made in examining the census figures. First, although there had been a movement of some Africans back to the homelands this cannot be taken to imply that they had been drawn back by greater economic opportunities. The economic development in the black homelands had been much slower than the government had originally anticipated,

[1] Quoted in *Africa Report*, vol. 14, no. 2, Feb. 1969, p. 21.

AFRICAN POPULATION IN 'HOMELANDS' AND 'WHITE'
AREAS OF SOUTH AFRICA, 1960 AND 1970[1]

	Africans in homelands		Africans in white areas	
	Number (millions)	Percentage of total	Number (millions)	Percentage of total
1960	4	37·5	6·8	62·5
1970	6·9	46·5	8	53·5

yet it persisted with its policy of removing from the white areas those Africans who were not economically active—the old, the women, and the children. If, as is probable, it was these who accounted for a large proportion of the Africans who returned to the homelands, then, according to Professor S. P. Cilliers, 'the number of economically active Bantu in the cities may have actually increased in which case we will not have made the white economy less dependent on black labour'.[2] Equally, if the proportion of economically inactive Africans in the homelands had increased, development would have been made even more difficult.

Other provisos concern the statistics themselves. Between 1960 and 1970 some boundary adjustments had been made between 'black' and 'white' areas by which some African townships which provide labour for the white urban areas had been included in the black areas. This accounts for about 300,000 Africans who without shifting their place of residence were included in the black areas in the 1970 census. Another query which hangs over the figures is that while the 1970 figures are likely to be more accurate than those of 1960, it is probable that there was still a large number of Africans who were illegally living in the white areas and therefore avoided being enumerated in the census.[3]

The government's failure to reduce the numbers of Africans in white areas was tacitly accepted by Vorster in 1969 when he advanced an argument which shifted the ground away from the old Nationalist claims. He argued that the number of Africans living in white areas was not the sole or even the main considera-

[1] Based on table in Merle Lipton's 'The South African Census and the Bantustan Policy', *The World Today* (London, Oxford University Press for the Royal Institute of International Affairs), vol. 28, no. 6, p. 259.
[2] Cilliers's views were reported in *Southern Africa*, 24 Oct. 1970, p. 228.
[3] See Lipton, op. cit., p. 260.

tion. 'Numbers', he said, 'are not the decisive factor . . . a political say is in fact the decisive factor.'[1] According to this argument, apartheid need not imply a physical separation of peoples but rather an attempt to provide separate political opportunities, by giving those Africans who lived in the white areas a vote in the homeland of their national group.

Obviously problems and uncertainties lay ahead for the Bantustan policy, but as South Africa moved into the 1970s the chances still seemed to be that the government would go ahead with the programme and in time grant independence to separate African states. In 1968 Christopher Hill wrote that 'South Africa has staked everything on the Bantustans. If they fail, then the whole of the Nationalist Party thinking has failed and many will regard separate development as a fraud. On the other hand, South Africa has much to gain by showing that she is genuinely prepared to grant independence to the Transkei, since by doing so she will demonstrate to the world that the policy of apartheid is based not just on oppression, but on a real desire to promote freedom for the races.'[2]

Hill's argument still seems the most persuasive. The Bantustans will not fulfil all the dreams of Verwoerd and his disciples, but to abandon the idea entirely would be to accept that apartheid, the policy of separation, has no final logical outcome, that by inference the United Party's pragmatic view of a white-dominated mixed society has been right all along, and that the chance of rehabilitation in the international community through this particular policy has been abandoned. To accept all this could be a mortal blow to the National Party.

The government went ahead creating political and administrative structures for the separate Bantu peoples. In September 1970 M. C. Botha announced that eight Bantu authorities had been established and that the South African Government would be able to negotiate with each of these authorities as the separate peoples advanced to their future destiny of independence.[3] In the Transkei, which remained the most politically advanced Bantustan, the second general election in 1968 furthered the South African Government's aims. Unlike the first election (1963), when the anti-

---

[1] H of A, 7 Feb. 1969, col. 360.
[2] Christopher Hill, 'African Political Units' in *Africa South of the Congo* (Royal African Society, 1968).
[3] H of A, 7 Sept. 1970, col. 3503.

Bantustan Democratic Party had gained a majority of the elected seats, this time Paramount Chief Kaizer Matanzima's pro-Bantustan Transkei National Independence Party won 28 elected seats against 14 by the Democratic Party.[1]

Following the 1966 International Court decision, the Bantustan system was introduced into South West Africa where six Bantu homelands were defined, with Ovamboland much the most populous.[2] The Ovambos make up over 45 per cent of the total South West African population, and as the great majority of them live in the homeland itself they make a model Bantustan.[3]

In the Republic itself one of the Government's greatest successes was to persuade the Zulus, who had held out longer than any other major group, to accept the Bantustan policy. The government must, however, retain some doubts about future relations with the Zulus as their leader, Chief Gatsha Buthelezi, a man of courage and independence of views, has openly criticized the government in the past.

Buthelezi's case in particular emphasizes that the Africans who have emerged as leaders within the Bantustan structure could be influential in promoting change in South Africa. Their position is much more secure than that of the African nationalist leaders. They are key figures in a government-designed structure and the government would endanger its whole policy if it failed to give them respect. Among these Bantustan leaders there is a variety of views but they share two characteristics which distinguish them clearly from the African nationalists. First, their authority has some support from a traditional base, and second, they are pre-

---

[1] IRR 1968, p. 142. Matanzima's party had held a majority in the previous Assembly because of support from the chiefs. The state of the parties after the 1968 election (1963 election figures in brackets) was:

	Chiefs	Elected Members	Total
Transkei National Independence Party	56 (56)	28 (15)	84 (71)
Democratic Party	8 (8)	14 (27)	22 (35)
Independent and Others	—	3 (3)	3 (3)

[2] Development of Self-Government for Native Nations of South West Africa Act, No. 54 of 1968.

[3] See Richard Dale, 'Ovamboland: Bantustan Without Tears?', *Africa Report*, vol. 14, no. 2, Feb. 1969, pp. 16–23.

pared to work within the framework of separate development. In December 1968 Chief Mangope, speaking at the Tswana Territorial Authority, said: 'We thank the Republican Government for what it has given the Tswana people. Even if it has its weaknesses and mistakes, I want people in the world to know that we have accepted separate development.' In the Transkei Matanzima said: 'We wholeheartedly endorse this policy as being the only policy whereby the different races in South Africa can live side by side in peace and harmony. This policy ensures each racial group full political rights and the maximum development and progress in its own part of our common fatherland.'[1]

A picture of the steady implementation of 'the grand design', at a pace suited to the development of the individual African peoples and accepted by their leaders, was one that the South African Government was eager to impress on the outside world. But the relations with the Bantustans were not always as smooth as the government claimed, and some of the misunderstandings which arose in these formative years suggest that there could be considerable friction in the future. The government was petulant in responding to demands and assertions from the Bantustans which were unpalatable to it. In 1968 a leading member of the Transkei governing party, Mr. M. H. Canca, moved that the South African Government be asked to do everything in its power to prepare the territory for independence in the shortest possible time. The Transkei Assembly passed the motion by a large majority, but the Minister of Bantu Administration and Development was far from encouraging. He said that the road to full independence was 'a long and difficult one', and he laid down seven prerequisites, including some that few existing states could match —'integrity of purpose in public affairs from the highest to the lowest official', and 'a democratic way of life and a sense of complete responsibility'.[2]

Other examples of disagreement between the government and the Transkei Assembly during 1968 concerned claims to land and requests for boundary changes. These could be major friction areas in the future. The first disagreement came when the Assembly requested that the districts of Elliott, Maclean, and Mount Currie and portions of the districts of Port St. John and Matatiele be transferred to the Transkei. The Republican Government replied that

---

[1] *Southern Africa*, 6 Dec. 1969, p. 310.   [2] IRR 1968, pp. 143–4.

continued representations about the transfer of those 'white' areas would tend to disturb good relations.[1] Another Assembly motion asked for the amalgamation of the Transkei and the Ciskei (a separate Bantustan) and the incorporation of the white-owned land between them. The Minister of Bantu Administration quashed this. He said that the two territories would never be joined physically and a wide strip of white-owned land would continue to separate them.[2]

In the early 1970s, therefore, the future of the Bantustans was still open to question, but the momentum of the government's policy in both internal and external affairs was towards further legal separation. Before the decade is out some of the Bantustans could join the old High Commission Territories as constitutionally independent states, but they would remain heavily dependent on the Republic for their well-being and survival.

By the late 1960s the South African Government was emphasizing more strongly than ever a direct link between its Bantustan policy and its relationship with other African states. 'Our African policy', said Muller, 'is in a large measure determined by, and indeed flows logically from our internal policy of separate development and separate freedoms for the various ethnic groups, which make up our country. In a nutshell, our aim is to assist the separate nations which inhabit South Africa to develop economically and constitutionally to their fullest possible potential. There is no ceiling to this development. The logical extension of this policy is that we should seek also to establish friendly relations and collaboration with the African states beyond our borders.'[3]

Strength in diversity and preparedness to work peacefully with black neighbours became constant themes of government statements. In 1968 Vorster said that among the changing circumstances that had helped South Africa was the emergence of independent black states on her borders. These people, he said, knew South Africa and were prepared to work with her. It was those who did not know the Republic that made the attacks.[4] With particular reference to the ex-High Commission Territories, Vorster completed the reversal of policy that had been in train since Malan's

[1] IRR 1968, pp. 127–8.   [2] IRR 1968, p. 138.
[3] *Southern Africa*, 6 Dec. 1969, p. 310.
[4] H of A, 23 Mar. 1968, cols. 2725 and 2727.

day. He said that South Africa would not have wanted to incorporate them even if the offer had been made. He had made clear 'that even if they [the British] wanted to give us the former protectorates tomorrow, we would not want them, because we are leading our own Black people along the road to independence. Why should we want these additional black states?'[1]

[1] H of A, 24 Apr. 1968, col. 4023.

16

THE SOUTHERN AFRICAN BLOC

During the early 1960s the South African Government had canvassed the idea of establishing closer links with its southern African neighbours. The possibility of a common market or commonwealth had been mentioned. In advancing these proposals the South Africans had always emphasized the advantages of economic and technical co-operation, but also implicit in the proposals was the retention of the political *status quo* inside the white-controlled Republic. The South African Government sought to increase the security and wealth of the Republic by surrounding her with dependent territories which would put political stability as well as economic and technical co-operation high on their list of priorities. The South African Government had said that its principal interest was not in the particular forms of government of the neighbouring states nor the colour of their rulers' skin, but in their behaviour—whether, for example, they would agree to peaceful co-operation and refuse to support or harbour the Republic's enemies. However, the Rhodesian UDI had confirmed a strong commitment to support for *white* neighbouring governments.

In the late 1960s the South African Government was able to use its economic and military strength to mould a bloc of southern African states in which the Republic was the dominant partner.[1] (As defined in this study the bloc consisted of the Republic of South Africa and South West Africa; the Portuguese territories of Angola and Mozambique; the old High Commission Territories which gained independence as Lesotho (ex Basutoland), Botswana (ex Bechuanaland), and Swaziland; and two of the territories of the old Central African Federation, Rhodesia (ex Southern Rhodesia), and Malawi (ex Nyasaland). Zambia (ex Northern Rhodesia),

[1] Larry Bowman, 'The Subordinate State System of Southern Africa', *International Studies Quarterly*, vol. 12, Sept. 1968, pp. 231–61.

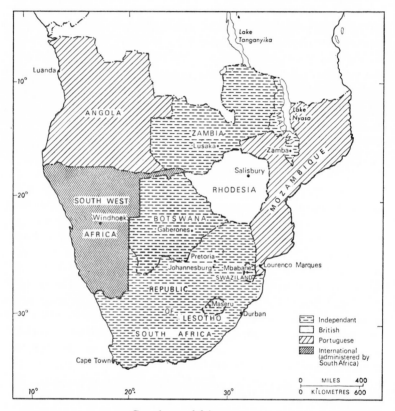

Southern Africa—1970

(Rhodesia (ex-Southern Rhodesia) declared UDI in 1965. Britain
continued to claim legal sovereignty.)

the third member of the old Federation, retained very strong links with the bloc but excluded itself by opposition to white minority rule.) Although the South Africans saw the bloc in part as a defensive grouping, it was not simply an extension of the old laager concept. While in part the South Africans hoped that it would help to buttress them against their enemies, they also saw it as a major link in the extension of the outward policy.

Ironically, the South African opportunity to use its resources more effectively came with the change of circumstances in the sub-continent following the British colonial withdrawal and the increased African nationalist activity against the white-controlled states. The developments that Malan had so feared in the early 1950s had in the event opened up a flexible situation which the South Africans were able to exploit. They were able to use their relatively great strength to make the neighbouring territories heavily dependent on them for economic development, political stability, and military security.

Even excluding the Republic, there is great disparity among the territories of the southern African bloc in terms of status, size, and development. Two are Portuguese colonial territories; another, Rhodesia, has been in constitutional limbo as the dispute with Britain has dragged on; while the remainder are small, newly independent 'black states'. Measured in terms of population and wealth, and still excluding the Republic, they varied, on 1965 figures, between Swaziland with a population of *c*. 380,000 and Mozambique with *c*. 7,000,000; between Botswana with a Gross Domestic Product of R28 million and Mozambique with R744 million. This disparity emphasizes that while there are good grounds for claiming that a 'bloc' of states exists, tied together by a network of common interests, important differences remain and from these differences arise forces for fission as well as fusion.

One of the clearest features of the bloc is the dominance of the white-controlled territories. In their relations with these territories the South Africans have been able to use the common commitment to white rule to cement other ties. Naturally, the black states do not share this commitment, but they acquiesce. They accept that there is little or nothing they can do and so practise a 'live and let live' policy. This is true also of defence co-operation, which has grown from the white governments' response to guerrilla attacks. They have moved closer together to create an informal but increasingly integrated response. Again the black states feel they have no choice but to accept the situation for their own safety, and have refused to become involved by providing bases or refuge for the guerrillas.

The most pervasive of the factors for co-operation are the economic ties which cover a wide range of activities including trade, the provision of capital, shared harbour, communication and banking facilities, and the movement of labour. All the territories participate in this economic activity although naturally the pattern of involvement is different in each case. In explaining the changing economic circumstances of southern Africa, H. R. Read isolated a number of factors—South Africa's 'outward policy'; the more open attitude of the Portuguese to investment in their territories; the break-up of the British Empire which brought independence for the Protectorates; the collapse of the Central African Federation; and finally UDI.[1] Read stated that before these changes there had been four distinct trading areas—(a) South Africa, South West Africa, and the High Commission Territories; (b) the Central African Federation; (c) Angola; (d) Mozambique— although naturally there was some inter-area trading. The late 1960s saw the break-up of the old trading patterns and the formation of a larger unit in which all the territories participated.

As in the past, the South Africans in searching for contacts with their neighbours gave greatest emphasis to economic and technical co-operation. The government disclaimed any ambition to impose a uniform pattern of political behaviour or to interfere in any way in the affairs of the neighbouring states. A South African view of the relationship was outlined by three economists, J. A. Lombard, J. J. Stadler, and P. J. van der Merwe. They wrote of 'systematic co-operation', which was 'a clear alternative to *isolation* on the one hand, and *integration* on the other hand. The idea of systematic co-operation is to obtain the best of both worlds of politics and economics respectively, or perhaps more reasonably, to obtain the optimum combination of political independence and economic viability for the various culturally homogeneous population groups.'[2] They argued for much greater economic integration

[1] *Southern Africa*, 14 Oct. 1968.
[2] J. A. Lombard, J. J. Stadler, P. J. van der Merwe, *The Concept of Economic Co-operation in Southern Africa* (Pretoria, Econburo (Pty.) Limited, 1968), p. 9.

in the sub-continent and in particular an increase in the flow of goods at the expense of labour. 'In short,' they wrote, 'without necessarily reducing the R3,641 million trade with the rest of the world, the *percentage* dependence on the rest of the world could be reduced by rapidly increasing the inter-regional trade at present valued at about R651 million. *This would be the target.*'[1]

Within this pattern of economic co-operation the white states, and especially the Republic, are dominant, as is indicated by the figures for Gross Domestic Products.

GROSS DOMESTIC PRODUCTS IN SOUTHERN AFRICA IN 1965
(IN R MILLION)[2]

South Africa (including South West Africa)	8,084
Mozambique	744
Rhodesia	706
Angola	603
Malawi	116
Swaziland	60
Lesotho	33
Botswana	28

The Republic of South Africa is the hub of southern African economic co-operation. As a major international trading state with links spreading to most parts of the globe, she is on a different economic plane to all the other territories. Measured in terms of trade, the Republic has roughly six times as much trade with the rest of the world as with her neighbours. Yet within the sub-continent South African trade with her neighbours represents roughly 80 per cent of the total.[3] This leaves the neighbouring territories in a dependent relationship, although naturally the degree of dependence varies.

The Republic's economic pre-eminence gives her a pre-eminence in all other spheres. Muller, after speaking of economic co-operation with other states, told the students of the University of Stellenbosch that South Africa was now taking 'her rightful role in Africa',[4] and Vorster was prompted to assert that South Africa was not just another African state but a leader in every

[1] ibid., p. 34.
[2] Based on a table in Lombard et al., op. cit., p. 22.   [3] ibid., p. 34.
[4] *Southern Africa*, 11 Mar. 1968, p. 162.

sphere. He foresaw southern Africa being more closely tied together by its opposition to communism, and its economic interdependence, which would continue to grow, irrespective of race,
as a simple matter of common sense.[1] In the case of the old High
Commission Territories, the British explained that while the
Territories would be granted political independence this did not
imply that they could be *economically* independent. The leaders of
the new states generally accepted this. Prince Dlamini of Swaziland said that 'Swaziland must be constrained by its geographical
and economic circumstances to follow a policy of enlightened self-
interest, relying upon a maximum of acumen and a minimum of
heroics.'[2]

The unrivalled position of South Africa and its ability to ex-
ploit economic strength to gain politically desirable ends is well
demonstrated by its use of aid. For the black states even relatively
small amounts of aid can be of great significance. Lesotho,
Swaziland, and Malawi quickly took advantage of the South
African offers. In Lesotho's case it included help with the supply
of electricity, a grant of £50,000 to expand the para-military
police, and co-operation in the Oxbow hydro-electric scheme. The
acceptance of aid by Malawi was politically even more significant
and the South African Government was prepared to pay a price
to gain Banda's co-operation. New trade and labour agreements
were signed. Malawi also received loans for a range of projects,
including R8 million for the building of the first stage of a new
capital at Lilongwe (a prestige project which the British refused to
support), and R11 million for a rail link to the Mozambique border
at Nacala. South African advisers were sent on request to help
departments of the Malawi Government.[3] 'Being a good African
does not mean cutting your economic throat',[4] declared President
Banda, who became a leading protagonist of contact with the
Republic and of accepting what she offered.

Drawing diplomatic capital from these links, the South African
Government said that they demonstrated that black states were not
uniformly opposed to contact with the Republic, and they showed
that South Africa was prepared for peaceful co-operation with

---

[1] ibid., 11 Nov. 1968.
[2] Quoted by Cockram, *Vorster's Foreign Policy*, p. 129.
[3] For an outline of the aid given, see Cockram, op. cit., ch. 9.
[4] Cockram, op. cit., p. 156.

any state, provided there was an acceptance of non-interference in each other's affairs. Ministerial visits were exchanged with Lesotho and Malawi, and in Malawi's case there was a formal exchange of diplomats. Chief Jonathan of Lesotho, another leading advocate of contact, visited South Africa to meet both Verwoerd and Vorster. Perhaps quite unconsciously Vorster revealed South Africa's dominant position in the relationship when he reported on his meeting. He had told Jonathan that South Africa was not prepared to hand out aid indiscriminately. 'I have offered him technical assistance, which he accepted. I have offered him advice, which he gladly accepted, and investigations which include the Oxbow scheme are already in progress.'[1]

In Malawi's case the South Africans had more to gain because Malawi was less dependent on the Republic. With this in mind, the South Africans subordinated their own preference for diplomatic contact through occasional visits by ministers and a roving am-bassador, and in September 1967 announced agreement with Malawi on an exchange of diplomats. It was a decision that met strong internal opposition from the 'verkramptes', especially when Muller confirmed that 'All diplomats regardless of their colour enjoy the same privileges and immunities everywhere in the world and in South Africa as well.'[2] He also announced that diplomatic suburbs were being established in Pretoria and Cape Town to house black and white diplomats. (The first Malawian mission was headed by a white man, Mr. P. A. Richardson, with a black deputy, Mr. Joseph Kachingwe.[3] Both lived in the diplomatic suburb.) The diplomatic exchange with Malawi was a major breakthrough for the government's 'outward policy', and Vorster followed it up by visiting Malawi in 1970, his first visit to a black state.

South Africa also established a closer relationship with the Portuguese colonial government, as witnessed by the opening of an underwater cable between Cape Town and Lisbon in 1969. The relationship included the commitment to white rule and common defence interests, but economic co-operation was again of central importance. The South Africans, who had failed to find oil inside their own boundaries, became heavily involved in exploiting Angolan oil. The clearest example of economic co-operation was, however, in hydro-electric schemes. One of these, on the Cunene

---

[1] H of A, 11 Apr. 1967, cols. 3957–8.
[2] H of A, 30 May 1968, col. 6321.   [3] IDAAF, Oct.–Dec. 1967, p. 9.

River which forms the boundary between Angola and South West Africa, will provide power and water for both territories. Another, and by far the largest of the hydro-electrical projects, is the Cabora Bassa dam on the Zambezi near Tete in Mozambique.[1] It is designed as one of the largest such schemes in the world, and in addition to its power output there are plans for a large-scale white settlement based on irrigation.

Cabora Bassa is being financed by an international consortium, ZAMCO, with French, West German, and South African interests. From the beginning the South Africans have had a large share in the project and this has steadily increased. When in December 1970, after strong pressure from anti-colonial and anti-apartheid groups, the Italians withdrew their interest, the South Africans took over the share and so finished with an estimated two-thirds of the total stake of £170 million.[2] South Africa's involvement is also vital because of her preparedness to buy a large portion of the power which will be generated. Without this guarantee the scheme could never have gone ahead. On completion of the first phase, which is planned for 1974, the output of electricity will be 1,200 megawatts, of which South Africa will take 1,000.

The South Africans argue that the hydro-electric schemes prove their point that southern Africa forms a natural unit in which resources can be tapped for the benefit of all. Dr. H. J. van Eck, Chairman of the Industrial Development Corporation, said: 'We can make electricity the most important single interlinking factor in Southern Africa. If we really want to help our neighbours, these are the lines along which we must direct our thinking. We can help them overcome one of the greatest problems that balk the economic growth of less-developed countries, namely the fact that without the prize advantages of large-scale production they cannot take off.'[3]

If the Cabora Bassa scheme is successful it will provide a relatively cheap, long-term source of electricity for South Africa, but what must be stressed is that the Republic has no immediate pressing need to develop this source of power. Already within her own borders she has built up a generating capacity based on

---

[1] For a clear, brief article, see William A. Hance, 'Cabora Bassa hydro project', *Africa Report*, May 1970, pp. 20–1.

[2] IDAAF, July–Dec. 1970 (Economic Section, p. 100).

[3] Quoted in Lombard et al., op. cit., p. 57.

thermal electricity which could satisfy the Republic's short and middle-term needs, while for the long-term future there are possibilities of developing nuclear energy.[1] Why therefore was the decision taken? Beyond the official emphasis on economic co-operation, it is also part of the South African Government's attempt to preserve stability in neighbouring states and to build a buffer of friendly, stable governments who will oppose revolutionary movements against the Republic. Muller stated that it was in South Africa's interest 'to have the Southern African continent prosperous and stable, to enable it to withstand communism'.[2] When Vorster explained the reasons for establishing diplomatic relations with Malawi he said that the government had noted with concern the way the communists had taken advantage of the British withdrawal east of Suez and their infiltration into Tanzania. There was a danger, he said, of the communists extending their influence from the east to the west coasts, of cutting Africa in two. 'That is why I found it necessary to establish diplomatic relations with Malawi.'[3]

The South African Government hopes to build political stability, first by underpinning the neighbouring white states, and second by satisfying the aspirations of the black states. 'If they do not eat,' said the industrialist Anton Rupert, 'we do not sleep.'[4] The African leaders recognized South Africa's aims and, despite their poverty and material weakness, it gave them some leverage in relations with the Republic. 'If South Africa and Rhodesia are going to survive,' said Banda, 'they must be surrounded by stable governments or otherwise they themselves are in danger. Remember that troublemakers survive where there is no stability—where there is economic chaos.'[5]

Participation in major projects outside the Republic's borders involves some but not major risks for the South Africans. They realize that whoever rules the neighbouring states there will be strong incentives to co-operate with the Republic, and that these incentives will be strengthened by the mutual development projects. In the case of the hydro-electric schemes, even if the worst were to happen and the power was cut off, it would be no

[1] ibid., pp. 57–9.   [2] Cockram, op. cit., p. 127.
[3] H of A, 23 Apr. 1969, col. 4577.
[4] Quoted by Vandenbosch, *South Africa and the World*, p. 144.
[5] Quoted by Cockram, op. cit., p. 142.

more that an inconvenience for the Republic. When Cabora Bassa
is completed it is estimated that it will supply about 8½ per cent of
South Africa's power needs in 1980 and less than 5 per cent in
1990. This leaves the South African Government in the enviable
position of being able to participate in these schemes, with every
chance of increasing its influence among its neighbours and yet
avoiding absolute reliance on them.

It was the political implications of southern African co-operation that most exercised South Africa's critics. They were incensed by the use being made of South Africa's economic strength.
They saw Cabora Bassa not in terms of megawatts of power, or
acres of irrigated land, but as a symbol of increasing white power
and solidarity. FRELIMO, the African nationalist movement in
Mozambique, which had been waging a guerrilla war against the
Portuguese for years, argued that the Cabora Bassa scheme would
reinforce Portuguese colonial rule. It would also extend South
Africa's influence, with the possibility of her forces being committed to fight if the dam were threatened.[1] They noted that the
irrigation scheme was designed to attract up to a million white
farmers, and feared that the Western states with a heavy capital
investment in the scheme would become even more committed
to retaining the *status quo*.

Rhodesia's UDI, as well as strengthening economic links,
clearly brought out the continuing commitment to white rule.
Neither the Portuguese nor the South Africans had wanted this
commitment to be spelt out so clearly. They were both eager to
build more acceptable international images: the Portuguese by
emphasizing their policy of integration, the South Africans by
concentrating attention on the Bantustans and their increasing
contact with their black neighbours. UDI made a difficult task
very much more difficult, but as the Rhodesians hung on to their
independence some advantages emerged for South Africa. As will
be discussed in the next chapter, the South Africans played a major
part in undermining United Nations economic sanctions against
Rhodesia. In doing this they helped to discredit the whole idea, so
that sanctions against the Republic became that much less likely.[2]
Also UDI pulled the southern African bloc together into a closer
economic unit as it reorganized itself to withstand the sanctions.

[1] Africa Bureau (London), Fact Sheet No. 1.   [2] See ch. 18, pp. 282–4.

Finally, in the diplomatic manœuvrings by which the British and the Rhodesians tried to reach a settlement, both turned to South Africa, recognizing her as the linchpin of the sub-continent, and using her both for communications and for arranging new contacts. In these moves and counter-moves a chapter was being completed in southern Africa's history. British imperial power was in its final hour. The three elements that had dominated white southern Africa—the British imperialists, the English-speaking settlers, and the Afrikaner nationalists—were jockeying against each other for the last time. If the ghosts of Kruger, Rhodes, and Milner haunted the scene, Milner's must have been in despair, Kruger's in triumph.

UDI did not create the southern African bloc, but it clarified, solidified, and defined its membership and the nature of the co-operation involved. It has been a touchstone of membership and has drawn, at least temporarily, the bloc's boundaries. To remain inside has involved either co-operation with Rhodesia or the negative response of abstaining from active hostility to her. Zambia's position since UDI made this clear. Zambia, because of her geographical position, her resources, and the economic and communications links built up over the century, is part of the 'natural' southern Africa as conceived by the South African Government. But Zambia refused to recognize UDI. As far as she has been able she has imposed sanctions against Rhodesia, and consciously tried to draw herself away from southern Africa by improving communications to the north (including the Chinese-built railway to the east coast) and by creating a network of new relations, particularly with Tanzania. When President Kaunda opened a new oil pipeline linking Zambia to the Tanzanian coast he explained the political background to the economic decision. 'We are landlocked, we are surrounded on the east, south and west by regimes basically opposed, if not hostile to the fundamental principles upon which our policies are based, our communications to the north and north-east, which provide the only reliable life-line, still have a capacity which falls below the requirement of the Nation. . . . The pipeline, therefore, removes one of our greatest sources of hardship.'[1]

Zambia was unable to cut herself off entirely from the neighbouring states of southern Africa, and one of the results of imposing

[1] *Africa Report* (Washington), vol. 13, no. 8, Nov. 1968, pp. 26–7.

sanctions against Rhodesia was that she was forced, at least temporarily, to turn to South Africa as the most convenient alternative source of supply. Zambia therefore retains strong economic links with southern Africa, but her hostility to the Smith government and her support for African nationalist guerrilla fighters have disqualified her from membership of the bloc.

The guerrilla fighters (called 'freedom fighters' by themselves, and 'terrorists' by the South Africans) have been organized by the various African nationalist movements of southern Africa. While the main attention of each nationalist movement was centred on the particular territory from which it sprang, and while there were rivalries between the movements, there was a sense in which the guerrillas presented an overall black military challenge to white southern Africa. The white rulers recognized this and it drew them closer together in their response to an identifiable, common enemy. There was, however, no formal agreement, or at least no publicly known agreement for military co-operation. In 1967 Vorster said: 'The question has often been put whether South Africa had a defence agreement with Portugal or Rhodesia against terrorists. The reply to this is "No". We are good friends and good friends do not need an agreement to combat murderers. Good friends know what their duty is when their neighbours' house is on fire.'[1]

The first signs of large-scale guerrilla activity were in the Portuguese territories of Angola and Mozambique. Beginning in 1961 in Angola, and 1964 in Mozambique, a protracted struggle developed in which over periods the guerrillas succeeded in occupying sections in the north of the two territories.[2] During the early years of the 1960s there was no direct guerrilla penetration of the Republic or South West Africa, but at this time the African nationalist parties were recruiting fighters and sending them out of the country for training. The first infiltration came in South West Africa in 1965 when guerrillas from the South West African People's Organization (SWAPO) entered Ovamboland. They established a base and, while undetected, trained recruits. Then in August 1966, after the guerrillas had launched their first attacks

[1] IDAAF, July–Sept. 1967, p. 51.
[2] For an account of the African nationalist activities in Portuguese territories see Gibson, *African Liberation Movements*, part 5.

on two trading stores, the South African police uncovered the base. In the clash which followed two guerrillas were killed and seven arrested. Some members of the group escaped and continued to mount raids, but by 1967 they had all been rounded up or driven out of the territory.[1] In the years that followed SWAPO continued to make sporadic attacks into South West Africa.[2]

One of the difficulties for the South African guerrilla bands was that from their camps in Zambia and Tanzania they were hundreds of miles away from the borders of South Africa, with large tracts of hostile territory to cross before reaching the Republic. The nationalist leaders were presented with the problem of having an increasing number of trained guerrilla fighters waiting in their camps with little prospect of a direct attack on South Africa itself. This in part prompted the ANC to combine with the Zimbabwe African Peoples' Union (ZAPU)[3] in some of the fighting that followed Rhodesia's UDI. Another reason for the joint action was that the nationalist leaders interpreted the situation as one in which the combined black forces were attacking white southern Africa in general. In a joint statement the ANC and ZAPU said that they had marched into Rhodesia 'as comrades-in-arms on a common route, each bound to its destination. It is the determination of these combined forces to fight the common enemy to the finish.'[4] In September 1967 they sent a joint appeal to the OAU for support in 'the struggle which is already raging for liberation', and asked that it be recognized that a full-scale war was being waged and that prisoners should be treated under the terms of the Geneva Convention.

The South Africans were also prepared to recognize a war situation. The chief of staff of the army said that the Republic must be in a state of war, while Vorster stated: 'I am not apologizing for the fact that I have issued instructions to the police to deal with the terrorists as one deals with an enemy in time of war. This is no child's play. These people come here to kill innocent women and children.'[5] Yet while they were prepared to acknowledge the war situation, they were not prepared to recognize the guerrillas as prisoners of war. For almost all white South Africans

[1] IRR 1967, pp. 59–61.   [2] See Gibson, op. cit., pp. 132–41.
[3] As in South Africa, there was a major split in the African nationalist movement. A group split away from ZAPU to form the Zimbabwe African National Union (ZANU). (See Barber, *Rhodesia*, ch. IX.)
[4] IDAAF, Oct.–Dec. 1967, p. 81.   [5] H of A, 25 Apr. 1968, col. 4079.

they were 'terrorists' and 'murderers' and were to be treated as such.

One of the South African fears was that the guerrillas might link up with and rejuvenate the remnants of the internal resistance movements. Both the ANC and the PAC hoped to achieve this, but while the ANC were prepared to combine with other groups in fighting outside South Africa, the PAC believed that they should concentrate immediately on penetrating into South Africa. Fewer PAC members had fled the Republic in the exodus and so its chances of rejuvenating internal activity seemed rather better than the ANC's, but the problem of the guerrilla fighters being hundreds of miles away from the Republic remained. At least one of the bands that attempted the hazardous journey met disaster when, in June 1968, Portuguese forces intercepted and destroyed a PAC unit deep in Mozambique on its way to South Africa.[1]

To counter these threats and to have further powers to deal directly with guerrilla activities the government introduced the Terrorism Act in 1967, adding further to the sweeping and severe powers already available to the executive, and the police in particular. When the Minister of Justice introduced the new legislation he admitted that it gave the government far-reaching powers, but said he felt he had no reason to make excuses for that.[2] Three years later Mr. P. C. Pelser, the Minister of Justice, repeated that no excuses were required because South Africa was fighting cunning and ruthless men who had been trained to lie and resist interrogation. They were planning a racial war for all southern Africa. There was, he estimated, a fully trained guerrilla manpower pool of 38,000–42,000 in camps in Zambia and Tanzania, and others in the 'pipeline' being trained not only in Africa but in China, Russia, and Cuba.[3]

In justifying the new legislation the government emphasized the dangers that were faced, but at other times they balanced this with assertions of confidence in South Africa's substantial military strength. Speaking of the guerrillas in 1966, P. W. Botha said: 'They are underestimating our determination and our military power; such attempts can only lead to the death of these people.' Then he extended the warning to those who were supporting the

---

[1] See Gibson, *African Liberation Movements*, p. 102.
[2] For an outline of the legislation see IRR 1967, pp. 61–4.
[3] *Southern Africa*, 19 Sept. 1970, p. 156.

guerrillas. South Africa, he said, was not seeking war, she wanted peace and constructive development, 'but the price of peace will be too high if it has to be maintained at the expense of our self-respect and freedom'.[1]

In recognizing the guerrillas as a common enemy the white governments co-ordinated some of their military activities. There were general consultations and exchanges of information between South Africa, Rhodesia, and the Portuguese authorities. The most obvious co-operation came between the Rhodesians and South Africans, with sections of South African police being sent to fight in Rhodesia. When the British Government, which still claimed legal sovereignty in Rhodesia, objected, Vorster replied that the police had been sent because it would be folly to wait until the guerrillas came into the Republic.[2] On another occasion he told a National Party meeting, 'We sent our policemen to Rhodesia to fight terrorists who were destined for South Africa. This action has nothing to do with the Rhodesian issue—all we are doing is pulling our own chestnuts out of the fire.'[3] In August 1968 Brigadier P. J. Venter, head of the Security Police, claimed that twenty-nine of the guerrillas so far killed in Rhodesia had positively been identified as South Africans, and that another fifty who had been killed or had died in the bush were also South Africans. He said that the African National Congress and the Pan-African Congress were backing different groups of guerrillas, who were both communist-trained. 'There is', he said, 'overwhelming proof that the terrorist war is a communist plot.'[4]

Rhodesia had become a cockpit for South Africa's own guerrilla war, and fighting there, if fighting had to be done, had advantages for the South Africans. If the Rhodesians, with small-scale South African military support, could counter the guerrillas, not only would a friendly neighbouring white government have been saved, but guerrilla warfare in southern Africa would have been discredited. These two objectives would have been achieved at little cost to the Republic, and without fighting on South African soil.

The fiercest fighting in Rhodesia came in short concentrated spells during 1967 and 1968, with both sides claiming substantial

[1] H of A, 29 Sept. 1966, col. 3236.
[2] *Die Transvaler* (Johannesburg), 9 Sept. 1967.
[3] *The Star* (Johannesburg), 7 Sept. 1968.
[4] IDAAF, July–Dec. 1968, p. 224.

successes. For example, after the fighting in August 1967 the ZAPU–ANC alliance claimed to have killed forty-three members of the government forces, while the Rhodesian Government said only seven had been killed. According to the government's reports one hundred and forty-five guerrillas and thirteen government troops and police had been killed by August 1968.[1] In July 1968 Constable D. du Toit was the first South African to be killed. John Gaunt, Rhodesia's accredited diplomatic representative in South Africa, spoke of 'a shot resounding around Southern Africa' uniting all her white people.[2]

Between 1966 and 1968 it looked as though the guerrillas would become a major threat. In March 1968 *Die Burger* reported that the latest invasion of Rhodesia had been on a determined and ambitious scale, and there were thousands more trained guerrillas waiting to attack. It continued: 'There was apparently a determined effort to obtain a grip over an area inside Rhodesia, in other words the beginning of a slow conquest according to the best rules of "revolutionary warfare". . . . Experience elsewhere has shown that when this stage is reached the task of the security force becomes immeasurably greater because it is no longer possible to say who is who.'[3]

In the same year the South Africans had renewed trouble in South West Africa and the Caprivi Strip. In October Mr. S. L. Muller, the Minister of Police, after admitting an attack upon a police vehicle and the arrest of thirty-three 'political agitators', including five chiefs and two 'terrorists', said that considerable guerrilla activity was taking place in part of the Caprivi Strip. 'The terrorists are moving from town to town and attempting to influence chiefs to co-operate with them.' The situation was made more difficult because the people of the area were illiterate and poor and 'not at all well disposed towards the whites'.[4]

After these clashes of 1968 the government forces in Rhodesia gained a predominance over the guerrillas. They achieved this by their ability to concentrate vastly superior fire power, their use of informers and defectors, their realization that guerrillas must be constantly harried, and their appreciation that by fear or promises

---

[1] John Day, 'The Rhodesian Nationalists and the Commonwealth African States', *Journal of Commonwealth Political Studies*, vol. VII, no. 2, July 1969, pp. 137–8.

[2] *The Guardian*, 26 July 1968.   [3] IDAAF, Apr.–June 1968, p. 174.

[4] IDAAF, July–Dec. 1968, p. 224.

the local population must be turned against the guerrillas. Edward Feit's comment that 'a government is as capable of learning as are the revolutionaries. They are as able to alter their method of attack as their opponents',[1] was made about the South African Government's response to the internal resistance movements, but it is equally apposite for the reaction to the guerrillas. The preparedness of the armed forces to learn and to retain a flexible attitude to the dangers faced, and their preparedness for quick, relatively small-scale action was mentioned in the 1967 Defence White Paper. This said that the permanent armed forces were organized to meet three main aims—first, to train, command, and control a 'citizen army' which could be mobilized rapidly in emergencies; second, to provide certain key operational units; and third, to develop a 'rapid strike' capability for immediate employment in times of crisis.[2]

To add to the advantages and efforts made by the white governments were the difficulties faced by the guerrillas. Much of the southern African terrain is unsuitable for tactics which have been used in other guerrilla wars. Most of the countryside is open, with few hideaway areas, and the rural population is too scattered for the guerrillas to lose themselves in a mass of people. In addition the external support for the nationalist movements was not always appropriate or consistent, and serious internal squabbles developed inside the movements. After 1968 the morale of the South African and Rhodesian guerrillas appears to have fallen sharply. When their combined operations had failed to produce quick successes the ANC and ZAPU fell to recriminations against each other, and the nationalist movements in other territories were reluctant to ally themselves with the ANC. The PAC efforts to infiltrate directly into South Africa had met no better results. The host governments in Zambia and Tanzania, and especially Zambia, showed increasing signs of restiveness about housing men

---

[1] Edward Feit, 'Urban Revolt in Southern Africa', *Journal of Modern African Studies*, vol. 8, no. 1, April 1970, pp. 55–72. An example of the training process was the major military exercise 'Sibasa' held in the Northern Transvaal in August 1968, in which simulated guerrilla attacks were repulsed. One important aspect of the operation was to convince the local population that it was in their interest to co-operate with the government forces (IDAAF, July–Dec. 1968, pp. 222–3).

[2] Printed annexure to Minutes of Proceedings of the House of Assembly, WPDD, 1967.

who, having been frustrated in their original intentions, could become trouble-makers.[1]

The problems faced by the guerrilla fighters, plus the increased strength of the governments' armed forces, had temporarily tipped the balance in favour of the governments. The *Strategic Survey* for 1970 of the Institute of Strategic Studies said of the fighting in Rhodesia that, while the guerrillas were well trained, 'the Rhodesian forces, with considerable South African help, more than held their own. Indeed, while the Portuguese remained in Mozambique, and Zambia continued to depend so heavily upon the electrical power produced at the Kariba Dam in Rhodesia, it seemed doubtful that ZANU and ZAPU could ever become more than a serious irritant to a Rhodesian regime which was prepared to spend heavily both upon its intelligence services and its armed forces.' The report was even gloomier from the guerrilla point of view about the impact in South Africa. 'During 1970', it stated, 'African guerrilla activity produced little concern or alarm in Pretoria.'[2]

Yet while the guerrilla movements had suffered serious setbacks they were still a major potential danger for the white governments, who remained alert, fearful of renewed activity, especially if the internal resistance movements were reactivated. In the Portuguese territories the nationalist guerrillas, despite internal conflicts, continued their operations. In Mozambique FRELIMO set itself the specific task of destroying the Cabora Bassa scheme and had some success in extending its activities to the Tete area near the dam site. Even though the South Africans were not directly involved in the fighting they must have viewed this development with considerable concern.

So far the southern African bloc has been presented as a reasonably cohesive unit, but major qualifications must be added. There was no formal commitment to membership, and although South Africa was in a very strong position she did not exercise direct control over the composition and behaviour of the governments of

---

[1] See Gibson, op. cit., part 2. Also John Day, op. cit., and Alan Rake, 'Black Guerrillas in Rhodesia', *Africa Report* (Washington), vol. 13, no. 9, Dec. 1968, pp. 23–6.

[2] *Strategic Survey 1970* (London, Institute of Strategic Studies, 1971), p. 58.

the neighbouring states. Among the white rulers the Rhodesians refused to make a settlement with Britain when the South Africans were eager that they should do so. In public, however, the South Africans were careful to avoid any suggestion of applying pressure. 'I am neither prepared', said Vorster, 'to twist Mr. Smith's arm nor prepared to dictate to him', for such action would be interference in Rhodesia's affairs and South Africa is opposed to such interference.[1] In 1969 Ian Smith dismissed reports of South African and Portuguese disquiet at the declaration of the Rhodesian Republic and took the opportunity of outlining his views of the relationship with South Africa. 'I have maintained', he said, 'closer association with the South African Government than any Prime Minister previously in our history. I can assure you that I have been kept completely in the picture as far as the feelings of these Governments are concerned. They don't interfere in our affairs and we don't interfere in theirs, but we do think aloud together.'[2]

The circumstances which created the southern African bloc were new and the pattern of relationships untried over a period. As the circumstances alter these relationships will be open to change. Furthermore, the common interests which were so prominent during the late 1960s tend to mask the variety of attitudes and policies found in the different territories. Considerable doubt must also cling to the future internal stability of the Portuguese territories and Rhodesia. The Rhodesians have overcome sanctions, and in doing so have rendered a service to South Africa by undermining the credibility of this form of international action. But the rapid growth of the African population in Rhodesia, with an almost stagnant white population, leaves open the question of whether the whites can sustain their position over the long term. Equally the Portuguese have survived so far against the most determined and aggressive of all the guerrilla armies, but the price has been high. Portugal, the least developed of European countries, has been forced to retain an expeditionary force of about 130,000 men in her African territories and has devoted about 45 per cent of her total budget to military expenditure.[3] It is not idle to ask such questions as: How long can the white Rhodesians retain their position against the great mass of African numbers? and How long

---

[1] H of A, 23 Apr. 1969, col. 4580.
[2] *The Guardian*, 19 June 1969.
[3] *Africa Report*, Nov. 1969, p. 16.

can the Portuguese keep up the immense effort involved in holding
on to their territories?

Behind their common bond of commitment to white rule, the
white governments have different racial policies. The Portuguese
policy of assimilation, even though it is being implemented very
slowly, follows a path directly opposite to apartheid, and even in
Rhodesia there is some African participation in government and a
recognition that the separation of the races imposed in South
Africa cannot be duplicated entirely in Rhodesia's circumstances.
Against this, however, there is no doubt of the determination of the
Rhodesians and Portuguese to retain control in 'civilized' hands,
which, for the Rhodesians at least, is interpreted as 'white hands'.

The small black states have no ideological commitment to the
bloc. They participate either because they feel they have no choice
or because they see direct material advantages. However, there are
differences in the range of options open to them and the choices
they have made. At one end of the scale whoever rules Lesotho
has little choice but to co-operate closely with the Republic. At
the other end Malawi has more choice, although even in this case
the country's poverty makes co-operation with South Africa very
tempting.

Against this Sir Seretse Khama of Botswana has been more
aloof towards South Africa and he has consistently criticized her
policies. He has opposed the use of violence against the Republic.
He has accepted continuing co-operation in areas which were
already well established before independence, but he has been
reluctant to accept aid and has said openly that he dislikes reliance upon a country which practises apartheid. Speaking at the
United Nations, he said that Botswana had no choice but to 'live
and let live', but he added, 'We are confident that we can co-exist
with the Republic of South Africa without sacrificing our national
interests or our fundamental principles. For we have made no
secret of our detestation of apartheid.' In speaking of diplomatic
relations he said that for obvious reasons Botswana had to have
contacts with South Africa, but for 'equally obvious reasons we
decline to consider an exchange of diplomatic representatives until
South Africa can fully guarantee that Botswana's representatives
will in *all* respects, at *all* times, and in *all* places be treated in the
same way as diplomats for other countries'. Equally, he said,
Botswana was not prepared to exchange diplomats with Portugal

7. Vorster during a visit to Port Elizabeth in 1971. In the background is Kaizer Matanzima, Prime Minister of the Transkei. *Cape Times*

8. Hilgard Muller, *c.* 1970.   *Cape Times*

and had accepted refugees from Angola. Seretse Khama condemned UDI and finished by saying that Botswana, as a 'healthy non-racial democracy . . . will present an effective and serious challenge to the credibility of South Africa's racial policies', which might force the South Africans either to abandon the Bantu homelands policy or surrender 'sovereignty to genuinely independent states', and it 'will add to the problem South Africa is already facing in reconciling its irrational racial policies with its desire for economic growth'.[1]

The South African Government, while continuing to make friendly overtures to Botswana, was concerned both about this open hostility to apartheid and about steps which demonstrated Botswana's independence of will. In 1970, when it was announced that Botswana was opening diplomatic relations with Russia, the South African Government gave the warning that Botswana was largely surrounded by South Africa and that the Republic did not favour this diplomatic development.[2] In the same year a dispute arose over a new road, built with American aid. This linked Zambia and Botswana at a point where, according to the Botswana Government, they had a common boundary. The South African Government, probably fearing that this would further break Botswana's reliance on the Republic and perhaps provide a route for the infiltration of African nationalists, at first disputed the Botswana claim to a common boundary with Zambia.[3] Later Muller disclaimed any intention of interfering in Botswana's affairs. It was, he said, purely a legal difference and if a road were built South Africa would also hope to use it.[4]

The area of manœuvre open to the Botswana Government must not be exaggerated. Although important mineral finds were made in Botswana during the late 1960s, they were unlikely to alter substantially the country's lack of wealth and her very heavy economic reliance upon South Africa. What concerned South Africa more than any increase in Botswana's material strength was having a neighbouring head of state who was prepared to declare that 'we are determined that no word or deed on Botswana's part will give comfort to the advocates of race supremacy'.[5]

[1] *Journal of Modern African Studies*, vol. 8, no. 1, Apr. 1970, pp. 123–8.
[2] IDAAF, Jan.–June 1970, p. 374.
[3] *Southern Africa*, 2 May 1970, p. 247.
[4] *Southern Africa*, 12 Sept. 1970, p. 147.
[5] IDAAF, July–Dec. 1970, p. 421.

When challenged, the South African Government says that its ambitions in southern Africa are confined to peaceful co-operation. It disclaims any thought of dominating other states however small they may be, or of practising any form of neo-colonialism. It recalls South Africa's traditional respect for international law, state sovereignty, and for the principle of non-interference in another's internal affairs. But these attitudes were moulded in very different circumstances from those which face South Africa in the sub-continent today. The concern with sovereignty had come from the old fear of British domination, the concern with non-interference was the product of post-war international pressures. In southern Africa in the late 1960s the Republic, far from being endangered itself, had, because of its dominant position, become a threat to others. 'Possibly our gravest weakness', wrote Leo Marquard, 'lies in our economic and military strength which may tempt us in two ways . . . to base our foreign policy on the concept of security in expansion, and to allow our nationalism to develop into imperialism.'[1]

Can the South African Government co-operate and grant aid to its neighbours without interfering in their affairs? Is aid, which is intended to help preserve the *status quo*, a form of interference? By helping President Banda to build a new capital at Lilongwe, and by investing heavily in the Portuguese territories, can the South Africans avoid deeper and deeper involvement in the internal affairs of these territories? The South Africans would deny the accusations implicit in these questions, but as their interests spread more widely in the sub-continent, as they invest more, send more advisers and set up more co-operative schemes, so their perception of South Africa's direct interests is likely to expand. They will argue, as they have argued in helping Rhodesia, that they are simply serving the Republic's interests, but what if these interests became defined as the stability of all southern Africa?

When Vorster offered a non-aggression pact to other African states in 1970 he said that this revealed that South Africa had no aggressive intentions.[2] Plainly it was conceived as part of the Republic's defence strategy, for if countries like Zambia and Tanzania were prepared to sign, the guerrillas would lose their

---

[1] Leo Marquard, *Our Foreign Policy*, Presidential Address to the South African Institute of Race Relations, 1969 (published by the Institute), p. 20.

[2] H of A, 15 Sept. 1970, col. 4207.

bases and training facilities. However, the public emphasis of the South Africans was on the guarantee that South Africa had no aggressive intents towards other African states. Speaking at the United Nations, Muller regretted that some African states had spurned South Africa's offer. 'I very much hope', he said, 'that they will reconsider their attitude, for I know of nothing more that South Africa can do or say to convince them that any fears they may have of aggressive intentions on our part are totally unfounded.'[1]

Here was Muller holding out the olive branch: re-emphasizing that South Africa's military intentions are purely defensive. But what is 'defensive' action? This is a particularly difficult question to answer when guerrilla warfare is involved, and the difficulty is increased because of South Africa's military predominance and range of interests in the sub-continent. Being the dominant military power is a unique position for her and it opens up unique temptations. Vorster, speaking about the guerrillas, warned those who were helping them that if men are trained to fight they usually finish up fighting. 'If you train a racehorse', he said, 'then you must let it run at some stage or another. It does not help you if it stands in the stable and eats hay from morning till night.'[2] If this can be said of the guerrillas then precisely the same thing can be said about the South African armed forces. Vorster's stable was full of horses ready to run. And with South Africa's expanding interests in southern Africa, it will appear increasingly logical for the South Africans to argue that they are protecting themselves and their own interest by military involvement in other territories. Would the South Africans stand idly by if the Cabora Bassa dam were threatened by guerrilla fighters? Would they stand idly by if there were a black rising in Rhodesia?[3]

The South African Government has already shown its willing-

---

[1] *Southern Africa*, 10 Oct. 1970.

[2] Senate Debate, 1 June 1967, col. 3615.

[3] I raised similar queries in a conversation I had with a senior South African official about Lesotho. At first he protested that South Africa would never interfere directly in Lesotho's affairs, as he said the government's behaviour at the time of the disputed Lesotho election in 1970 had shown. But when I pressed him about what South Africa would do if there was a long period of internal fighting and instability in Lesotho, he accepted that that might be considered a different situation and the South African Government might be forced to involve itself. Non-interference, he said, was based on the assumption that there was stability in Lesotho.

ness to accept 'defensive' assignments outside its own borders by
sending troops into Rhodesia, and there has been pressure on the
government to extend direct support to the Portuguese forces. If
guerrilla warfare develops further the South Africans, again
drawing a leaf from the Israeli book, may be tempted to make
strikes against neighbouring territories which harbour guerrilla
camps. Botha, the Defence Minister, threatened precisely this in
1968,[1] and in 1970 Vorster stated that if guerrillas invaded South
Africa from other countries, 'we shall resist them. If they take to
flight we shall chase them and we shall do so right into those
countries from which they came.'[2] These threats were particularly
directed at Zambia (Vorster once warned Kaunda that South
Africa 'will hit him so hard he will never forget it'[3]), but they were
matched by offers of friendship, if only Kaunda and his government would accept mutually beneficial co-operation. In 1968
Muller said that Kaunda knew South Africa was prepared to
co-operate with her neighbours, and it was high time he realized
'that he is sounding a discordant note in Southern Africa, where
good neighbourliness is being practised'. It was in his own interests
to reconsider his attitude for the good of his people.[4]

The South African Government now has considerable military
power, but this has to be set in the context of continuing constraints on its use. The South African Government is more eager
than ever to overcome diplomatic hostility and to become an
accepted and respected member of the international community.
Military action outside the Republic's borders could endanger
the whole enterprise. Larger-scale military action might even be
the one factor that would persuade the ever-reluctant major powers
to take direct action against the Republic. These constraints are
there and are recognized by the South African Government, but
they co-exist with the expanding interest and involvement in
southern Africa. In the same way that the South African Government judges the development of the bloc in terms of the preservation and prosperity of the white society, so it will judge the
question of military action against any perceived dangers to that
society. In the past the South Africans have shown an independent,
defiant attitude to external views, and a preparedness to reject
those values which challenge white supremacy. There is no reason

---

[1] H of A, 3 Apr. 1968, col. 3328.   [2] H of A, 15 Sept. 1970, col. 4208.
[3] Quoted by Cockram, op. cit., p. 152.   [4] H of A, 30 May 1968, col. 6324.

to believe that they will change their commitment in the future. Like its predecessors, Vorster's government saw continued white control of the state as a 'core interest' to be defended at all costs.[1]

[1] ' "Core" values and interests can be described as those kinds of goals for which most people are willing to make ultimate sacrifices. They are usually stated in the form of basic "principles" of foreign policy and become articles of faith which a society accepts uncritically.' K. J. Holsti, *International Politics* (Englewood Cliffs, New Jersey, Prentice Hall, 1967), p. 132.

17

DIALOGUE IN AFRICA

The South Africans' objective was to develop outwards from the sub-continent by building up contacts and friendships throughout Africa. This helps to explain the particular frustration they felt at Kaunda's obduracy. Yet, while Kaunda was not prepared to respond overtly to South Africa's offers of friendship, he realized the limitations placed on his country by her geographical and economic circumstances. In an exchange of confidential letters with Vorster the possibility of discussion between the two governments was mentioned. In 1971 Vorster revealed this correspondence, 'to expose President Kaunda of Zambia as a double-talker'. He challenged Kaunda to honour his promise of talks, and coupled this with a general invitation to any African leader to have discussions 'on an equal footing'.[1] (The Zambian Government denied that Kaunda had ever suggested talks, and said the proposal had come from South Africa.) In revealing the correspondence Vorster may have hoped to discredit a leading critic of the Republic. If Kaunda lost office his replacement might be less hostile towards South Africa, and Zambia might be prepared to take her 'natural' place in the southern African group of states. Another possible reason for the disclosure was to encourage those black states which believed that it was better to talk than to fight with South Africa. If it could be shown that Kaunda had established a personal dialogue with South Africa it would encourage others to follow.

The controversial issue of establishing a peaceful 'dialogue' with South Africa came into the open in November 1970 when President Houphouet-Boigny of the Ivory Coast declared: 'We will not achieve the solution to the problem of apartheid in South Africa by resorting to force of arms. We must open talks with this coun-

[1] IDAAF, Jan.–June 1971, p. 427.

try.'[1] A dialogue already existed between the Republic and the small states of southern Africa, but it was Houphouet-Boigny's declaration that sparked off the major controversy. The behaviour of the southern African states could be explained in terms of their dependence on the Republic. There was no such explanation for the Ivory Coast. The South Africans took the point immediately. The old unanimous hostile front of the 'middle belt' states had publicly been broken. New opportunities were opening up to extend the 'outward policy'.

Balanced against this South African interpretation was the explanation given by those black states which favoured a dialogue. In the broadest terms their argument was that as the tactics already used to attack apartheid had not succeeded, there was no point in continuing with them. As an alternative, peaceful contact could be used as a means of convincing and persuading the South Africans to change their policies. The common thread which bound together the advocates of a dialogue was their contention that a dialogue was the best way to bring change in the Republic's racial policies. Yet there were differences of emphasis among them. Some rejected all proposals to use force against South Africa, while others, like Dr. Busia of Ghana, said that a 'dialogue and armed pressure are not incompatible'.

Obviously the South Africans rejected this view. For them a dialogue would serve not to bring radical change to the Republic but to provide the opportunity to co-operate on economic and technical matters, and to explain existing policies. Vorster stated that 'As far as the policy of separate development is concerned, it can be discussed and I take it as a matter of course that it will be discussed . . . more nonsense has been written and spoken about the policy of separate development than any subject I know of. I will gladly take the opportunity to explain the policy for what it is and not what people think.'[2] On another occasion he said that he would only enter into dialogue on the basis that 'there is no interference with South Africa's domestic policy of apartheid'.[3]

The OAU summit conference of June 1971 voted by a majority of twenty-eight states to six (with five abstentions and two absent)

---

[1] *Africa* (Africa Journal Ltd., London), 2 July 1971, p. 14. There have been suggestions that French influence was behind Houphouet–Boigny's move, but I have no evidence of this.

[2] *The Times*, 24 June 1971.   [3] IDAAF, July–Dec. 1970, p. 383.

that there was no basis for a dialogue.[1] More significant than the result of the vote was the fact that a dialogue had been debated at all. It would have been unthinkable a few years before. It became 'thinkable' because the methods already tried to bring radical change in South Africa had failed. 'For seven years', said Houphouet-Boigny, 'we have had nothing but grand and violent speeches, with tragic and sometimes ridiculous results. We cannot make threats without the means to apply them.'[2] The advocates of dialogue asserted that sanctions had failed to depose Smith in Rhodesia, a direct black military confrontation was impracticable, and even the guerrilla fighters had had little success. 'What we appear to be doing so far,' said Busia, 'is to send our African brothers to slaughter.'[3] With these past failures in mind, the advocates of dialogue argued that it was only through contact, through the peaceful demonstration of black men's capacity, and through encouragement to those who were searching for change inside South Africa, that the racial barriers could be broken.

Another factor which stimulated the dialogue argument was the serious internal difficulties and political instability of many African states. This caused major international concern and undermined the 'myth of innocence'.[4] Also the internal political conflicts had seriously reduced the capacity of the black governments to take action outside their own borders.[5] The period of crises within the black states coincided with and helped to reinforce the increasing confidence in South Africa. The South African Government sought to take advantage of this. It preached again its preparedness to co-operate on a live-and-let-live basis, and in 1970 Vorster offered the black states the non-aggression pact. He said that 'on behalf of our country . . . I am prepared to enter into a non-aggression pact with any black state, irrespective

---

[1] The six states which voted in favour of dialogue were the Ivory Coast, Gabon, Lesotho, Madagascar, Malawi, Mauritius. The five abstentions were Dahomey, Niger, Togo, Swaziland, Upper Volta. The Central African Republic and Uganda were absent. (John Barratt, 'Dialogue in Africa—A New Approach', *South Africa International*, vol. 2, no. 2, Oct. 1971, pp. 99–109.)

[2] Barratt, op. cit., p. 102.

[3] ibid.   [4] See ch. 10, p. 142.

[5] South Africa has also been accused of secret involvement in Black Africa's troubles. There were accusations that South Africa gave help to the Biafrans in their attempt to break away from Nigeria, and South African agents were said to be involved in the murder of Tom Mboya in Kenya. I have no evidence to support or refute the accusations.

of whether they are our immediate neighbours or black states further up such as Tanzania, Zambia and other states of Africa.'[1] With past failures and present difficulties in mind the South African appeal for co-operation was a seductive one, but few were immediately prepared to follow the Ivory Coast. The old militant spirit was still alive. Dr. Okoi Arikpo, Nigeria's Minister of External Affairs, said that the non-aggression pact was 'absolutely unacceptable'. If South Africa did not accept the right of Africans to political freedom, 'then she must not expect peace with the Africans'. The most telling rejection came from President Nyerere of Tanzania: 'Our conflict is not that of two states quarrelling about a border or something of that nature. The conflict is about apartheid versus humanity and about our right to freedom. . . . If the right to self-determination does not exist for the blacks of Southern Africa then it does not exist for Tanzania. This is the root cause of the conflict between the free states of Africa and the apartheid of South Africa.'[2]

Although few were prepared publicly to support a dialogue, there was an increasing ambivalence among the black states. This can be detected in the Lusaka Manifesto, which was issued after a meeting of fourteen states convened by Zambia and Tanzania. The manifesto comes out uncompromisingly against apartheid and states that it is impossible to abandon the cause of liberating the black people of southern Africa. But there was uncertainty about how 'liberation' could be achieved. 'We would prefer', it stated, 'to negotiate rather than destroy, to talk rather than kill. If peaceful progress to emancipation were possible, or if changed circumstances were to make it possible in the future, we would urge our brothers in the resistance movements to use peaceful methods of struggle even at the cost of some compromise on the timing of change.' But was peaceful progress to emancipation possible? The manifesto did not make it absolutely clear. It could be, and was, interpreted in different ways. Muller said that he was 'impressed by the spirit of the manifesto . . . apart from the realization which is beginning to appear from it, the modesty of the people in regard to their own achievements, or lack of achievements, and the fact that they deny that they are opposed to the whites simply because they are whites'.[3]

[1] H of A, 15 Sept. 1970, col. 4207.   [2] IDAAF, July–Nov. 1970, p. 383.
[3] H of A, 7 May 1969, col. 5450.

While the broad 'dialogue' debate was developing, the South
Africans worked steadily, piece by piece, to extend their relations
with the black states. 'We are', said Muller, 'in direct contact with
considerably more African governments than I am prepared and in
a position to disclose at this juncture.'[1] South Africa's chief hope
was that in a changing climate, in which the old principles of
implacable hostility and determination to isolate the Republic were
under question, individual black states would be prepared to make
contacts and accept aid. At first this contact might be covert, but
with time more open contacts could be made. The development
of relations with the Malagasy Republic is a good example of the
pattern South Africa hoped would emerge. After informal, secret
contacts the Malagasy Government came out openly in favour of
co-operation. In January 1970 President Philibert Tsiranana said
that although Malagasy was opposed to apartheid she would
establish trade and social relations with South Africa. In November 1970 it was announced that South Africa would grant Malagasy
a loan of R2,320,000 to finance airport improvements. Also
export credit facilities were agreed to help with the building of a
large hotel and casino.[2] Later in that same month Dr. Muller
paid an official visit to Malagasy. He came, he said, to finalize
negotiations, but 'this is not the end. It is a beginning. It is a mile-
stone which will be followed by many others.'[3]

Nyerere's appeal for support in the continuing struggle of
apartheid versus humanity was the old fundamentalist voice of
black Africa, but it was now not the only voice. The new one,
although not yet strong, was there to challenge. It called for an
acceptance of a less than perfect world, of learning to live with
unpleasant realities, of emphasizing material as well as moral
issues, of achieving slow progress by compromise. The South
African Government's hope was that the new voice of the dialogue
would succeed, that material interests and *realpolitik* would overcome past ideals and ideological commitments, that the mile-
stones which had been laid in Malagasy and Malawi would stretch
up through Africa as the Republic used its wealth and strength to
fulfil the old ambitions of making South Africa secure for the
white man and making her a leading African state.

[1] ibid.   [2] IDAAF, July–Dec. 1970, p. 385.
[3] *Southern Africa*, 28 Nov. 1970, p. 291.

18

THE LIMITS OF INTERNATIONAL
CO-OPERATION

By the late 1960s hostility towards South Africa had become institutionalized within the United Nations. In addition to the regular discussions of South African affairs in the General Assembly and the Security Council, and special conferences and gatherings on apartheid, there were three permanent United Nations bodies which concentrated on South African affairs. These were the United Nations Special Committee on Apartheid, the Unit on Apartheid, and the United Nations Council for Namibia (South West Africa).

The United Nations Special Committee on Apartheid had been set up in 1962. Its brief is 'to keep the racial policies of the Government of South Africa under review when the Assembly is not in session' and 'to report either to the Assembly or the Security Council or to both, as may be appropriate from time to time'. The Committee makes annual reports to the General Assembly and makes recommendations about action which the Assembly should take over apartheid. The Unit on Apartheid was created in 1966 to help the work of the Apartheid Committee. The third United Nations group is the Council for Namibia. It was established in May 1967 as the Council for South West Africa, but the name was changed to 'Namibia' in the following month.[1] The Council was charged 'to administer South West Africa until independence' and 'to undertake certain planning measures and to organize training for South West Africans'. A United Nations Commissioner was appointed for Namibia to whom the Council could entrust executive and administrative

---

[1] 'Namibia' is the name chosen by the African nationalist party, the South West African People's Organization (SWAPO), and is now generally used by the United Nations. Not surprisingly, the South African Government have continued to use 'South West Africa'.

tasks. This post was filled on an acting basis by the Legal Counsel of the United Nations.

In the United Nations attitudes towards international legal obligations reflected, as ever, the different views of what *should* happen. 'We do not consider ourselves bound by law created by Afro-Asians at will', said Vorster.[1] In contrast, the most militant of South Africa's opponents were inclined to believe that a General Assembly resolution, or even a firm conviction of right, was an adequate base for action against the Republic. The Western powers, and even Russia on occasion, were more circumspect and tried to balance Assembly resolutions against other considerations, such as limits imposed by the organization's Charter, Security Council resolutions, and the International Court's decisions. A characteristic clash came in 1968 during an attempt to oust South Africa from the United Nations Conference on Trade and Development (UNCTAD). When the United States delegate, supported this time by Russia, pointed out the legal difficulties and complexities of such a step, he was accused of bringing in 'logic and law' to confuse the committee, who 'are going to do the right thing, whether it is legal or not'.[2]

The South African Government retained an ambivalent attitude towards the United Nations. The precise point of the government's attitude-scale which was emphasized at any time depended both upon particular circumstances and the audience to whom the remarks were directed. Three speeches by Muller demonstrate this. One was made in London in 1969 at the South Africa Club Dinner. Muller was on his way back to the Republic after a visit to the United Nations—a frustrating and exasperating experience for any South African. The frustration broke through Muller's usually bland exterior. He said: 'Finding itself impotent in many vital questions, the organization [the United Nations] has become a mirror of the growing international disorder. Designed to uphold the rule of law and to advance a sense of order, it is itself in danger of becoming one of the agents of discord and strife.' Turning to South West Africa, he said that the United Nations 'seems to make its own laws as it goes along' and appears to have no interest in the welfare of the people of the territory, but rather to pursue a vendetta against South Africa. And he concluded:

[1] Quoted by Cockram, *Vorster's Foreign Policy*, p. 24.
[2] Cockram, op. cit., p. 47.

'Looking around this distracted and dangerous world one wonders what a strange perversity it is that drives people to spend so much time and energy on the domestic affairs of South Africa when all around them, and often near at hand, there are grave convulsions and threats to public order and peace itself.'[1]

In the previous year, when Muller had spoken in the House of Assembly in a debate on an opposition motion about the United Nations, he was intent on explaining within South Africa why the government was retaining membership of the organization. South Africa, he said, was adopting a wait-and-see attitude. The importance of the United Nations was recognized, but at the same time it must never be seen as a super-government and the Republic was concerned about aspects of its behaviour, such as the hostile report of the Secretary General and 'small, insignificant states being allowed in, all with equal votes'.[2] He repeated South Africa's continued rejection of any interference in internal affairs, but he ended on a positive note related to the 'outward policy', saying that South Africa was no longer prepared merely to defend a position, she would go out and assert herself.[3]

On other occasions Muller could even find himself defending the United Nations, or at least its usefulness to South Africa. When in 1969 he was once again being questioned about the purpose of retaining membership, he said that the United Nations is 'the best, the largest international forum where we can state our case in a businesslike and positive way', and 'where contacts can be made'. Muller also pointed out that the United Nations gave access to specialized international agencies such as the World Bank and the International Atomic Energy Agency. He concluded that 'as long as we regard it in our interest, and as long as South Africa's honour is not impugned, we shall remain in the United Nations and co-operate'.[4]

Although the government had this range of views about the

---

[1] *Southern Africa*, 1 Nov. 1969.

[2] H of A, 16 Feb. 1968, col. 712.   [3] ibid., col. 714.

[4] H of A, 7 May 1969, col. 5443. According to the 1968 opinion poll the government's decision to retain membership was supported by a majority of white South Africans, but it was only a small majority. In answer to the question 'Do you or don't you think South Africa should withdraw her membership from the United Nations?', 37·9 per cent thought that South Africa should withdraw while 43·9 per cent thought she should retain membership (18·2 per cent said 'Don't know'). Public Opinion Survey undertaken by Market Research Africa, Johannesburg, for the South African Morning Group of Newspapers.

United Nations, what stands out clearly is that it was intent on holding on to membership despite all the hostility. One reason for this was the negative one of frustrating possible United Nations action against the Republic. Another was the more positive reason, which developed strongly during the late 1960s, of seizing any opportunity to extend diplomatic contacts. In this field the chance offered at the United Nations for informal and secret contacts was very important for the South Africans, who, after leaving the Commonwealth, had few similar opportunities.

Despite the continued verbal hostility, the concrete action taken by the United Nations against South Africa remained very limited. The arms ban remained, although widely breached. There were some small-scale aid schemes, such as the Trust Fund for South Africa which provided assistance for the victims of apartheid, and there was an education and training programme for Africans who had fled from the white-controlled territories of southern Africa. This was a poor harvest from the generous scattering of the United Nations' verbal seeds. U Thant, the Secretary General, recognized this. In his Annual Report in 1970 he wrote that it was with heavy heart that he noted how ineffective the organization's efforts had been to eliminate the 'continuing affront to human dignity'. 'What is needed', he said, 'is the political will on the part of the member-states to take effective measures which would induce South Africa to renounce its policies.'[1]

As in the past, South West Africa was a major issue at the United Nations. Despite the setback at the International Court, South Africa's militant opponents were determined to assert that the Republic had lost the right to administer the territory. In October 1966 the General Assembly resolved that, as the Republic had failed to fulfil its obligations under the mandate, its rights to administer the territory were thereby terminated and the territory had become a direct responsibility of the United Nations. The South African Government refused even to debate the issue because it did 'not want to create even an impression that it considers itself bound by that unlawful resolution'.[2] Muller reasserted South Africa's traditional stand: that while recognizing that South West Africa had a separate identity and status in inter-

---

[1] *Southern Africa*, 26 Sept. 1970.
[2] Vorster, H of A, 2 May 1967, col. 5221.

national law, and while respecting the terms of the old mandate, the South African Government had no obligations whatsoever to the United Nations in its administration of the territory, and it was within South Africa's power to annex the territory if it so decided.

In 1969 the Security Council, with Britain and France abstaining, endorsed the General Assembly's resolution of 1966 and called on South Africa to withdraw by October. In January 1970 a further Council resolution condemned the refusal to withdraw. The point had been reached where not only did the international organization and the South African Government use different names for the territory—Namibia and South West Africa—but they started from different assumptions about who was the lawful administering authority. When African nationalist guerrillas who had been captured in the territory were tried in Pretoria under the Republic's Terrorism Act, the General Assembly resolved that the Republic had acted illegally as its writ did not run in Namibia. A call was made for the release of the guerrillas, and at the trial the defence counsel argued that South African courts had no competence in the case. The Pretoria court rejected this, convicted the guerrillas, and sentenced them to long terms of imprisonment.[1] The Security Council then took up the issue and in March 1968 passed a resolution condemning South Africa's flagrant defiance of the earlier resolution. United Nations members were asked to co-operate in the implementation of the resolution, and a threat was held out that the Council would take 'effective steps or measures' if the Republic did not comply. But just how serious was this threat? From the beginning the United States, the United Kingdom, France, and Canada had made clear that in supporting the resolution they were not committed to a particular form of action. They were, as ever, opposed to the use of force.[2] In fact, nothing came of the resolutions. The South African Government ignored them; there was no United Nations action other than verbal remonstrance; the guerrillas lay in prison.

Whatever approach is made to the South West Africa question, there is a great gulf between what the opposing sides say they are doing, or going to do, and their actual behaviour. From the United Nations side this has been clear from the strongly worded but vain resolutions threatening action, and the unfulfilled threats

[1] IRR 1968, p. 59.   [2] IRR 1968, p. 304.

about the Pretoria trial. It has also been clear in the futile attempts which have been made to create a United Nations administration in Namibia. The South African Government would obviously have been hostile to any United Nations Council set up to administer the territory, but the list of states appointed to the Council in 1967—Chile, Colombia, Guyana, India, Indonesia, Nigeria, Pakistan, Turkey, the United Arab Republic, Yugoslavia, and Zambia—must have made it even more hostile. In March 1968 the Council announced that it had decided to visit Namibia during April. The plan was that the full Council would stay about nine days and then leave behind Mr. Constantin Stravropolos, the legal counsel, to set up a United Nations administration. They reached Lusaka in Zambia, but no further. The South African Government refused entry to South West Africa, and as no airline could be found to fly the Council to the territory the attempt was abandoned. The failure underlined again the gap between the protestations made in the United Nations and the reality of power on the ground.[1]

While the United Nations and its agencies suffered from credibility gaps over Namibia, there were also substantial differences between the South African Government's statements and its behaviour. The South Africans have always disclaimed any intention of annexing the territory, and have said that they recognize its separate identity in international law. In 1967 Muller said there was no intention of absorbing the territory. 'Anyone who accuses South Africa today of imperialistic designs on South West Africa can only be doing it out of malicious intent because the facts clearly contradict such an allegation.'[2] Yet in practice the South African Government, while exercising caution to avoid giving good reason for outside intervention, virtually treated South West Africa as a part of the Republic. The extension of the Bantustan policy was followed by the South West Africa Affairs Act of 1969, which left only a paper-thin distinction between the territory and the Republic proper. Before this Act, the South West Africa Legislative Assembly (an all-white body) had enjoyed wider powers than the provinces within the Republic itself.[3] But the Act transferred to Pretoria responsibility for a number of subjects, including Coloured affairs, the administration of

---

[1] IRR 1968, p. 302.   [2] H of A, 19 Apr. 1967, col. 4525.
[3] The provinces are the Cape, Natal, Orange Free State, and the Transvaal

justice, and labour affairs.[1] It was a clear indication that, notwithstanding international opinion, the South African Government was able and determined to dictate the pattern of government and administration to the territory.

The conflicting claims to the territory continued to be advanced in legal terms. In 1970 the dispute was back with the International Court of Justice. This time it was the Security Council which initiated the case.[2] The Court was asked to give an *advisory* ruling on: 'What are the legal consequences for states of the continued presence of South Africa in Namibia notwithstanding the Security Council resolution 276 (1970)?' This resolution had strongly condemned South Africa's refusal to comply with General Assembly and Security Council resolutions on Namibia. It declared South Africa's presence in the territory and all its acts there to be illegal, and called on all states to refrain from dealing with the Republic as far as the territory was concerned. The South African Government had naturally ignored this resolution, but agreed to be represented again at the court case. Muller explained that although the government had withdrawn its consent from the Court's compulsory jurisdiction in 1967, only an advisory opinion had been sought this time.[3]

John Dugard, commenting on the case, suggested that the Security Council had two objectives in mind: first, to call a temporary halt to ineffective rhetoric; and second, to provide a legal base for future action. The instigators of the case hoped that the court would confirm, either explicitly or by implication, that the Republic had lost its legal right to administer the territory and instead confirm that resolutions of the General Assembly and Security Council were legally sound, for both France and Britain had questioned the legality of the United Nations actions.[4]

The South Africans introduced an early surprise, suggesting that a referendum be organized, under joint United Nations and South African supervision, to test opinion among the people of

---

[1] IRR 1969, p. 306. The central government's powers before the 1969 Act included defence and security, police, foreign affairs, native affairs, transport, information, immigration, customs and excise, currency, and banking and audit.

[2] Finland instigated the case, while the United Kingdom, Russia, and Poland abstained.

[3] *Southern Africa*, 12 Sept. 1970.

[4] John Dugard, 'South-West Africa returns to the International Court', *New Nation* (Pretoria), Feb. 1971, pp. 6–7.

the territory about their choice of administration. The suggestion was rejected, but the South Africans continued to argue that support from the inhabitants was one of their claims to the territory. When the President of the Court, Sir Muhammed Zafrullah Khan, questioned South Africa's title if, as the South African Government contended, the League of Nations mandate had lapsed, E. M. Grosshopf, of the South African team, replied that even if the mandate had lapsed, South Africa could claim the territory by right of conquest, by long occupation, by continuation of the sacred trust agreed in 1920, and, most important of all, because the administration was for the benefit of all the inhabitants who wanted the South Africans to remain.[1]

In June 1971 the Court found by 13 votes to 2 that South Africa's presence in Namibia was illegal and that South Africa was under obligation to withdraw its administration. In rejecting the court's findings Vorster said that 'the opinions of the majority were clearly politically motivated however they tried to clothe them in legal language'. The court's ruling was 'the culmination of a systematic process of erosion of the authority and prestige of the International Court'. The court had been packed by South Africa's opponents so 'the majority opinion is not only entirely untenable, but is clearly and demonstrably the result of political manœuvring instead of objective jurisprudence'. South Africa, he said, rejected the advisory opinion because 'it is our duty to administer South West Africa so as to promote the well-being and progress of its inhabitants. We will carry out this duty with a view to self-determination for all the population groups.'[2]

In 1946 Smuts had said of South West Africa: 'We have the fullest authority and we have exercised it and whether you call it sovereignty or not it seems to be just a juggling with words, introducing lawyers' technical language into the matter. The facts are quite clear; we have the power.'[3] Over the years which followed there had been no substantial shift either in the South African attitude or in the 'power' situation.

If the ineffectiveness of international organizations had been confined to the United Nations there would have been a strong

---

[1] *Today's News*, 19 Mar. 1971 (published by the South African Director of Information, London).

[2] *Today's News*, 24 June 1971.   [3] H of A, 15 Mar. 1946, col. 3674.

case for suggesting that it was the behaviour of the major powers, and more particularly the Western powers, that had undermined all international efforts. Without doubt their reluctance to disturb the *status quo* and their eagerness to preserve economic links were impediments to action, but even the black states of the Organization of African Unity cannot escape criticism for ineffectiveness and inefficiency in their confrontation with the Republic.

From the beginning the OAU had pledged its support for those who were struggling to liberate Africans from the white-dominated governments of southern Africa. Each of the members was 'obliged' to make an annual contribution to a fund to support the liberation movement. By 1971 there were forty-one members of OAU and the annual contributions to the fund should have totalled £900,000. In 1970 only twelve states paid their contributions, and the total receipts were under £400,000, including £100,000 arrears paid by Libya. Some African countries, including Malawi, Sierra Leone, and Senegal, had never paid. By the end of 1970 the total debt was £3 million with little chance that this would ever be collected. Only three African states, Tanzania, Uganda, and Zambia, were up to date with their payments. The bulk of the fund went to liberation movements in Portuguese Guinea, Mozambique, and Angola, the three areas in which there was active guerrilla fighting. Little was left to support the movements in other areas. One of the liberation movement leaders cynically commented that 'Independent Africa continuously assures us of support and then expects us to fight with words.'

Some African states explained their failure to pay by criticizing the ineffectiveness of the liberation movements and the OAU Liberation Committee. Following these criticisms, the 1969 OAU summit meeting set up a seven-nation investigation committee, under Mr. Youssouf Sylla of Senegal, to investigate the work of the Liberation Committee. Little progress was made by Sylla's committee, which lamely excused itself by saying that only fourteen African states had completed a questionnaire which it had circulated.[1] It has even been argued that tough words with very limited action may well have favoured the Republic, by creating a credibility gap in the international organization and by forewarning the South Africans of any action that may be taken. This latter point was made by some of the liberation movements at the OAU.

[1] *The Guardian*, 20 Feb. 1971.

They claimed that militant statements by African states had encouraged the South African Government to undertake massive rearmament, and so make a difficult task even more difficult.

The chief United Nations threat to South Africa in the early 1960s had been the imposition of economic sanctions, and the action following Rhodesia's UDI became a test case for such sanctions. They were imposed on South Africa's doorstep and provided that combination of forces that the South African Government had always feared—international action supported by the Western powers. Verwoerd, in recognizing the danger, said: 'The whole situation is most delicate and dangerous for all who are or may become implicated, and so it is wise to say as little as possible.' But while discretion was wise he felt obliged to add that 'I say quite unambiguously that we believe that majority rule there, which means Black rule over Whites in Rhodesia, will lead to destruction and chaos.'[1]

The South Africans realized that many of their militant opponents saw Rhodesian sanctions as a prelude to sanctions against the Republic. The British protested that they had no intention of involving South Africa, but such protests had to be measured against the contradictions of British policy. After the initial British euphoria, when it was assumed that limited action would quickly overthrow Smith, it became plain that if sanctions were to be effective the loopholes being used by the Rhodesians would have to be blocked. By far the largest of these loopholes was provided by South Africa.

Information about trade and financial transactions between Rhodesia and South Africa has not been published since UDI, and so it is impossible to quantify with any accuracy the flow of commercial and trading contacts. R. B. Sutcliffe made a rough calculation based on a comparison of Rhodesia's export figures with the import figures claimed by countries importing from Rhodesia other than South Africa and Mozambique. (Mozambique, like South Africa, does not publish figures.) According to Sutcliffe's calculations about 26 per cent of Rhodesia's exports went to South Africa and Mozambique in 1965. The proportion rose steadily in the following years—35 per cent in 1966, 65 per

[1] H of A, 25 Jan. 1966, cols. 49–50.

cent in 1967, and an estimated 85 per cent in 1969.[1] A substantial part of this Rhodesian trade will simply be passing through the two neighbouring states, using the 'middleman' facilities to circumvent sanctions. As Sutcliffe emphasizes, these can only be taken as rough figures, and no distinction is drawn between the Republic and Mozambique in allocating the proportion of trade. But even if the figures are very rough, they certainly indicate the extent to which the Rhodesians have relied on South Africa. The Rhodesians have freely admitted this. Mr. Lardner Burke, the Rhodesian Minister of Justice, Law and Order, said in 1967: 'As Rhodesians we will let South Africa know that we will never let them down. We can never say thank you enough for what South Africa has done since UDI.'[2]

The Rhodesians' thanks could be extended to the many governments who turned a blind eye when their nationals broke sanctions by trading directly or indirectly with Rhodesia. The British Government did make a genuine effort to impose sanctions, but its policy of continuing them against Rhodesia while refusing to take steps against the Republic was plainly self-defeating. In the early stages the South Africans could never be sure that the British would not try to remedy this by extending sanctions to the Republic.[3] The British failed to resolve the contradictions in their policy. From the beginning the imposition of sanctions had been full of compromises. They were applied piecemeal and had little immediate impact on most white Rhodesians. There was no quick hammer-blow which might have undermined white confidence. The Smith government had enough breathing space before each British move to counter its full effect and to keep up white morale. Also, the British always held on to the hope that a negotiated, compromise settlement was possible. The application of sanctions

[1] R. B. Sutcliffe, 'The Political Economy of Rhodesian Sanctions', *Journal of Commonwealth Political Studies* (Leicester University Press), vol. 12, no. 2, July 1966, pp. 113–25.

[2] IDAAF, July–Sept. 1967, p. 44.

[3] An accurate estimate of the costs that might have been involved is impossible to calculate. According to a *Daily Telegraph* article which was said to be based on a confidential British Government report, if sanctions had been extended to South Africa it could have increased unemployment in Britain by 40,000 and resulted in an export loss of £100 million in the first year, an increase of about £100 million in the cost of imports, and the loss of another £100 million as invisibles. Quoted by Kenneth P. Young, *Rhodesia and Independence* (London, J. M. Dent and Sons Ltd., 1969), p. 502.

was always tempered by this hope, and in the attempts to reach a negotiated settlement the Republic was again an important link. The public stand of the South African Government never faltered. It claimed that the dispute was a domestic one between Britain and Rhodesia in which outsiders, and particularly the United Nations, should not be involved. The government stated its readiness to give whatever help it could towards a peaceful solution, but it was not prepared to favour or to exert pressures on either side. In reality, of course, the South African behaviour strongly favoured the Rhodesians.

The Rhodesian experience reinforced the already strong doubts about the effectiveness of the United Nations in organizing international action against South Africa, and the reluctance of the major Western trading states to impose sanctions. Working through the United Nations, Britain had attempted to use economic measures to achieve political ends. Although the sanctions certainly hurt the Rhodesian economy, they failed, at least in the short term, to produce the desired political results. On the basis of this experience it was asked, first, whether it was possible to organize economic action against South Africa, and second, even if some economic pressure could be brought to bear, whether this would change the white government's determination to press ahead with its racial policies. To both questions the lessons drawn from Rhodesia gave answers which were favourable to the South African Government. The Rhodesian situation had underlined the intransigence of southern Africa's white rulers as well as the difficulties of organizing and co-ordinating international action against them. It left the international organization more uncertain than ever about how to translate hostile words into effective action, or whether indeed most states were prepared to do more than use hostile words.

19

THE AMBIVALENCE OF WESTERN CONTACTS

In the years between 1964 and 1970, the lifetime of Harold Wilson's Labour government in Britain, relations between the British and South African Governments were probably more strained than at any time since the formation of the Union in 1910. In the first place the South Africans had a general mistrust of socialist governments. Mr B. J. Schoeman, the Minister of Transport, spoke of 'the abhorrent policy of socialism in that country and its spineless handling of the trade unions'.[1] This general mistrust was given particular point by the Rhodesian situation and by the Labour government's refusal to sell arms to the Republic. The arms decision contrasted with that of the previous Conservative government. The Conservative view had been that: 'It is unreasonable to think that we can have a total embargo on arms to South Africa and still expect that country to continue with the Simonstown Agreement.'[2]

With the closure of the Suez Canal, and the appearance for the first time of Russian warships in the Indian Ocean, the South Africans believed that the case for combined Western defence of the sea routes was stronger than ever. Following the canal closure there was substantial increase in the already important trade which passed around the Cape. In the eighteen months following the closure more than 10,000 ships were re-routed around Africa.[3] South African harbours handled record amounts of cargo, and in

[1] *Southern Africa*, 20 Sept. 1969, p. 150.
[2] R. A. Butler in 1964, quoted by Spence, *The Strategic Significance of Southern Africa*, p. 17.
[3] The principal trading nations which used the harbours during the eighteen-month period were Britain, 3,000 ships; Holland, 1,170; and the United States, 725 (*Report*, June 1969, p. 12). In the six-month period after the closure of Suez 54 warships docked at South African ports, of which 46 were British, 4 French, 3 Portuguese, and 1 Belgian (IDAAF Special Report, *The British Embargo on Arms for South Africa*, Mar. 1968, p. 5).

addition to the re-routing, the development of giant tankers which were too large for the Suez Canal meant a permanent increase in traffic. By 1970 one fifth of Western Europe's oil was using the Cape route.

At a time when Britain was trying to cut her defence expenditure east of Suez, the South African Government accepted that it would take a larger share in sea defence. This was formalized in 1967 by a revision of the Simonstown Agreement. Botha announced that mutually acceptable terms had been worked out by which the British naval presence would be reduced and the Chief of the South African Navy would assume 'greater responsibilities for the defence of the sea route round the Cape in time of war'.[1] But having accepted this additional responsibility, the South Africans thought that the British should respond by supplying arms.

Despite the Labour government's initial decision to impose the ban, the South Africans had never abandoned hope that it would change its mind, and they had been encouraged in this because the arms ban had not been absolute. Replacement parts and ammunition for existing equipment had continued to be supplied.[2] Early in 1967 the South Africans sent the British Government an extensive 'shopping list' of arms which were required over the next ten years. The total value was estimated at £200 million, with immediate orders worth about £75 million.

The British promised an early reply but then dragged their feet until a complex set of circumstances forced a decision late in 1967. This was an especially bad year for the British economy and the government was forced into devaluation. There were, therefore, pressing economic arguments to accept the valuable arms order. In addition, some cabinet members, including George Brown, the Foreign Secretary, and Denis Healey, the Minister of Defence,

---

[1] H of A, 2 Feb. 1967, col. 511. The British withdrew the Commander in Chief, South Atlantic, and the frigate which had permanently been stationed at Simonstown. Responsibility for the area on the British side now fell on the Commander in Chief, Home Fleet, with a British Commodore at Simonstown to liaise with the South Africans.

[2] See Abdul S. Minty, *South Africa's Defence Strategy* (London, Anti-Apartheid Movement, 1969), p. 3. Minty notes that spares and ammunition continued to be supplied for all weapons previously sold. He also mentions (a) the sale of £400,000 worth of motor chassis for armoured cars and army lorries in 1965, (b) the supply of partly charged shells which could pass as practice ammunition, and (c) licences granted for production of military goods in South Africa, including Rolls-Royce engines for Impala aircraft.

accepted the argument that the arms sales would help Western defence interests in the southern oceans. George Brown wrote that while it was unthinkable for a British Government to supply arms for internal use for the imposition of apartheid, 'the question of the external defence of South Africa, and the protection of those waters, so essential for ourselves in view of the closing of the Suez Canal and the consequent dependence by us commercially upon that route, especially in face of the growing Russian advance in the Indian Ocean, was another matter'.[1]

In the arms negotiations with Britain the South Africans tried to use both the stick and the carrot. The carrot consisted of the economic benefits of the sale, the prospects of increased defence co-operation, and help in finding a Rhodesian settlement. The stick was made up of threats to withdraw from the Simonstown Agreement, to remove other defence co-operation such as flyover rights, and to reduce the import of other British goods. To the South Africans these arguments were compelling, but in December 1967 Mr. Harold Wilson, the British Prime Minister, announced that the arms ban would stand.

The South Africans, who had watched British behaviour with increasing exasperation, were incensed. Vorster reacted immediately and angrily, saying: 'We now know, after a long time of stalling and hedging, where we stand with the Wilson Government and in the coming year I will look anew at the Simonstown Agreement in that light. The British decision will not, however, leave us defenceless and we shall certainly not forget those friends who supply us now or when the storm clouds are past.'[2] Referring to Wilson, Vorster said that he would be mistaken if he thought that co-operation could be one-sided and that the moral obligations which flow from contractual relations could be exchanged for political expediency. P. W. Botha, the Defence Minister, who was among the most enthusiastic wavers of the stick, said: 'The United Kingdom Government cannot continue to rely on our benevolent acquiescence to the use of our airfields, on the naval base at Simonstown, or any of our other harbour facilities in peace or war, except when we deem it in the interests of South Africa to make them available.'[3]

[1] George Brown, *In My Way* (Penguin, 1972), p. 167.
[2] IDAAF supplementary report, *The British Embargo on Arms for South Africa*, Mar. 1968, p. 4.
[3] H of A, 20 Feb. 1968, col. 869.

Although the Labour government had been tempted, there were good reasons why it avoided the gesture of friendship to the Republic implied by the sale of arms. In Britain there was considerable opposition to the sale especially in the Labour Party itself, and after the devaluation the government was internally in a weak position. Abroad, South Africa's many critics would have branded Britain as a friend of racialists. Also there were genuine doubts whether the economic advantages of the sale would outweigh other disadvantages: whether, for example, other African states would boycott British goods. Also in terms of diplomatic contacts there might be considerable problems. If the Russians and Chinese wanted influence around the Indian Ocean, might not Britain make their task easier by agreeing to sell arms to the Republic? Then there were doubts about the military purpose of the Russian naval presence. Were they really a danger to the shipping lanes? If the Russians did want a naval confrontation in the Indian Ocean, would a few frigates supplied to South Africa make any material difference? Spence concluded that 'talk of denying strategic areas to the Soviets is to underestimate the difficulties (and the risks) involved in a situation where the *use* as distinct from the *display* of force can provoke escalation'.[1]

Botha thrust aside the British uncertainties about Russian and Chinese activities. The Russians would not have sent their vessels these enormous distances unless it was part of a pattern of communist expansion. He saw it as a build-up similar to the early stages of Soviet naval expansion in the Mediterranean, and when it came to questions about the precise defence issues involved Botha stated that, far from vague and woolly fears, the Republic had very clear ideas. 'It does not mean', he said, 'an aimless patrolling of endless stretches of sea, but the active protection of terminal points, i.e. the harbours, the passive protection of convoys, namely by re-routing them, and of ships at sea by means of the application of security measures and the active protection of convoys and ships at sea when a real threat to such convoys and ships arises.'[2] On another occasion he said the Republic had excellent facilities for ships and aircraft, and geographically was ideally suited to protect the southern oceans. 'South Africa is in itself an aircraft carrier from which . . . protection can be afforded;

[1] Spence, *The Strategic Significance of Southern Africa*, p. 30.
[2] H of A, 27 May 1968, col. 6030.

we have the necessary command and communications systems which are indispensable to the control of operations of merchant shipping in the southern oceans.'[1]

Undoubtedly the South Africans believed strongly in the need for a combined Western defence of the Cape route, but they hoped that by playing heavily on the strategic importance of southern Africa they could gain more than military aid. When they asked Britain for arms to defend the Cape route they were, said President Nyerere of Tanzania, asking for 'a badge of respectability'. And Spence has written that the South African Government 'would interpret closer military liaison with Britain as a tacit admission that the latter would in the last analysis be protecting South African interests (and this would by definition include the integrity of the regime) as well as its own in any protracted struggle with the Communist forces in the area.'[2]

Diplomatic relations with Britain improved sharply with the electoral victory of the Conservative Party in 1970. Among other things, the Conservatives offered a better chance of a Rhodesian settlement, but the improvement was most clearly marked when the Heath government, resisting strong Commonwealth pressure and considerable pressure in Britain itself, announced that in principle it was prepared to resume the sale of arms for external defence. The British Government further announced that under the terms of the Simonstown Agreement it was legally obliged to sell Wasp helicopters for the frigates supplied under the Agreement.[3] The South African Government was delighted. The circle of arms suppliers would be extended, there was a chance of future defence co-operation, and the British 'badge of respectability' would make it easier for others to break the ban and establish closer relations with the Republic.

While the British had hesitated and vacillated, the French had seized the opportunity to sell arms to South Africa. It was a point George Brown had been quick to make in arguing for the resumption of British sales. French aircraft and helicopters and three Daphne-type submarines were bought by the South Africans as

[1] Quoted by Spence, *The Strategic Significance of Southern Africa*, p. 30.
[2] Spence, op. cit., p. 42.
[3] See Gordon Lawrie, 'Britain's Obligations under the Simonstown Agreements: A Critique of the Opinion of the Law Officers of the Crown', *International Affairs*, vol. 47, no. 4, Oct. 1971, pp. 708–28.

part of a growing relationship between the two countries. But there was no indication that the French were prepared to extend their activities to play the role that the South Africans expected of Britain. They viewed the bilateral relationship with South Africa primarily as a business affair. There was no suggestion that they would become involved in defence agreements covering the southern African sub-continent or the surrounding oceans. Perhaps it was the absence of historical and emotional commitment that blunted the edge of international criticism, for the French escaped relatively unscathed from defying the arms ban. As the British ruefully noted, similar behaviour by them brought the whole international community hammering at their door.

The Americans had neither the traditional ties of the British nor the panache of the French, but generally they adopted a more hostile diplomatic stance towards South Africa than either. The United States supported the arms ban and disagreed with the British and French Governments whenever they breached it. South Africa's relations with the United States have never been close. While the two governments could see advantages in limited co-operation, there has always been reluctance on the American side to become too involved. The South Africans on their side were eager for diplomatic friendship, as Muller explained in 1966: 'We acknowledge and we honour the United States as the leader of the Free World today. . . . It is the policy of this Government to steer clear of points of friction with the United States as much as possible . . . but to concentrate on points of common interest.' He mentioned the common stand against communism, the increasing American interest in Africa, and the cultural and trade ties that already existed.[1] He also saw better relations with the United States as one of the fruits of successful Bantustan and outward policies. 'What I do believe,' he said, 'is that as we sort out and solve our colour policies here in South Africa, and as our relations with our neighbouring Black states improve, as they are doing, so the United States will also develop more appreciation for South Africa and for the attempts which we are making to solve a very difficult problem.'[2]

The incidents which revealed the tension with the United

[1] H of A, 23 Sept. 1966, cols. 2804–5.
[2] H of A ,23 Sept. 1966, col. 2805.

States were often relatively insignificant in themselves. The South Africans would be offended because the Americans invited non-whites to an embassy party; a black American tennis player would be refused an entry visa; there would be confusion about shore leave for American seamen. For example, in February 1967 the aircraft carrier *Independence*, with its racially mixed crew, called at Cape Town. A series of shore parties and entertainments had been arranged, but inevitably, as this was South Africa, the entertainments were racially segregated. At the last moment the captain, on instructions from the United States, refused the crew shore leave because of the segregation. The decision caused a minor diplomatic storm in Cape Town harbour.[1]

While there was tension between the two governments, it was largely suppressed tension. At the United Nations American representatives like Adlai Stevenson and Arthur Goldberg spoke out against apartheid, but the United States Government wanted to avoid involvement in another international crisis area. In the words of the Secretary of State, William Rogers, the Americans saw southern Africa as a 'low profile' area. This reflected a shift in American thinking from the early 1960s when African affairs had seemed to be of increasing international importance and when the white castle in the south had seemed in danger of immediate collapse. The uncertainty of the American attitude also stemmed from clashing interests within the United States. There has been a conflict between the ideals of racial equality and self-determination, and the established military and economic interests.[2] Added to the material interests have been right-wing ideological commitments which have produced a lobby sympathetic to white South Africa. According to Vernon McKay this gained in strength during the 1960s. He suggested that while the United States Government remained publicly hostile to the whites of southern Africa, there was growing sympathy for them stimulated by organizations like the American–Southern African Council. This sympathy extended to Rhodesia as well as South Africa. McKay thought it

[1] IRR 1967, pp. 86–7.
[2] See Larry Bowman, 'South Africa's Southern Strategy, and its Implications for the United States', *International Affairs*, vol. 47, no. 1, Jan. 1971, pp. 19–30. The military interest included a satellite tracking station, refuelling and resupply facilities for ships and aircraft, and a general concern to counter communist expansion.

was based in part on anti-British sentiment and in part on the
'domino theory'—that if one stable country in southern Africa
fell all the others would come tumbling after, leaving a situation
of chaos and confusion which would be in nobody's interest,
least of all that of the United States.[1]

One difficulty which South African ministers and officials
complained about in their relations with the United States was
that they were never sure which of the many American voices
represented United States policy.[2] The policy is articulated by a
range of people from the President downwards. To whom, asked
the South Africans, should they listen most carefully, for certainly
the Americans did not always speak with one voice. For example,
South African officials often draw a contrast between the Pentagon,
which is said to be generally co-operative, and the State Department, which is hostile and unsympathetic. Speaking about
American policy Vorster said: 'If I only knew what it was. Candidly,
we don't know what it is. However, the little we know about
United States policy towards South Africa, we don't understand
at all. We fail to understand why the State Department adopts
this attitude towards us. Presumably it is on account of our domestic policy, which is exclusively our own affair.'[3]

Although United States policy was difficult to pin down, a
broad official attitude emerged which was less involved and had
more verbal hostility than that of the British Government but
differed little from the British in its aims. The Americans searched
for a path which would avoid difficulties and complications. They
favoured change but not at the expense of major disorder. They
rejected the use of force or breaking off all contact with the
Republic. They disliked racial discrimination but were doubtful if
any radical change could be achieved in the short term. They were
sympathetic to the opponents of apartheid but did not want to
become too directly involved themselves. They wanted to avoid a
general conflict situation in southern Africa, partly because of their
experience in Asia and the danger of a major power clash, and
partly because of their existing economic and military interests.
The Americans no longer believed that dramatic change was

---

[1] Vernon McKay in William A. Hance (ed.), *Southern Africa and the United
States* (New York, Columbia University Press, 1968), p. 24.
[2] Private conversation with South African officials.
[3] Quoted by Cockram, *Vorster's Foreign Policy*, p. 193.

inevitable and adopted an attitude of 'wait and see what long-term social and economic changes will bring'.

American ambivalence and their 'low profile' attitude to southern Africa was made plain in 1970 by William Rogers, and by President Nixon in his 'State of the World' message. In their statements high ideals clash with perceived realities, the calls for change are tempered by the refusal to become too involved, the moral support for the black African cause is balanced by a stake in the existing order.

Rogers's statement came after a quick visit to ten African countries, but not including southern Africa. Regarding the Republic, 'this rich, troubled land', he could see no advantage in breaking off contacts, but quickly added that this did not imply 'any acceptance or condoning of its discriminatory system'.[1] In what he saw as a conflict situation between the white governments and the non-white majorities, he identified with the majority cause. 'The modern world demands', he said, 'a community of nations based on respect for fundamental rights. . . . These are not only moral and legal principles, they are powerful and ultimately irresistible political forces. We take our stand on the side of these forces of fundamental human rights in Southern Africa as we do at home and elsewhere.' But what did this statement imply? What practical consequences would follow, and what were these 'fundamental rights', and 'irresistible political forces'? An incident which had arisen two years earlier when Vice-President Humphrey was visiting Zambia probably puts the practical situation in better perspective. President Kaunda told Humphrey that a 'catastrophe' in southern Africa was 'inevitable' unless the United States 'acts, and acts quickly'. Humphrey publicly replied: 'We are not timid . . . we are with you in policy. We are with you in fact.' But then, according to Bruce Oudes, Humphrey told reporters that Kaunda was overstating the case and also overstating what the United States could do about it.[2]

Nixon's report combined Rogers's fine words and Humphrey's acceptance of American limitations. The President said that 'for moral as well as historical reasons, the United States stands firmly for the principle of racial equality and self-determination'.

[1] IDAAF, Jan.–June 1970, p. 351.
[2] Bruce Oudes, 'Was Rogers' African Tour a Bad Trip?', *African Report*, Apr. 1970, p. 24.

But he went on to say that the 1960s had shown how intractable the racial problem had proved to be. 'These tensions are deeply rooted in the history of the region, and thus in the psychology of both Black and White.' Although the problem had to be solved there was the dilemma of how this could best be done. He rejected violence, for 'violence and the counter-violence it inevitably provokes will only make more difficult the task of those on both sides working for progress on racial questions'. He therefore welcomed the Lusaka Manifesto of African leaders which he said called for a peaceful settlement of the tension in southern Africa.[1] But he had interpreted the Manifesto to suit American policy. While the leaders who met at Lusaka had stated that they preferred a peaceful settlement, they also said that if the liberation of the people of southern Africa could not be achieved by peaceful methods other methods would have to be used, and that in fact this situation had already been reached with the increasing guerrilla warfare in southern Africa.

While still resenting the continued hostility of the Americans, the South African Government realized by the late 1960s that it had at least achieved what it had set out to do in the darkest days of the early 1960s. It had not gained diplomatic friendship, and the Americans had retained the arms ban, but the United States Government had been persuaded that radical change was *not* inevitable, that change would only come in the long term, and that in such circumstances it was in American interests to avoid a deep involvement in action against South Africa or to encourage violence as a means of achieving change.

So far this chapter has concentrated on South Africa's relations with other governments, but in the long term the most important external influences may not be these formal links but economic, social, and cultural contacts. A wide-ranging debate developed inside and outside South Africa about the impact of such contacts. Inside the Republic there were the white fears of the effects of Western permissiveness and contact with black states on the existing values of the white society. Outside South Africa, and based on the assumption that change was desirable, the questions were phrased in terms of whether change could be best achieved by greater contact or by isolating South Africa.

[1] *Rand Daily Mail*, 2 Mar. 1970.

The isolationists argued that by refusing contacts, white South Africans would be made to realize both the strength of external opposition and that it was only by abandoning their present racial policies that they could hope for friendship and co-operation from others. When playwrights like Peter Weiss and Robert Bolt refused to have their works performed before segregated audiences they intended not only to show their own personal opposition to segregation, but to add their weight to the wider isolationist cause. Another isolationist argument was that existing contacts helped to support the present racial structure. The Reverend David Head and Mrs. Laura Ross made this point at a meeting of Barclays Bank shareholders early in 1971. As anti-apartheid representatives who had obtained shares in the bank to make their views felt, they argued that the bank's involvement in the Republic lent a respectability which the South African Government craved and, therefore, reinforced apartheid. The bank, they argued, was seen to support the opponents of the blacks.[1]

Against the isolationists were those who argued that it was by increased contact that change could be brought about most quickly and effectively. One claim was that through contact South Africans would be introduced to new ideas and attitudes, that they would absorb many of these ideas almost unconsciously, and that in having contact with different social structures they would be encouraged to introduce change themselves. Isolation, it was argued, would only breed recalcitrance. President Nixon declared that 'The United States believes that the outside world can and should use its contacts with Southern Africa to promote and speed that change. We do not, therefore, believe that the isolation of the white regimes serves African interests, or our own or that of ultimate justice. A combination of contact and moral pressure serves all three.'[2]

A unique attempt to foster change by contact was made by the Polaroid Company of America early in 1971. After complaints by its black employees in the United States about its activities in South Africa the company sent an investigating team of two black men and two whites to the Republic. Following the team's report the company decided that it would remain in South Africa but consciously work for change. It announced a programme which involved discontinuing the sale of products to the South African

---

[1] *The Guardian* 14 Jan. 1971.   [2] IDAAF, Jan.–June 1971, p. 430.

Government, a substantial improvement in the salaries and other benefits of non-white employees, the training of non-whites for responsible posts, and the allocation of some company profits for the education of blacks.[1] The company said it hoped that its lead would be followed by others, for in isolation it would be a pointless gesture.

The change-by-contact advocates have usually carried the day in terms of economic relationships. There are some who believe that the invisible hand of economic growth will break down racial barriers whether the South African Government likes it or not. Increasingly the argument was heard from the governments and firms which favoured continued contacts with the Republic that it was by helping to develop and expand the economy that socio-political change would be achieved. This argument is a seductive one for South Africa's trading partners. It has the double attraction of offering continuing economic benefits while at the same time undermining a social structure which is internationally disliked. These views are, however, challenged by others who believe that economic development is constantly reinforcing white supremacy. They point out that the South African economy has developed steadily throughout the post-war period without breaking down the racial barriers.[2] The evidence supports this latter view—that rapid economic expansion does not necessarily break down racial barriers. There is no invisible economic hand inevitably forcing a particular pattern of social change. Those who believe that there is ignore the importance of political decisions in socio-economic development, and the 'caste' nature of South African society. Doubtless with economic expansion the range of jobs open to a particular caste will change, the non-whites will have more chance of skilled jobs and draw higher wages, because of the shortage of white labour. Blacks will take over jobs previously done by Coloureds, and the Coloureds will take over white jobs, but the racial structure of the society need not change. Horwitz's

[1] ibid. (Economic Section, p. 114E). The company increased African salaries so that senior workers were earning R180–R190 per month. It donated R35,000 to an education trust—the American–South African Education Trust—with Chief Gatha Buthelezi as chairman, and a gift of R10,500 to the Association for the Educational and Cultural Advancement of Africans in South Africa.

[2] For the opposing views see *African Affairs* (1970)—Frederick Johnstone, 'White Prosperity and White Supremacy in South Africa Today' (vol. 69, no. 275, pp. 124–40) and D. Hobart Houghton (vol. 69, no. 277, pp. 379–80).

point still stands. The 'political factor' in South Africa 'has always had an ultimate—a way of life to preserve and to promote. The polity has always sought its ideal and its ideology—the white man's supremacy. The network of economic development had to follow accordingly.'[1]

The most successful area of activity for those who advocate the isolation of South Africa has been in sport. Inside the Republic apartheid has always been rigorously applied to sport. Whites and non-whites have neither been allowed to play in the same sides nor to compete against each other. South Africa's representative teams have always been all-white, and, with the exception of a few Maori rugby players, non-white sportsmen have not been allowed into the country to compete against white South Africans or to enter 'open' competitions. This sports apartheid brought increasing criticism and opposition outside South Africa and by 1970 most of South Africa's international sporting links had either been broken or were under severe strain.

South Africa's greatest sporting disappointment was the withdrawal of her invitation to the Mexico Olympic Games in 1968. The South Africans had not been invited to the previous games in Tokyo because at that time the government had insisted that separate white and non-white teams would have to be sent. The possibility of South Africa being readmitted in 1968 came after Vorster had announced that South Africa was prepared to send a single, racially mixed team. The team would travel together as one party, and would be selected by a committee made up half of whites and half of non-whites. But in the trials for the Olympic team inside the Republic whites and non-whites were not allowed to compete against each other, so that internal apartheid would not

[1] Horwitz, *The Political Economy of South Africa*, p. 12. Adam's attitude-survey among the white power-élite generally supports Horwitz's judgement. Although there is a clear division on the question of retaining job reservation (49 per cent for retaining it and 46 per cent against), the division reflects language groups more than business interests: 77 per cent of the English-speaking businessmen were against retaining it, but 73 per cent of the Afrikaner businessmen favoured its retention (*South Africa: Sociological Perspectives*, p. 87). Among his conclusions Adam thought that the apartheid structure might favour business as well as government and be favoured by both political parties because: (*a*) the level of private profits would be substantially lower in a more open society where 'exploitation of labour divisions along racial lines would be more difficult' (p. 84); and (*b*) the Bantustans provide cheap labour pools, with people dependent on white benevolence (p. 88).

be broken. After a report by a fact-finding group from the International Olympic Committee (IOC) which visited the Republic, a majority of member-states voted for South Africa's participation and an invitation was issued. However, this decision was greeted with so much opposition, with threats of withdrawal from Afro-Asian states and plans for demonstrations against the South Africans, that the invitation was subsequently withdrawn. Mr. Avery Brundage, the IOC President, said: 'We thought the safety of the South African team and the success of the games were in grave doubt.'[1] Vorster's bitter comment was that 'If what is happening now is to be the pattern according to which matters will be arranged in the world in future, then . . . it is not necessary for us to hold Olympic Games; then we should arrange tree-climbing events, for then we are in the jungle.'[2]

The failure to gain admission to the Mexico Games was all the more galling because, by white South African standards, the government had made considerable concessions. The states which threatened to boycott the Games had argued that the concessions would have made no difference to apartheid in sport, but they might have been more real than the government had imagined. A unique situation might have been created of white and non-white South Africans uniting together in an international endeavour and receiving support at home across the races. The chance disappeared, and after that the government's policy tended, at least temporarily, to become more rigid in the face of continuing external hostility, and increasing 'verkrampte' criticism at home. Vorster was determined to retain a tough as well as a flexible image, and under pressure the toughness began to gain on the flexibility. He asserted that 'the communists and the Afro-Asians are blackmailing various countries to refuse to play with us. . . . What they really want to do is to exert physical pressure on us through sport.' And he repeated his fears that the permissive society 'can be more destructive than the actual physical assault upon South Africa'.[3]

In terms of white public opinion the South African Government had a delicate balance to maintain on this question of sport and race. There is considerable sporting enthusiasm in South Africa and pride in her achievements. The South Africans are

[1] IRR 1968, p. 298. For accounts of the decisions relating to Olympic entry see IRR 1967, pp. 320–2 and 1968, pp. 295–9. Also Cockram, op. cit., ch. 14.
[2] H of A, 24 Apr. 1968, col. 4071.   [3] The Times, 2 June 1970.

eager to test their abilities against international rivals, but for most of them the eagerness stops short of challenging the structure of social apartheid. The government had therefore the task of showing enough flexibility to encourage international sporting contacts and yet not so much that apartheid was seen to be endangered. This was particularly difficult because the range of white opinion on this issue was greater than on most which involve race.[1]

The government's sensitivity was shown in the Basil D'Oliveira case. This case indicates that when in doubt the government veered on the side of caution. D'Oliveira, a Coloured player born and brought up in South Africa but resident in Britain, was chosen to play for the English cricket team which was to tour the Republic in 1968/9. D'Oliveira was not among those originally selected for the team and the English selectors were strongly criticized for being afraid to offend the South African authorities by choosing him. However, when a member of the party fell out D'Oliveira was asked to fill his place. Following D'Oliveira's late selection Vorster, after some hesitation, decided that the English touring team would not be welcome in the Republic. He said that 'the team which was coming to South Africa was no longer a sports team, that it was no longer the team of the MCC,[2] but that it had become the team of . . . the political enemies of South Africa. For that reason . . . I had the courage of my convictions to declare in public that under those circumstances this team, with D'Oliveira included, would not be welcome in South Africa.'[3] Vorster had 'the courage of his convictions' because he feared, first, the impact on apartheid of an outstanding Coloured cricketer being given equal treatment with whites, and second, criticism among whites if the government was thought to be weakening.[4]

Following the 'D'Oliveira affair' the South African cricket tour of England in 1970 was cancelled. This cancellation came after a dispute among MCC members, threats of massive demonstrations against the South African cricketers, and pressure from the Labour

[1] See results of opinion polls on this, ch. 14, p. 224 n.
[2] The Marylebone Cricket Club (MCC) is the governing body of English cricket.
[3] H of A, 21 Apr. 1969, col. 4405.
[4] Munger, who has some access to government leaders in South Africa, wrote that D'Oliveira would be allowed to play in the Republic (E. Munger, 'New White Politics in South Africa' in Hance (ed.), *Southern Africa and the United States*, p. 72). This suggests that the government changed its mind as the controversy developed.

government for the tour to be cancelled. The threat of major demonstrations was no idle one, for the South African rugby tour of Britain in the previous winter had set off a series of major anti-apartheid demonstrations.

The South African Government has argued that sport should be outside politics, and that the organization of sport in the Republic was a matter exclusively for South Africans. The attempts to isolate the Republic from international sport were said to be made by political opponents and not by the sporting bodies themselves. In a speech of April 1967 in which he outlined the new approach to international sport Vorster said: 'Above all I want to request that this matter would not be dragged into politics', but later in the same speech he said that separate development was South Africa's policy, and 'therefore also applies to the field of sport'.[1] The contradiction is clear. Separate development (apartheid) is a policy which rests on political decisions. Racial separation in sport is as much a political decision as setting up the Bantustans or retaining an exclusively white House of Assembly.

The South African reaction to her increasing isolation in sport has been mixed. One response was a refusal to contemplate change. Vorster stated bluntly: 'If the choice is between taking part in international sport and our way of life which we have developed in this country over generations, then naturally the majority of our people will say that we have no choice in the matter whatsoever.'[2] Later he stressed that South Africa was a multi-national state, that white teams represented the white nation, and that other national groups should organize their own teams. 'I do not', he said, 'hold out the prospect of anything which is not in accordance with the principle that mixed sport shall not be practised here in South Africa.'[3]

In contrast there were signs, especially among sportsmen and those who governed sporting bodies, that the policy of isolation was having at least some effect. Late in 1970 the South African Rugby Board decided to form a multi-racial National Rugby Advisory Council, consisting of representatives from white and non-white bodies, and the South African Cricket Board of Control proposed that in future South African teams abroad should be non-racial and selected on merit.

---

[1] H of A, 11 Apr. 1967, cols. 3959–60.
[2] *The Times*, 2 June 1970.   [3] H of A, 23 Apr. 1971, col. 5068.

The isolation versus increased contact debate underlines the uncertainties that still surrounded South Africa's relations with the outside world at the beginning of the 1970s. There remains a broad international consensus that the existing social structure of the Republic is unsatisfactory. Yet this consensus has, to a greater or lesser degree, existed throughout the post-war years, and for all the denunciations of international bodies and attempts to organize external pressure, the white minority has retained its exclusive control. External pressures may well have induced changes inside South Africa, but they have not destroyed the essentially racial character of the society or the white man's dominance. Why then retain the pressure? Is it because in the long term radical change can be induced from outside? Is there still the hope of stimulating changes in attitudes within South Africa? Is it because radical changes are slowly taking place in the Republic and external pressures are helping these along? Is apartheid so abhorrent that even if there is little chance of any quick change the stand of principle has to be maintained? Is it because South Africa is a symbol for all men of the injustice of racialism? Or is it because individual states cannot afford to lose face in the international community by dropping their hostile stance towards the Republic? Is it largely a façade that is kept up because nobody is prepared to recognize the reality that international pressure on South Africa has been unsuccesful, and will continue to be unsuccessful?

Whatever the views of the outside world, Vorster's government in 1970 seemed as determined as Verwoerd's had been in earlier years 'to maintain white supremacy for all time to come over our own people and our own country, by force if necessary'.[1] South Africa's foreign policy was directed to that end.

[1] Statement by Verwoerd, H of A, 5 Feb. 1965, col. 636.

20

THE BROAD GOALS OF
SOUTH AFRICA'S FOREIGN POLICY

The broad goals of a state's foreign policy are usually taken to include (*a*) the state's survival; (*b*) the preservation and promotion of particular values; (*c*) wealth maximization; and (*d*) the ability to influence other states.[1] These goals cannot be clearly separated and sometimes act counter to each other, but they provide a useful base for drawing together some general conclusions about South Africa's foreign policy.[2] In doing this, the close relationship between domestic and external policies is re-emphasized.

A feature of South Africa's political development has been the distinction drawn by the government between 'the nation' (seen as a group of people sharing common values, characteristics, and loyalties, and having a sense of identity) and 'the state' (seen as the geographical area over which the government claims sovereignty). The distinction existed, at least implicitly, under the United Party government, for Smuts was committed to retaining control of the state in white hands while creating a sense of white South African nationalism based on reconciliation between Boer and Briton and loyalty to the Crown. The United Party's policy towards non-whites was imprecise; it could be argued that the question of extending the concept of South African nationalism to exclude the non-whites was left open, but at best this was a remote possibility. In practice both the United and National Parties were committed to ensuring the survival of a *white-controlled state*.

The National Party was clearer in its racial policy. It dismissed

[1] P. Reynolds, *An Introduction to International Politics* (London, Longman, 1971), gives the first three of these (p. 49).

[2] Roy Jones, *Analysing Foreign Policy* (London, Routledge and Kegan Paul, 1970), rightly points out that although statesmen may have broad objectives they more usually follow policies with specific objectives (p. 28). However, examining broad goals is a useful way of drawing together conclusions for policy pursued over a period.

any possibility, even in a remote future, of the non-whites gaining full citizenship or playing a part in the government. There was to be no attempt to foster national integration on the basis of the existing state and the concept of a single South African nationalism. In addition to the broad division between white and non-white, the National Party drew further divisions within the races. One of these was in the white society—the division between Afrikaners and English-speakers—and in its early days of office, as it sought to consolidate Afrikaner control of the government, the National Party was prepared to emphasize this division. Although later it became relatively less important, and was certainly given less emphasis by the government, the division never disappeared entirely. Fears that Afrikaner values could be swamped by alien or liberal or permissive ideas continued to be harboured.

By the early 1960s, with Afrikaner control of government firmly established and the non-white challenge intensified, the National Party government began to preach a 'white nationalism' (the Afrikaners remained the 'core' of the white nation). The government projected a view of South Africa as a multi-national state, consisting of the white nation and several non-white nations. Control of the South African state would remain for all time in white hands, but the possibility was held out of cutting away parts of the existing state to provide separate, and in time sovereign, independent homelands for the black nations. (The equity of the division is a separate issue, and the Indian and Coloured peoples had no homeland outside the white state.) The government argued that the future surrender of sovereignty over part of the existing state was a logical extension of its multi-national policy and therefore came from free choice, but it can also be interpreted as an attempt to defend the white nation by providing an outlet for black frustration and a counter to international hostility.

The points to be emphasized are, first, that 'the state' which was to be defended was ruled exclusively by white men, and, second, that the values which were preserved and promoted were those of the white society (or sometimes a particular group within the white society). Among these values those which proclaimed the right of the white man to exclusive control of the state created strong hostility inside and outside South Africa. In an attempt to defend the white position one of the original aims of the apartheid policy was to reduce substantially the number of non-whites living in the white state. Verwoerd had argued that while there were dangers in having small black states on the borders, there were even more dangers in retaining a dissatisfied black majority within the white state. This aspect of the policy did not succeed. The numbers of non-whites living and working within 'white' South Africa continued to increase so that the whites remained a minority and an increasingly small minority. The government continued, as in the past, to represent and defend the values and privileges of this minority, and so the chronic problem of internal security against the non-whites persisted. The government steadily increased the resources and legislative powers directed to counter the danger of internal revolution.

It was this situation inside South Africa which largely shaped external relations, and created the main external dangers for the government. Throughout the post-war period strong international criticism and hostility was directed at the government's racial policies. There was a broad international consensus in which the claims of the South African Government were rejected. Instead the emphasis was placed on the concentration of power in white hands, and what was seen by the critics as the ruthless and systematic denial of basic human rights to the non-white majority. In what Wallace has described as 'the social restraints provided by the international system' ('international opinion, or "world opinion"; international mores, or shared values on acceptable and unacceptable behaviour; and international law')[1] the South African Government was under strong pressure. It was constantly forced to look over its shoulder for external reactions to internal policies. It lived with the danger of external and internal opponents combining to challenge the existing order.

The broad international consensus criticizing South Africa's policies did not extend to a consensus on what should or could be done to remedy the situation. The South African Government protested that the attacks were unfair and distorted the situation. It accused other governments of exercising more discrimination than was found in South Africa, and claimed that it pursued policies which benefited all the peoples of South Africa. Furthermore the South African Government argued that it was wrong to perceive international relations in terms of morals and ideals.

---

[1] William Wallace, *Foreign Policy and the Political Process* (London, Macmillan, 1971), p. 19.

The emphasis should rather be on material interest and *realpolitik*.

This emphasis on material ties was important in South Africa's attempts to influence other states. At best 'influence' is an ill-defined term, but what was clear to the South Africans was that their chances were poor of persuading others to accept their values on racial issues. In contrast their economic strength (and their potential military importance) gave many Western states a stake in the continuing stability and prosperity of the country. It gave the South Africans the opportunity to extend their influence both among the Western states and in Africa, especially southern Africa, by offering technical and economic aid.

In terms of international law the situation was not so clear-cut. Attempts were made to reinforce the 'moral' attacks on South Africa with legal backing, but the South African Government also used the law, with its tendency to emphasize the *status quo*, as a means of defending its international position. In particular it emphasized state sovereignty, and the right of governments to decide internal policy without external interference.

While the clash of values resulted in increasing diplomatic hostility, the practical action taken against South Africa was very limited indeed. A variety of reasons helps to explain this. Some of these reasons were found in South Africa's general international environment—the importance of existing economic contacts, the limited ability of international organizations to persuade sovereign states to take combined action, the internal weakness revealed by the new black states, the relative strength of South Africa within the African continent, and the geographical circumstances by which South Africa was remote from the main areas of East–West confrontation and yet had strategic importance for the West in relation to the Cape route.

Another general constraint on effective international action was that while many governments were prepared to denounce South Africa, their policies towards her were dictated by the pursuit of particular interests and not the implementation of a widely accepted international morality. It confirmed Warner Levi's view that 'national interests overpower morality'.[1] Leading opponents of South Africa attempted to translate the general disapproval

[1] Warner Levi, 'The Relative Irrelevance of Moral Norms in International Politics' in James Rosenau, *International Politics and Foreign Policy* (New York, Free Press, 1969), pp. 191–8.

into precise issues that would directly involve state interests. For example, President Kaunda tried to persuade the Western states that a major racial conflict involving all southern Africa was imminent. On their side the South Africans attempted to avoid disputes on precise issues, and to ensure that the direct interests of other states, particularly African neighbours and major Western states, were served by preserving stability in southern Africa. Again economic contacts were important in achieving this end. Ironically in the early 1960s South Africa's extensive foreign economic links were seen by some of her opponents as a potential source of weakness and not of strength. These opponents argued that South Africa was so dependent on the links that if they could be endangered the government would be forced into major internal social change. Vigorous attempts were made to organize economic sanctions, but there was always marked reluctance, particularly on the part of South Africa's main trading partners, to take any action. The experience of the white Rhodesians, who, with extensive South African support, successfully resisted sanctions, appeared to kill whatever chance there may have been of this form of action against the Republic.

Allied to their general circumstances, the South Africans took particular steps to defend their position. Under Smuts, security was sought within the Commonwealth. In its early years of office the National Party remained in the Commonwealth and also tried to secure membership of a Western alliance. This attempt was based partly upon fear of communism—for the South African Government a blanket term which was often extended to cover almost all its opponents. It was also based on the hope of committing other governments to retaining the existing order in Africa. The Western states, with the exception of Britain which had established military interests in southern Africa, refused to be drawn into a formal defence agreement. This failure to secure an alliance became of particular significance in the early 1960s when the white state found itself surrounded by dangers and virtually friendless. But the South African Government, reflecting the values of the white society, was so strongly committed to retaining white dominance that instead of searching for compromise policies which might have attracted some international support, it went ahead with its apartheid policies. It accepted diplomatic isolation, including losing membership of the Commonwealth. Verwoerd, with his granite response, refused all suggestions of sharing power with non-whites within the existing state. While this intransigence may have created difficulty for South Africa in gaining diplomatic sympathy, it made those who had the strongest contacts with her pause to assess the price to be paid of trying to impose radical change on a recalcitrant foe. Also, in response to the dangers, there was a rapid expansion of the armed forces, so that when the colonial withdrawal from Africa was complete (Portugal excepted) the Republic was the most powerful military state in Africa.

As the immediate dangers of the early 1960s disappeared, the South African Government found itself in a substantially stronger position than had been anticipated, especially in Africa. The colonial withdrawal had thrown up opportunities as well as dangers, and the South Africans set out to seize these by using their economic and military strength. The dangers of the newly independent and hostile black states combining together in a military challenge, or persuading other more powerful states to take action against the Republic, gradually receded.

Although diplomatic isolation increased and the danger remained of major guerrilla activity spreading from the Portuguese territories or Rhodesia, South Africa was able to use her relatively great resources to extend her influence, especially among her neighbours. A bloc of southern African states emerged, drawn around the powerful Republic. In one sense this bloc can be seen as a white defensive group, clustering together to counter economic sanctions and guerrilla attacks, and drawing in those small black states which had no choice but to co-operate. In another sense it can be seen as a projection outwards of South Africa's strength by the establishment of a group of dependent states which could offer the Republic substantial economic and military advantages. The emergence of the bloc was the clearest indication of a new period of confidence in South Africa's foreign policy—'the outward policy'. The established objectives of extending influence in Africa by the use of economic and technical contacts, the search for new economic opportunities, the creation of a defensive group against external attacks, and the hopes of gaining international respectability and acceptance, were all to be found in the outward policy. But they were sought in a new set of circumstances, which were more favourable to South Africa. Because of the government's increased resources and the more favourable pattern of international developments, South Africa's foreign policy revealed a new vigour and confidence.

The importance of South Africa's economic strength has been stressed, and yet no white South African government (especially the National Party government) aimed simply at 'wealth maximization'. There was a complex political-economic interrelationship in which continued economic growth was pursued so long as it did not challenge white supremacy. In the face of economic developments the government frequently modified the detailed implementation of apartheid, and in the broadest terms economic growth continued to draw the races together in a working relationship. Yet this was not allowed to undermine the caste nature of South African society. Social and political divisions between the races were increasingly reinforced, and when economic considerations were seen as a challenge to these divisions the government rejected the economic considerations. Both within and outside South Africa there were those who argued that continued economic growth would undermine the government's attempts to maintain a racially structured society, but the evidence of the years between 1945 and 1970 indicate that the white government was able to use economic growth to reinforce its position both internally and externally.

Despite almost universal moral condemnation and diplomatic hostility, the white South African state survived the years between 1945 and 1970. There was usually little room for the government to seize an international initiative. It was constantly forced back on to the defensive, but the white state had survived and its particular values were still being promoted as the Republic entered the 1970s.

SELECT BIBLIOGRAPHY

The bibliography is restricted to books and articles specifically related to South Africa's foreign policy. The place of publication is London unless otherwise stated.

BOOKS AND PAMPHLETS

Adam, Heribert. *South Africa: Sociological Perspectives.* Oxford University Press, 1971.

Austin, Dennis. *Britain and South Africa.* Oxford University Press, for the Royal Institute of International Affairs, 1966.

Ballinger, Margaret. *From Union to Apartheid.* Cape Town, Juta, 1969.

Barratt, John. 'The Department of Foreign Affairs' in Dennis Worrall (ed.), *South Africa: Government and Politics.* Pretoria, J. L. van Schaik, 1971.

Benson, Mary. *Tshekedi Khama.* Faber and Faber, 1960.

—— *South Africa: The Struggle for a Birthright.* Penguin, 1966.

Black, Joseph E., and Thompson, Kenneth W. (eds.), *Foreign Policies in a World of Change.* New York, Harper & Row, 1963.

Booth, R. *The Armed Forces of African States.* Institute for Strategic Studies, 1970.

Brookes, Edgar H. *Apartheid.* Routledge and Kegan Paul, 1968.

Brown, Douglas. *Against the World: A Study of White South African Attitudes.* Collins, 1966.

Calvocoressi, Peter. *South Africa and World Opinion.* Oxford University Press for the Institute of Race Relations, 1961.

Carter, Gwendolen M. *The Politics of Inequality: South Africa since 1948.* Thames and Hudson, 3rd edn. 1963.

—— *Five African States: Responses to Diversity.* Ithaca, N.Y., Cornell University Press, 1963.

Carter, Gwendolen, Karis, Thomas, and Stultz, Newell. *South Africa's Transkei: The Politics of Domestic Colonialism.* Evanston, Illinois, Northwestern University Press, 1967.

Červenka, Z. *The Organization of African Unity.* C. Hurst and Co., 1968.

Cockram, Gail. *Vorster's Foreign Policy.* Pretoria and Cape Town, Academica, 1970.

De Villiers, René. 'Afrikaner Nationalism' in *The Oxford History of South Africa* (ed. Wilson and Thompson), *Vol. II: South Africa 1870–1966.* Oxford, Clarendon Press, 1971.

Eayrs, James (ed.). *The Commonwealth and Suez: A Documentary Survey.* Oxford University Press, 1964.

Emerson, Rupert. *Africa and United States Policy.* Englewood Cliffs, New Jersey, Prentice-Hall, 1967.

Feit, Edward. *South Africa: The Dynamics of the African National Congress.* Oxford University Press for the Institute of Race Relations, 1962.

—— *African Opposition in South Africa.* Hoover Institute, Stanford University Press, California, 1967.

First, Ruth. *South West Africa.* Penguin, 1963.

Gibson, Richard. *African Liberation Movements.* Oxford University Press for the Institute of Race Relations, 1972.

Hailey, Lord. *The Republic of South Africa and the High Commission Territories.* Oxford University Press, 1963.

Halpern, Jack. *South Africa's Hostages.* Penguin, 1965.

Hance, William (ed.). *Southern Africa and the United States.* New York, Columbia University Press, 1968.

Hancock, Sir Keith. *Smuts: Vol. I, The Sanguine Years 1870–1919. Smuts: Vol. II, The Fields of Force.* Cambridge University Press, 2 vols. 1962, 1968.

Hepple, Alexander. *South Africa: A Political and Economic History.* Pall Mall Press, 1966.

—— *Verwoerd.* Penguin, 1967.

Hill, Christopher. *Bantustans.* Oxford University Press for the Institute of Race Relations, 1964.

Horrell, Muriel. *A Survey of Race Relations in South Africa.* Annual publication of South African Institute of Race Relations.

Horwitz, Ralph. *The Political Economy of South Africa.* Weidenfeld and Nicolson, 1967.

Houghton, D. Hobart. *The South African Economy.* Cape Town and London, Oxford University Press, 2nd edn. 1967.

Imishue, R. W. *South West Africa.* Pall Mall Press, 1966.

Lombard, J. A., Stadler, J. J., and Van der Merwe, P. J. *The Concept of Economic Co-operation in Southern Africa.* Pretoria, Econburo, 1968.

Louw, Eric. *The Case for South Africa.* New York, Macfadden, 1963.

McKay, Vernon. *Africa in World Politics.* New York, Harper and Row, 1963.

Malan, D. F. *Foreign Policy of the Union of South Africa.* Pretoria, State Information Department, 1948.

Miller, J. D. B. *The Commonwealth and the World.* Duckworth, 1958.

Mansergh, Nicholas (ed.), *Documents and Speeches on British Commonwealth Affairs 1931–1952.* 2 vols. Oxford University Press for the Royal Institute of International Affairs, 1952.

—— *Documents and Speeches on Commonwealth Affairs 1952–1962.* Oxford University Press for the Royal Institute of International Affairs, 1963.

—— *South Africa 1906–1961: The Price of Magnanimity.* Allen and Unwin, 1962.

—— *Commonwealth Perspectives*. Durham, N.C., Duke University Press, and Cambridge University Press, 1958.

—— *The Commonwealth Experience*. Weidenfeld and Nicolson, 1969.

Marquard, Leo. *The Peoples and Policies of South Africa*. Oxford University Press, 1952; 4th edn. 1969.

—— *Our Foreign Policy*. South African Institute of Race Relations, 1969.

Menzies, Sir Robert. *Afternoon Light*. Cassell, 1967.

Minty, Abdul S. *South Africa's Defence Strategy*. Anti-Apartheid Movement, 1969.

Munger, Edwin S. *Notes on the Formation of South African Foreign Policy*. Pasadena, California, Castle Press, 1965.

—— *Bechuanaland: Pan-African Outpost or Bantu Homeland?* Oxford University Press for the Institute of Race Relations, 1965.

—— *Afrikaner and African Nationalism*. Oxford University Press for the Institute of Race Relations, 1967.

Nicholls, Heaton. *South Africa in My Time*. Allen and Unwin, 1961.

Paton, Alan. *Hofmeyr*. Cape Town and London, Oxford University Press, 1965.

Patterson, Sheila. *The Last Trek: A Study of the Boer People and the Afrikaner Nation*. Routledge and Kegan Paul, 1957.

Potholm, Christian P., and Dale, Richard (eds.). *Southern Africa in Perspective*. New York, The Free Press, 1972.

Segal, Ronald (ed.). *Sanctions Against South Africa*. Penguin, 1964.

Smuts, Jan Christian. *Jan Christian Smuts*. Cassell, 1952.

Spence, Jack E. *Republic Under Pressure*. Oxford University Press for the Royal Institute of International Affairs, 1965.

—— *The Strategic Significance of Southern Africa*. Royal United Services Institution, 1970.

—— 'South Africa and the Modern World' (in *Oxford History of South Africa*, Vol. II).

Stevens, Richard P. *Lesotho, Botswana and Swaziland*. Pall Mall Press, 1967.

Thompson, Leonard. *Politics in the Republic of South Africa*. Boston, Little, Brown, 1966.

Van den Berghe, Pierre. *South Africa: A Study in Conflict*. Middletown, Conn., Wesleyan University Press, 1965.

Vandenbosch, A. *South Africa and the World: The Foreign Policy of Apartheid*. Lexington, Ky., University of Kentucky Press, 1970.

Van Wyk, J. T. *The United Nations, South West Africa and the Law*. University of Cape Town, 1968.

Vatcher, William Henry. *White Laager: The Rise of Afrikaner Nationalism*. Pall Mall Press, 1965.

Walker, Eric. *A History of South Africa*. Longmans, 1964.

Walshe, A. P. *The Rise of African Nationalism in South Africa*. C. Hurst, 1970.

Wellington, John H. *South West Africa and Its Human Issues*. Oxford, Clarendon Press, 1967.

Wilson, Monica, and Thompson, Leonard (eds.). *The Oxford History of South Africa*. Oxford, Clarendon Press, Vol. I (to 1870), 1969; Vol. II (1870–1966), 1971.

Worrall, Denis (ed.). *South Africa: Government and Politics*. Pretoria, J. L. van Schaik, 1971.

JOURNAL AND PERIODICAL ARTICLES

Austin, Dennis. 'White Power', *Journal of Commonwealth Political Studies*, July 1968.

Barratt, John. 'The Outward Movement in South Africa's Foreign Relations', South African Institute of International Affairs, *Newsletter No. 3*, 1969.

—— 'South Africa and the United Nations', *Newsletter No. 1*, 1969.

—— 'Dialogue in Africa: A New Approach', *South Africa International*, vol. 2, no. 2, Oct. 1971.

Bowman, Larry. 'The Subordinate State Systems of Southern Africa', *International Studies Quarterly*, vol. 12, Sept. 1968.

—— 'South Africa's Southern African Strategy, and its implications for the United States', *International Affairs*, vol. 47, no. 1, Jan. 1971.

Dagut, Merton. 'The South African Economy through the Sixties', *Southern Africa*, 3 Jan. 1970.

Dale, Richard. 'South Africa and the International Community', *World Politics*, vol. XVIII, Jan. 1966.

—— 'Ovamboland: Bantustan without Tears?', *Africa Report*, vol. 14, no. 2, Feb. 1969.

D'Amato, Anthony. 'The Bantustan Proposals for South-West Africa', *Journal of Modern African Studies*, vol. 4, Oct. 1966.

Day, John. 'The Rhodesian African Nationalists and the Commonwealth African States', *Journal of Commonwealth Political Studies*, vol. VII, no. 2, July 1969.

de Kiewiet, C. W. 'The World and Pretoria', *Africa Report*, vol. 14, no. 2, Feb. 1969, and *South Africa International*, vol. 1, no. 1, July 1970.

Dugard, C. J. R. 'The Legal Effect of United Nations Resolutions on Apartheid', *South African Law Journal*, vol. 83, Feb. 1966.

—— 'The Simonstown Agreements: South Africa, Britain and the United Nations', *South African Law Journal*, vol. 85, May 1968.

—— 'South West Africa Returns to the International Court', *New Nation*, Feb. 1971.

Feit, Edward. 'Urban Revolt in South Africa: a case study', *Journal of Modern African Studies*, vol. 8, no. 1, Apr. 1970.

Gervasi, Sean. 'South Africa's Economic Expansionism', *Sechaba*, vol. 5, no. 6, June 1971.

Hance, William A. 'Cabora Bassa Hydro Project', *African Report*, vol. 15, no. 5, May 1970.

Hill, Christopher R. 'UDI and South African Foreign Policy', *Journal of Commonwealth Political Studies*, vol. VII, no. 2, July 1969.

Johnstone, Frederick. 'White Prosperity and White Supremacy in South Africa Today', *African Affairs*, vol. 69, Apr. 1970.

Kennan, George F. 'Hazardous Courses in Southern Africa', *Southern Africa International*, vol. 1, no. 4, Apr. 1971.

Lawrie, G. C. 'South Africa's World Position', *Journal of Modern African Studies*, vol. 2, no. 1, 1964.

—— 'The Simonstown Agreements: South Africa, Britain and the Commonwealth', *South African Law Journal*, vol. 85, part 2, May 1968.

—— 'Britain's Obligations under the Simonstown Agreement', *International Affairs*, vol. 47, no. 4, Oct. 1971.

Miller, J. D. B. 'South Africa's Departure', *Journal of Commonwealth Political Studies*, vol. 1, 1961–3.

Muller, Hilgard. 'Some Aspects of South Africa's Foreign Policy', South African Institute of International Affairs, *Newsletter No. 4*, 1969.

Munger, Edwin S. 'South Africa: Are there silver linings?', *Foreign Affairs*, vol. 47, no. 2, Jan. 1969.

O'Meara, Patrick. 'Tensions in the Nationalist Party', *African Report*, vol. 14, no. 2, Feb. 1969.

Rake, Alan. 'Black Guerrillas in Rhodesia', *African Report*, vol. 13, no. 9, Dec. 1968.

Robson, Peter. 'Economic Integration in Southern Africa', *Journal of Modern African Studies*, vol. 5, Dec. 1967.

Sadie, J. L. 'An Economic Mission for Southern Africa', *South Africa International*, vol. 1, no. 4, Apr. 1971.

Spence, J. E. 'South Africa's "New Look" Foreign Policy', *World Today*, vol. 24, no. 4, 1968.

—— 'Tradition and Change in South African Foreign Policy', *Journal of Commonwealth Political Studies*, vol. 1, 1961–3.

—— 'British Policy Towards the High Commission Territories', *Journal of Modern African Studies*, vol. 2, 1964.

Stultz, Newell. 'The Politics of Security: South Africa under Verwoerd', *Journal of Modern African Studies*, vol. 7, no. 1, 1969.

Sutcliffe, R. B. 'The Political Economy of Rhodesian Sanctions', *Journal of Commonwealth Political Studies*, vol. 12, no. 2, July 1969.

Taylor, F. 'United States Private Investment in Africa', *Africa Report*, vol. 14, no. 1, Jan. 1969.

Umozurike, U. O. 'International Law and Namibia', *Journal of Modern African Studies*, vol. 8, no. 4, Dec. 1970.

Uys, Stanley. 'South Africa Shifts', *African Report*, vol. 15, no. 8, Nov. 1970.

von Maltitz, A. A. 'South African Minerals and their Importance to World Industry', *South Africa International*, vol. 1, no. 4, Apr. 1971.

Vosloo, Ben, and Lever, Jeffrey. 'Student Outlook at Stellenbosch', *New Nation*, Feb. 1971.

Welsh, David. 'Urbanization and the Solidarity of Afrikaner Nationalism', *Journal of Modern African Studies*, vol. 7, no. 2, 1969.

INDEX

INDEX